# THE
# MUSHROOM
# TRAILGUIDE

# THE
# MUSHROOM
# TRAILGUIDE

*Phyllis G. Glick*
*Illustrations by the Author*

HOLT, RINEHART AND WINSTON
*New York*

Copyright © 1979 by Phyllis G. Glick

Published by Holt, Rinehart and Winston,
383 Madison Avenue, New York,
New York 10017

Published simultaneously in Canada
by Holt, Rinehart and Winston of
Canada, Limited.

**Library of Congress Cataloging in Publication Data**

Glick, Phyllis G., 1924–
    The mushroom trailguide.

    Includes index.
    1. Mushrooms—Identification.   2. Mushrooms—
North America—Identification.   I. Title.
QK617.J63        589'.222'097        78-18424
ISBN Hardbound: 0-03-018306-5
ISBN Paperback: 0-03-018301-4

FIRST EDITION

*Designer: Madelaine Caldiero*

Printed in the United States of America
10 9 8 7 6 5 4 3 2 1

# CONTENTS

# FOREWORD

Interest in mushrooms and related fungi has grown tremendously during the past few years. Obviously some of this interest derives from the rediscovery of hallucinogenic compounds in some of these fungi, but this factor alone does not explain the whole story. The use of native fungi as sources of food has shown a great increase during this period, particularly here in North America. Also, there is an increasing number of individuals whose interest stems from their desire to learn more about these organisms—their names (most of these fungi are so poorly known that they have no common names); their contribution to the welfare of man, other than as a source of food, as well as the problems they cause; and an ever-increasing appreciation by many of their exquisite beauty and charm.

Because of the considerable variety of mushrooms and other fleshy fungi, and, especially, because the composition of the flora is still rather poorly known in so many parts of this country, no single reference will prove adequate for the identification of all of the fungi encountered on a walk through the woods, and frustration often prevails. Furthermore, the paucity of readily usable and constant characters that can be seen by the naked eye makes positive identification of many mushrooms—without the aid of a microscope—considerably more difficult than of many other groups of plants. The necessity of accurate identification of these fungi is essential, if collected for the table, due to the fact that there are some species that contain compounds that are toxic, even lethal, to man. Thus it behooves everyone interested in these fungi to develop a thorough familiarity with them and to be absolutely certain of their correct identification.

This trailguide, with its clear, concise, yet diagnostic descriptions and the numerous line drawings with an abundance of labels highlighting the distinctive features of each species, will be a useful companion on your hikes in the woods or on backpacking trips. Take it with you! Use it and enjoy it! Try its recipes! And become, like so many others, familiar with the stimulating and challenging world of the fleshy fungi.

—Harry D. Thiers, Ph.D.
*Professor of Botany*
*San Francisco State University*

# HOW
# TO USE
# THIS BOOK

Wild mushrooms are one of the most fascinating aspects of nature. It's like a treasure hunt to seek them out. Then it's like solving a mystery as you look for the clues that will tell you which mushroom you have found. Finally, you celebrate your success by dining on your gourmet finds.

The two questions most frequently asked about a mushroom are "What is it?" and "Can I eat it?" This book is designed to answer both. With this book, you will be able to (1) recognize which genus (or group) a mushroom belongs to and then (2) determine whether it is an edible or a poisonous species.

There are several thousand species of wild mushrooms in North America, so no one book can describe them all. Learning the edible and poisonous ones is the logical place to start, especially since these include most of the common and important species. Not included in this book are the vast number of mushrooms labeled *inedible,* meaning they are too tough or tasteless or terrible tasting to eat or they are untested—there are many small mushrooms about which little is known.

The sheer number of mushrooms seems overwhelming to the beginner. But who says you have to learn them all? Learn to recognize one at a time and soon you will know quite a few. Once you learn a mushroom, you'll recognize it as quickly as the face of a friend. As for those you don't know, don't worry about them. Even the experts aren't embarrassed to admit they're stumped quite frequently.

**MUSHROOM NAMES AREN'T AS DIFFICULT AS THEY LOOK** Few mushrooms have common names, so the scientific name is the one you must learn. It consists of two names (the genus and species), such as *Morchella esculenta,* just as a person has two names, such as *John Smith.* But in mushrooms, the last name is placed first: *Smith John.* The first name of a mushroom, i.e., *Morchella,* is comparable to a person's last name; it is the genus (plural: genera) and refers to a group of closely related mushrooms. The second name, i.e., *esculenta,* is comparable to a person's first name and designates the species or individual. Thus a genus is made up of closely related species, just as a family is made up of closely related individuals.

If you can tell quickly which genus a mushroom belongs to, the biggest part of the identification is done, and this book is specially designed to help you do this.

In the past 25 years, many mushrooms have been reclassified and their genera names changed. Many of the older mushroom guides use names that are no longer current. In this book, the current names are used, with the other ones shown in parentheses. One comforting thing is that the species name rarely changes, thus if you know a mushroom by a genus name that has been changed, you can still locate the mushroom by looking up its species name. Mycologists, themselves, differ on how to classify many species, and the nomenclature can be expected to keep changing for many years.

## HOW DO YOU TELL AN EDIBLE MUSHROOM FROM A POISONOUS ONE?  There are no generalities to guide you. The only way is to identify each specimen by genus and species. Forget all the rules of thumb that supposedly tell you if a mushroom is poisonous. None of them work. Some people say if you can peel a mushroom, it is safe to eat. Not so. Or that if it turns a spoon black, it is poisonous. Not so. Many mushroom poisonings have resulted from people following such erroneous beliefs. No rule is the only rule.

To identify a mushroom, you must first find one. And here the fun begins. Little equipment is needed, even for a daylong foray:

· You'll want some kind of basket to hold your treasure. You'll see people collecting in all kinds of containers, from cardboard boxes to plastic pails, but the best is a roomy, loosely woven basket (no lid) that will permit free air circulation.

· Take along a long-bladed instrument so you can dig up the entire mushroom, including the below-ground portions, which are vital for proper identification. Everything from a jackknife to a dandelion digger is used.

· You'll also need a roll of waxed paper or waxed-paper bags (or brown paper bags or old envelopes) to hold your mushrooms. Do not use plastic bags; they cause the mushrooms to sweat and start to decay. If using a roll of waxed paper, tear off a generous piece, roll the mushroom up in it, twist the ends shut, and stand vertically in the basket. For fragile species, carry several small containers. Wrap the specimen in waxed paper and place in container so it won't crush.

· You'll enjoy having a magnifying glass (with 10X lens) to reveal the delicate beauty of a mushroom and make it easier to see small identifying clues.

· A police whistle is handy to keep in touch with your wandering companions. It's easy to lose your sense of direction when walking head down in the woods. Some people work out a code: One blast on the whistle means "Where are you?" Two blasts means "Come here, I want to show you something interesting." Three blasts means "Help! I'm lost! Find me!"

· The proper way is to carry a notebook and promptly record the habitat and characteristics of each species as you find it. This requires a diligence hard to maintain in the excitement of finding mushrooms, but such record keeping greatly facilitates learning and identification.

As you collect, carefully package your mushrooms, putting only one species in a bag. Never mix two or more together. If they are very dirty, gently remove as much dirt as you can without destroying any part of the mushroom—you'll need every clue to identify it. Occasionally rearrange your basket to ensure that none of your specimens is crushed.

When collecting a mushroom that you know (positively) and want to take home to eat, clean it right then, cutting off the dirty stem end and brushing off all the dirt. That way it will arrive home in good edible condition. If you fail to clean it at picking time, jostling in the basket will distribute the dirt all over the mushroom by the time you get it home.

Never leave mushrooms in a hot, closed car. They are highly perishable. When you get home, sort them out and refrigerate in waxed paper or brown paper bags. Eat promptly before they deteriorate. Freeze, can, or dry the excess.

**HOW TO IDENTIFY A MUSHROOM**   Study all parts of a mushroom before deciding what you've found. All the clues must fit together since mushrooms have their similarities and their differences. Here's where you find out how good a Sherlock Holmes you are. It's best if you have 4 or 5 specimens in various stages of growth so you can study the variations within a species. Size in mushrooms—as in people—is extremely variable. The illustrations in this book are all drawn to the same scale, roughly half size, to help you judge the relative size of each species. Measurements given are for the average specimen with extra-large variations shown in parentheses, i.e., 3–6 (12) in. Color varies tremendously, depending on whether the mushroom is young or old, wet or dry, growing in sun or shade. Heavy rains may wash off the veil or ring or scales—or they may have been brushed off by an animal or as the mushroom pushed up through the earth. Expect variation but don't force a mushroom into identification. The basic clues must match. Also always note where a mushroom is growing and match this with the description. Habitat is an invaluable clue.

Mushrooms can be divided into two groups: gilled and nongilled. The latter are quite distinctive and easy to identify—good ones for a beginner. They come in a variety of shapes and sizes. Some look like ocean coral or a round ball or a tiny cup or a group of small icicles hanging from a tree. Others have the familiar umbrella-shaped cap and stem with a spongelike layer on the undersurface of the cap. To identify them, turn to page 160, study the picture keys until you find the correct genus, then turn to the pages describing the various species and carefully compare the illustrations and descriptions with your mystery mushroom. If no page number is listed in the keys for a genus, this means its species are inedible or untested, and thus not included in this book.

Gilled mushrooms are like the commercial mushrooms you buy in the supermarket. They have a stem and a cap and on the undersurface of the cap have gills—thin, finlike structures radiating from stem to cap edge like spokes on a wheel.

The first step in identifying a gilled mushroom is to make a spore print. Spores are the microscopic "seeds" of the mushroom. They are produced on the surface of the gills and sift down to the ground in a fine powder. In a thick deposit, they have a distinctive color that is a great aid in identifying a mushroom.

**TO MAKE A SPORE PRINT**   Cut off the cap of a fresh mushroom and place the cap gills down on a piece of white paper. Cover with a glass or bowl to keep it moist and protect it from air currents that would blow away the spores. Putting a tiny drop of water on top of the cap or moistening the inside of the bowl will keep the cap moist and facilitate spore dispersement. If a cap is too young or too old or has been refrigerated, it will not release spores. In 1 to 5 hours or overnight, the spores will fall onto the paper, forming a pattern of the gills. If the spore color is pale, scrape the spores into a thicker pile to intensify the color. Looking at them through a magnifying glass helps too, especially with white spores. Spore prints can be made of nongilled fungi, but usually they can be identified without knowing spore color.

Sometimes you can determine spore color in the field. Often spores will be deposited around the top of a mushroom stem or on the leaves or duff directly beneath the mushroom—or even on the cap of a smaller mushroom growing directly beneath it. Spores also coat the gills of many species at maturity.

You can also start a spore print in the field. Press a small piece of white paper against the gills of one cap and put it gills down in a bag in your basket. By the time you get home, enough spores will have fallen on the paper to reveal their color.

Gilled mushrooms fall into one of 6 spore color groups: (1) whitish to yellowish to lilac, (2) green, (3) pink to salmon, (4) yellow brown to rusty brown, (5) dark brown to purplish brown, and (6) blackish. Thus, for example, when a mushroom has a blackish spore print, you can ignore all the other groups and concentrate on only the 4 genera having black spore prints, greatly simplifying your hunt.

When you have determined the color of a spore print, turn to the picture keys for gilled mushrooms, pages 12–21, locate the correct spore color group, and carry on from there.

**OTHER AIDS**   Identification is easier when you learn to recognize mushrooms by their silhouettes, just as you recognize a friend down the street by his silhouette long before you see his face. The illustrations in this book are drawn to show you typical silhouettes. The niceties of shading have been eliminated so you will concentrate on the overall look of a genus. Once learned, you will be able to know instantly that the mushroom at your feet is a *Russula* even before you stoop to pick it. Or even to recognize a *Lepiota* from the car as you drive along.

Cut mushroom in half lengthwise to determine whether the gills are attached to the stem. If the cap is dry, moisten your finger and touch the cap to feel whether it is slimy or sticky when wet.

**JOIN A GROUP** One of the best ways to learn mushrooms is to join (or form) your own mycological society. Write to the North American Mycological Society, 4245 Redinger Road, Portsmouth, Ohio 45662, for addresses of nearby societies or inquire at your local community college or university. There are amateur mycologists in almost every community, so hunt them up and join them on forays.

**HOW TO STAY OUT OF TROUBLE** Never eat any mushroom if you are not 100% sure of its identification. A gamble could result in anything from mild stomach malaise to death. "When in doubt, throw it out."
· Identify each specimen separately, even those growing close together. Poisonous and edible specimens grow side by side and can easily be mixed together.
· Avoid all "LBM"s—those Little Brown Mushrooms that are very common, hard to identify, and often very poisonous. Be safe; don't eat any of them.
· Eat only fresh, young, insect-free specimens. Unfortunately, many people are so thrilled to gather a bagful of wild mushrooms that they eat all they find, rotten or otherwise. Use the same discrimination with mushrooms as you would in selecting fresh vegetables in the market. You wouldn't eat a rotten, wormy tomato, so don't eat a rotten, wormy mushroom. Throw out any that are discolored, mushy soft, or furry with mold.
· Because some people are allergic to certain mushrooms—even the supermarket ones—it is vital when trying a mushroom for the first time to eat (1) only a small amount, (2) only once that day, and (3) only one kind at a time. Don't overindulge with any mushroom. Some have a cumulative effect, and overeating will make you sick while a moderate portion will not. The very young (under 8 years old), the very old (over 80), and the chronically ill are particularly sensitive; even safe mushrooms can be harmful to them. Since no one can predict a person's individual food idiosyncrasies or the accuracy of his identifications, the author and the publisher of this book cannot accept responsibility for any untoward effects you may experience in eating any fleshy fungi.
· Never break off or pull up a mushroom, but always dig up the underground parts, scrutinizing the surrounding soil for any telltale cup remnants.
· Double-check that you haven't found a poisonous *Amanita* when you find a mushroom with (1) a ring on the stem, or (2) a cup at the base, or (3) warts or scales on the cap, or (4) a swollen base.
· Double-check the identification of any white-capped mushroom or any growing on dung. Many are toxic, and it's easy to mistake them for edible species.
· Always slice puffballs from top to bottom before eating to make sure they are still pure white and that you haven't gathered an *Amanita* button by mistake.

· Don't foray on private land without permission or within National Parks and Monuments areas where all flora and fauna are protected by law.

**COOK THEM RIGHT** To clean a mushroom, wipe with a damp cloth rather than wash, so it won't soak up too much water. Different species require different cooking methods. Some can be sautéed quickly; others require long, slow stewing. Specific cooking methods for the different genera are outlined on the pages describing them. Any surplus mushrooms can be frozen, dried, or canned for later use.

*Frozen:* Sauté or blanch mushrooms, cool, freeze in plastic containers.

*Dried:* Clean with dry cloth. Slice ¼ in. thick or leave small caps whole and (1) string and hang in the sun or a sunny, airy room till dry, or (2) arrange in a single layer on screening over a heat register, hot plate, or fruit dryer, in the sun, under an infrared lamp, or in oven with pilot light on and door open several inches, turning frequently till dry. Store in airtight containers. To rejuvenate, wash in several changes of water (getting rid of any remaining dirt), then soak in hot water, milk, or cream 15–30 minutes.

*Powdered:* Put dried caps through the blender and use the powder as seasoning.

*Canned:* Wash, cut into small pieces. Blanch for 3 minutes in boiling water, adding 1 teaspoon vinegar to each quart water. Pack hot in clean, hot containers, adding 1 teaspoon salt per quart. Cover with the cooking water. Adjust lids and process in pressure canner, per manufacturer's instructions.

*Pickled:* A wide variety of pickling baths may be used. Boil 1 cup vinegar and 3 tablespoons oil with seasonings of your choice, such as (1) salt, sugar, bay leaves, sliced garlic, fresh herbs, or (2) packaged mixed pickling spices and salt, or (3) garlic, fresh herbs, coriander, peppercorns. Add mushrooms and simmer 15–20 minutes. Pour into sterilized jars, seal, serve after 2 weeks. Or refrigerate for several days, and serve.

*Marinated:* Toss sliced mushroom caps in strong French vinaigrette dressing made with olive oil, lemon juice or vinegar, fresh herbs, and a splash of brandy (optional). Refrigerate overnight and serve.

*Sautéed:* Melt butter (or half butter and half olive oil) in skillet, add coarsely chopped garlic, parsley, fresh herbs of your choice, and brown. Add sliced mushrooms, sprinkle with salt, pepper. Reduce heat and cook slowly, stirring and shaking pan occasionally, till tender. (Herbs can be omitted and mushrooms seasoned at end with lemon juice—some people like nutmeg, too.)

*Creamed:* Sauté minced onion in butter until soft and golden brown. Add sliced mushrooms and sauté until tender. Reserve liquid. In separate pan, melt 3 tablespoons butter and stir in 3 tablespoons flour to make a white sauce. Add mushroom liquid plus enough water to make 1 cup. Season. Stir constantly until thickened. Add a few squirts lemon juice, then enrich with 1 egg yolk beaten into 1 cup cream. Reheat. Add mushrooms.

*Mushroom paste:* Sauté mushrooms, season to taste, blend to a paste in blender, moistening with stock as necessary. Freeze in small containers. Use when rich mushroom flavor is desired.

*Soup:* Simmer whole mushrooms in enough water or stock to cover amply for 5 minutes with salt, pepper. Make a white sauce, using a ratio of 2 tablespoons each, butter and flour, to 2 cups milk. Strain the mushrooms, reserving the water and adding it gradually to the white sauce. Chop the mushrooms finely, add to the liquid mixture, re-season and reheat. Can be enriched with butter and cream just before serving.

*Variation:* Instead of simmering mushrooms in water, sauté them, chopped, in butter as the first step.

*Blender soup:* Partially cook mushrooms in butter and oil with chopped shallots and parsley. Put through blender, then simmer 15 minutes in sufficient stock to make a thick soup. (If you have lots of mushrooms, no thickening is necessary, but if you wish to thicken, add a piece of bread, moistened in stock, to mushrooms in blender.) Just before serving, enrich with heavy cream. Reheat.

*Mushroom loaf:* Substitute mushrooms for meat in any meat loaf recipe using bread crumbs. Let stand 10 minutes before slicing. Good hot or chilled. Or use half mushrooms, half meat.

*With breakfast bacon:* Add sliced mushrooms to bacon when it's half fried. Cook till moisture evaporates. Serve with scrambled eggs.

*Quick mushroom spread:* Chop raw mushrooms and shallots (or garlic or scallions or chives) with sprigs of parsley or other fresh herbs. Moisten with olive oil and lemon juice, season with salt, pepper. Mix well. Serve on thin pieces of toast or crackers.

Finally, don't feel that mushrooms must be eaten to be enjoyed. Many mushroom collectors never eat their finds—to them the joy is in hunting and identifying them. The more you learn about mushrooms, the more you will enjoy them—and the more you will realize how much more there is to learn about "the world of wonder at your feet" (motto of the North American Mycological Society).

# PARTS OF A GILLED MUSHROOM

The aboveground portion of a mushroom is not the plant itself but the fruiting body whose purpose is to produce spores, the "seeds" of the mushroom. The plant proper is below ground, a network of fine threads, called *mycelium,* often not visible to the naked eye. The spores are produced on the surface of the gills, the thin finlike structures on the undersurface of the cap. The stem supports the cap and keeps it in a horizontal position so the spores can fall free of the gills at maturity. The cap protects the gills. The mushroom lasts only a short time, but the mycelium may last for many years.

In youth, in some species, the gills are covered and protected by a membrane called the *partial veil.* As the cap expands, this veil breaks. Pieces of it remain as a "ring" on the stem or as fragments hanging from the cap edge.

In some species, the young mushroom in its oval "button" stage is completely enveloped and protected by a membrane called the *universal veil.* As the stem elongates, this veil breaks. Pieces of it remain around the stem base as a "cup" and/or as scales or warts on the cap.

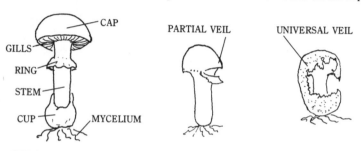

CAP

GILLS

RING

STEM

CUP   MYCELIUM

PARTIAL VEIL

UNIVERSAL VEIL

---

## *Gill Attachment (cross section)*

| NOT ATTACHED TO STEM, ENDING JUST SHORT OF IT | ATTACHED DIRECTLY TO STEM | NOTCHED JUST BEFORE REACHING STEM | EXTENDING DOWN STEM |

---

## *Cap Shapes*

ROUNDED   CONIC   BELL-SHAPED   KNOBBED

FLAT   DEPRESSED   FUNNEL   PITTED

# PICTURE KEYS,
# GILLED MUSHROOMS

# How to use these picture keys for gilled mushrooms

First, make a spore print, page 6, to establish spore color. Then turn to the appropriate picture key on this or the following pages. (Picture keys for nongilled mushrooms are on pages 160–161.) Decide whether your mushrooom belongs in Group I, II, or III, then look for the genus that resembles it and turn to the page listed to continue your comparison. You may have to study several genera before finding the correct one. If no page number is listed for a genus, this means it is inedible or untested and not included in this book.

**I   Gills not attached to stem. Cap easily detached from stem.**

- White spores
- Cap may have scales or warts
- Cap edge may be grooved
- Gills white to pale
- With or without ring on stem
- Cup or remnants at stem base
- On ground

AMANITA, PP. 24–29

- White spores
- Very slimy overall
- Ring slimy, often disappears
- No cup at stem base
- On ground

LIMACELLA

- White spores
- Small to very large
- Cap dry, scaly
- Ring sometimes movable, may disappear
- No cup, but stem base may be enlarged
- On ground

LEPIOTA, PP. 30–35
LEUCOAGARICUS, PP. 36–37, AS ABOVE EXCEPT
SMOOTH CAP, STEM

*Green Spores*

- The only mushroom with green spores
- Very large
- Cap scaly
- Ring large, may partially disappear
- No cup, but stem base is enlarged
- On ground

CHLOROPHYLLUM MOLYBDITES, PP. 36–37

**II  Gills attached to stem. Stem thin, different in structure from cap (tougher or more fragile), not easily detached from cap.**

- White to buff spores
- Cap soft, smooth, moist
- Cap edge inrolled in youth
- Stem brittle to fibrous
- On humus, needles, rotted wood

COLLYBIA, PP. 38–41

FLAMMULINA, PP. 38–41, AS ABOVE EXCEPT DARK-BROWN VELVETY STEM, SLIMY CAP

- White to buff spores   .
- Cap dry, leathery
- Dried cap revives when moistened
- Cap edge incurved in youth
- Stem tough, pliable
- In grass, leaves, needles

MARASMIUS, PP. 42–43

- White spores
- Small, dainty, fragile
- Cap more or less bell-shaped
- Cap edge grooved, straight, not inrolled, in youth
- Stem fragile, often hollow
- Often clustered on wood, needles, humus

MYCENA

- White to yellowish spores·
- Small, delicate, yellow to orangy
- Cap thin, depressed in center, becoming funnel-shaped
- Cap edge inrolled at first
- Gills extend down stem, far apart
- Stem brittle to fibrous, not pliant
- On wood, moss, soil

OMPHALINA

- White spores
- Small, fragile, yellow to orangy
- Entire dried plant revives in water
- Cap smooth, rounded, sometimes depressed
- Cap edge often grooved
- Gills often extend down stem
- Stem thin, pliant, dark brown over lower part with fine, short hairs at base
- Often clustered on decayed wood, needles, humus

XEROMPHALINA

III   **Gills attached to stem. Cap and stem of same structure, not easily separated.**

- White spores
- Cap medium to large, rounded, may flatten in age
- Gills usually notched at junction with stem
- Stem fleshy, stout
- On ground

TRICHOLOMA, PP. 44–47

TRICHOLOMOPSIS, PP. 48–49, AS ABOVE EXCEPT ON WOOD

MELANOLEUCA, PP. 50–51, AS ABOVE EXCEPT MORE SLENDER, STIFF STATURE

- White to cream to yellow spores
- Medium to large, often brightly colored
- Brittle, shatters easily
- Cap rounded to saucer-shaped
- Stem looks and breaks like piece of chalk
- On soil

RUSSULA, PP. 52–59

- White to yellowish spores
- Cap rounded to funnel-shaped
- Gills usually extend down stem slightly
- Gills exude milky or colored juice when cut
- Stem short, thick
- On soil under trees

LACTARIUS, PP. 60–65

- White spores
- Small, often brightly colored
- Cap conic to flat, often slimy
- Gills waxy looking and feeling, far apart, extend down stem, wedge-shaped in cross section
- On ground or duff

HYGROPHORUS, PP. 66–71

- White spores
- Cap white, gray, or black; may fade in drying
- Gills may stain yellow, blue, black
- Soapy feeling to cap, gills
- Gills may extend slightly down stem
- Stem rather thick
- On ground, sometimes clustered

LYOPHYLLUM, PP. 70–71

- White to buff spores
- Small to large, often fleshy
- Cap depressed in age, often funnel-shaped
- Gills often extend down stem
- Stem brittle or fibrous, not pliant
- On soil, needles, wood

CLITOCYBE, PP. 72–77

LEUCOPAXILLUS, AS ABOVE EXCEPT VERY LARGE; CHALKY-WHITE GILLS, STEM; WHITE MOLD COVERING BASE

**III continued**

- White to pale lilac spores
- Purplish to flesh color
- Gills far apart, waxy looking
- Stem fibrous
- Variable habitat
LACCARIA, PP. 76–77

- White spores
- Cap hairy to scaly
- Ring on stem
- On ground
ARMILLARIA, PP. 78–81
ARMILLARIELLA, PP. 78, 82–83, AS ABOVE EXCEPT
GROWS ON WOOD; ONE SPECIES DOES NOT HAVE RING

- White spores
- Large, fleshy, dingy colored
- Double veil and ring
- Gills extend down stem
- On ground under trees
CATATHELASMA, PP. 84–85

- White spores
- Grainy-mealy coating on cap, stem
- Veil fragments on cap edge
- Ring or remnants on stem
- On ground or decayed wood
CYSTODERMA, PP. 86–87

- White spores
- Cap tough, leathery
- Gills with sawtooth edges
- Stem short or absent, may be off-center
- On wood, often clustered
LENTINUS, LENTINELLUS, PP. 86–87
PANUS, PANELLUS, AS ABOVE EXCEPT GILLS HAVE
SMOOTH EDGES
SCHIZOPHYLLUM, SMALL, FAN-SHAPED, HAIRY; NO STEM

- White to buff to lilac spores
- Cap soft, fleshy, not woody, dull-colored
- Gill edges smooth
- Stem usually off-center or absent
- Clustered on wood or buried wood
PLEUROTUS, PP. 88–91
OMPHALOTUS, PP. 90–91, AS ABOVE EXCEPT ORANGE
OVERALL

**I Gills not attached to stem. Cap easily detached from stem.**

· Pink to salmon spores
· Cap silky, bell-shaped to rounded
· Gills whitish, aging pink to salmon
· No ring on stem
· Sacklike cup at stem base
· On wood, debris, rich ground
VOLVARIELLA, PP. 92–93

· Pink to salmon spores
· Cap soft, fleshy, rounded, aging flat
· Edge incurved in youth
· Gills whitish, aging pink to salmon
· No ring on stem
· No cup at base
· On wood, sawdust
PLUTEUS, PP. 94–95

**II Gills attached to stem. Stem thin, different in structure from cap (tougher or more fragile), not easily detached from cap.**

· Pink spores
· Small, delicate
· Cap bell-shaped to rounded, often with knob
· Cap edge straight, pressed tight against stem when young; often grooved when wet
· Stem pithy to hollow, never bluish
· On ground
NOLANEA

· Pink spores
· Small, often bluish, sometimes scaly
· Cap thin, rounded, often with pit in center
· Cap edge incurved in youth
· Stem slender, brittle, polished
· On ground, wood, wet areas
LEPTONIA

· Pink spores
· Tiny, dull-colored
· Cap thin, with hollow in center
· Cap edge incurved
· Stem soon hollow, often larger at top
ECCILIA

**III   Gills attached to stem. Cap and stem of same structure, not easily separated.**

- Salmon-pink spores
- Cap fleshy, often with polished sheen, cracked edge
- Gills age salmon pink
- Stem pallid, often grooved
- On ground

ENTOLOMA, PP. 96–97

- Pinkish-buff spores
- Often lilac, pinkish, buff, whitish
- Cap rounded, becoming upturned, wavy
- Gills notched at stem
- Stem stout, often bulbous
- No ring or cup
- On soil, decaying matter

LEPISTA, PP. 98–99

- Pink to salmon spores
- Whitish to grayish with kid-glove texture
- Cap rounded, becoming flat or depressed
- Gills extend down stem
- Gills whitish, aging pale pink
- On ground

CLITOPILUS, PP. 100–101

- Light-reddish spores
- Cap densely hairy, irregular
- Stem off-center or absent
- Cap attached at sides or on top to wood
- Disagreeable odor
- In groups on decaying wood

PHYLLOTOPSIS (CLAUDOPUS)

**I  Gills not attached to stem. Cap easily detached from stem.**

· Rusty-brown spores
· Cap egg-yolk yellow, soft, slimy; edge grooved
· Stem long, slimy, fragile
· Usually in clusters on dung, manured grass
BOLBITIUS

**II  Gills attached to stem. Stem thin, different in structure from cap (tougher or more fragile), not easily detached from cap.**

· Rusty-brown spores
· Cap small, conic to rounded, edge often grooved
· Stem long, thin, brittle
· May have veil, ring
· In deep moss or on wood, often clustered
GALERINA, PP. 102–103
TUBARIA, AS ABOVE EXCEPT CAP OFTEN HAS PIT IN
CENTER; GILLS RUN DOWN STEM; ON STICKS, DEBRIS

· Bright rusty-brown spores
· Cap tiny, fragile; conic to rounded
· Stem long, thin, may stain blue
· Sometimes veil, ring
· In grass or moss
CONOCYBE, PP. 102–103

**III  Gills attached to stem. Cap and stem of same structure, not easily separated.**

· Dull-brown spores
· Cap pointed to rounded, knobbed, edge split
· Usually streaked with hairy fibers
· Gills attached or notched at stem, age dark
· May have hairy veil, ring
· On soil in woods
INOCYBE, PP. 104–105

· Yellowish-brown spores
· Cap dull-colored, rounded, wavy; slimy to tacky
· Cap edge incurved in youth
· Gills age color of spores
· Sometimes hairy veil, ring
· Stem fleshy, dry, powdery white
· On soil
HEBELOMA, PP. 106–107

· Dark-brown spores
· Cap whitish to dull brown
· Gills whitish, aging spore color
· Usually ring on stem
· Stem fleshy, whitish to brownish
· In grass, wood mulch, needles
AGROCYBE, PP. 108–109

· Dull-brown spores
· Cap small, rounded to fan-shaped; rubbery
· Stem absent or off-center. Clustered on wood
CREPIDOTUS

**III   continued**

- Rusty-brown spores
- Cap fleshy, rounded, often knobbed
- Cobwebby when young
- Gills age rusty brown with spores
- Stem base enlarged or bulbous
- On soil in woods

CORTINARIUS, PP. 110–115

- Pale yellowish-brown spores
- Cap golden to orangy, mealy-powdery coating, veil remnants fringing edge
- Gills age cinnamon brown
- Ring large, flaring
- Stem buff; granular like cap
- On soil under conifers, hardwoods

TOGARIA, PP. 116–117

- Pale rusty-brown spores
- Cap tan to orange brown, rounded to flat, wrinkled
- Gills age rusty
- Ring large, white, movable, may disappear
- Stem dingy to tan; base enlarged
- On ground under conifers, hardwoods

ROZITES, PP. 116–117

- Yellow-brown spores
- Cap yellowish to brownish; rounded, becoming depressed; edge tightly inrolled
- Gills extend down stem; porelike at base; often bruise brown; easily separated from cap
- Stem may be off-center or absent
- Near or on wood

PAXILLUS, PP. 118–119

- Brownish-olive spores
- Cap rounded, becoming flat to upturned; velvety
- Looks like Bolete except for gills
- Gills extend down stem; bruise bluish
- On ground under conifers, hardwoods

PHYLLOPORUS, PP. 120–121

- Orangy-brown to red-brown spores
- Brightly colored, orange to yellowish
- Cap rounded, flattening in age
- Gills attached or extending down stem
- Often with cobwebby veil, ring
- On wood or buried wood

GYMNOPILUS, PP. 120–121

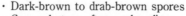

- Dark-brown to drab-brown spores
- Cap and stem often scaly, slimy
- Gills age color of spores
- Most species have ring
- Clustered on wood, decaying matter

PHOLIOTA, PP. 122–127

**I  Gills not attached to stem. Cap easily detached from stem.**

- Chocolate-brown spores
- Cap white to brown to gray brown
- Ring on stem
- Gills pinkish, aging chocolate brown
- No cup at base
- On ground

AGARICUS, PP. 128–139

**II  Gills attached to stem. Stem thin, different in structure from cap (tougher or more fragile), not easily detached from cap.**

- Purple-brown to chocolate-brown spores
- Very small
- Cap conic to flat, often with knob
- Cap edge incurved in youth
- Gills age brown or purplish
- Sometimes with ring
- Stem tall, thin, sometimes stains blue
- On dung, soil, wood debris

PSILOCYBE, PP. 138–139

**III  Gills attached to stem. Cap and stem of same structure, not easily separated.**

- Purplish-brown spores
- Cap bowl-shaped, often sulphur to reddish yellow
- Cap edge incurved when young
- Veil remnants on cap edge
- Rarely a ring
- Usually clustered on wood

NAEMATOLOMA, PP. 140–141

- Purple-brown spores
- Cap slimy when wet
- Ring on stem
- Not in clusters
- On manure, rich ground

STROPHARIA, PP. 142–143

**I   Gills not attached to stem. Cap easily detached from stem.**

- Black spores
- Cap oval to conic to bell-shaped
- Cap folded like umbrella against stem in youth
- Cap edge wrinkled or ribbed
- Gills dissolving into black, inky liquid
- Stem thin, easily detached from cap
- On wood, dung, humus, ground
COPRINUS, PP. 144–147

**II   Gills attached to stem. Stem thin, different in structure from cap (tougher or more fragile), not easily detached from cap.**

- Blackish spores
- Cap conic to bell-shaped, never flattened
- Gills pale, becoming mottled with spores
- Stem pale, thin, rigid
- On dung or manured grass
PANAEOLUS, PP. 148–149

**III   Gills attached to stem. Cap and stem of same structure, not easily separated**

- Brown-black spores, tinged purplish
- Small, fragile, dull-colored
- Cap conic to round to nearly flat
- Gills pale, aging dark
- Stem thin, fragile
- On wood, humus, grass
PSATHYRELLA, PP. 150–151

- Smoky-black spores
- Gills thick, far apart, extend down stem, age grayish
- Veil thin, hairy
- Under conifers
GOMPHIDIUS, PP. 152–155: WHITE FLESH, SLIMY CAP AND VEIL
CHROOGOMPHUS, PP. 152–153, 156–157: COLORED FLESH, DRY TO STICKY CAP AND VEIL

# GILLED MUSHROOMS

**AMANITA** This famous—or infamous—genus includes the most poisonous mushrooms in the world. It is imperative that you learn to avoid them; they cause the majority of mushroom fatalities. Fortunately, they are easy to recognize. Always check for these 4 characteristics: (1) In the young button stage, when it is a small, round ball, an *Amanita* is completely enclosed in an outer membrane—the universal veil. As the cap expands and the stem elongates, this veil breaks. If it is tough, it simply splits open, and the mushroom grows through the crack, the membrane remaining at the base of the stem as a conspicuous cup enveloping the stem base. If the membrane is fragile, it fragments, leaving pieces sticking to the top of the cap plus ridges or grooves on the stem base. If you pull a mushroom out of the ground, this membrane might be left behind and a crucial clue overlooked. Thus it is necessary to always dig up the entire mushroom base, scrutinizing the surrounding soil for any telltale tissue that would alert you. (2) On most species, a second membrane—the partial veil—covers and protects the young gills, extending from cap edge to stem. As the cap expands, the veil breaks away from the cap edge, remaining on the stem, often hanging around it like a little skirt. This is called a ring. Not all *Amanitas* have a ring. (3) Gills are white or palely colored; they are not attached to the stem; cap and stem are easily separated. (4) Spores are white. Representative species are described here. *Limacella* also has white spores and gills not attached to stem but is very slimy—so slippery you can hardly pick it up. The only other genus having a cup at the base is *Volvariella,* but it has pink spores and no ring.

EDIBILITY: A few species are considered edible in Europe, but the situation is very different here in North America where many more species flourish, including poisonous species closely related to edible ones, and many that are little known. Thus the rule in North America is DO NOT EAT ANY *AMANITAS:* to do so is playing mushroom roulette.

*Amanita verna;* destroying angel: White spores. Deadly poisonous.
CAP: 3–5 in. broad. Pure white with no veil remains. Rounded, aging flat. Smooth. Slimy. Edge unfurrowed.
GILLS: White. Crowded. Not attached to stem.
VEIL: White, membranous, leaving skirtlike ring, may almost disappear.
STEM: 4–10 in. tall. White, swollen base encased in loose cup.
WHERE & WHEN: Scattered under hardwoods, mixed woods, in clearings, lawns; spring, summer in eastern, southern U.S., Pacific Northwest.
*A. virosa:* Very similar but growing in summer, fall, eastern North America, Pacific Coast. Deadly poisonous.
*A. bisporigera:* Similar but more slender, smaller; summer, eastern and southern U.S. Deadly poisonous.

*Amanita phalloides;* death cap: White spores. Deadly poisonous.
CAP: 3–6 in. broad. Yellowish green to greenish, to dingy; paler on edge. Round, slimy. Smooth with no veil remains. Edge not furrowed.
GILLS: White. Close together. Not attached to stem.
VEIL: Membranous, leaving large skirtlike ring hanging around stem.
STEM: 3–5½ in. tall. White. Smooth. Encased in conspicuous cup.
WHERE & WHEN: Alone or in groups under oak and conifers; summer, fall.

# AMANITA

GENUS CHARACTERISTICS
· White spores
· Cap may have scales or warts
· Cap edge may be grooved
· Gills white to pale, not attached to stem
· With or without ring on stem
· Cup or remnants at stem base
· On ground

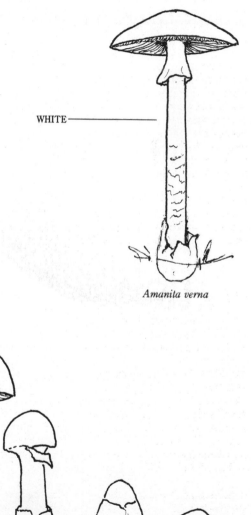

WHITE

*Amanita verna*

GREENISH

WHITE

WHITE

*Amanita phalloides*

*Amanita pantherina:* White spores. Poisonous, sometimes with hallucinogenic properties.

CAP: 2–5 (12) in. broad. Pale tan to dark brown with whitish soft patches and warts, remains of the universal veil. Usually yellowish to buff at edge. Round, aging nearly flat with furrowed edge, often fringed with veil fragments. Slimy. Flesh white except buff just under surface.

GILLS: White. Crowded with finely scalloped edges. Not attached to stem.

VEIL: Membranous, leaving a series of regular patches on cap edge and membranous, hanging ring on stem.

STEM: 2–5 in. tall. White, nearly smooth above ring, hairy below. Enlarging to egg-shaped base. No cup but a collarlike band just above bulb and a thin cottony layer on bulb that may rub off in dirt.

WHERE & WHEN: Several to many under conifers and mixed woods; spring–fall.

*Amanita muscaria:* White spores. Poisonous, sometimes with hallucinogenic properties.

CAP: 3–9 (12) in. broad. Several different colored varieties, ranging from red to orange to yellow to white. All adorned with whitish patches or warts of veil tissue. Round, flattening in age to upturned. Edge furrowed. Slimy. Flesh white.

GILLS: White to creamy with minutely hairy edges. Crowded. Not attached to stem.

VEIL: White, membranous, fragile, leaving ring on stem or remnants hanging from cap edge.

STEM: 3–6 in. tall. White covered with silky hairs. Enlarging toward bulbous base. No cup but 2 or 3 ridges above bulb.

WHERE & WHEN: Scattered under hardwoods, conifers; summer–fall.

*Amanita brunnescens:* White spores. Poisonous.

CAP: 1–4 (6) in. broad. Dark grayish brown, sometimes aging nearly white. Usually adorned with white cottony patches. Round, aging flat. Edge faintly furrowed. Slimy. Flesh white, staining reddish brown.

GILLS: White. Close together. Not attached to stem.

VEIL: White, membranous, breaking irregularly and hanging in shreds from cap, sometimes pulling away from stem entirely.

STEM: 2–5 in. tall. White. Smooth above ring, hairy below. Enlarging downward to large oval bulb, which is split or cleft. No cup but veil remains sometimes adhere in irregular patches or form an obscure collar around top of bulb.

WHERE & WHEN: Scattered under hardwoods and mixed woods; summer, fall in eastern North America.

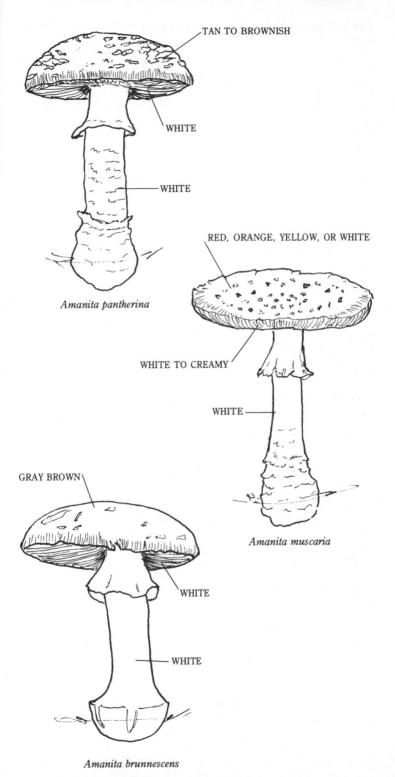

TAN TO BROWNISH

WHITE

WHITE

*Amanita pantherina*

RED, ORANGE, YELLOW, OR WHITE

WHITE TO CREAMY

WHITE

*Amanita muscaria*

GRAY BROWN

WHITE

WHITE

*Amanita brunnescens*

*Amanita caesarea;* Caesar's mushroom: White spores. Edible but don't.
CAP: 2–6 (12) in. broad. Orange to orange red, shading to bright yellow on edge. Conical, aging rounded, sometimes with low knob. Smooth with no warts or veil fragments. Edge with long furrows. Slimy. Flesh white, but yellowish just under cap, firm.
GILLS: Yellow. Close together. Not attached to stem.
VEIL: Yellow to orange, soft, membranous, leaving skirtlike ring.
STEM: 3–8 in. tall. Yellow. Smooth. Hairless to finely cottony. Dry. Hollow. Base encased in large white, membranous cup.
WHERE & WHEN: Scattered or in rings under hardwoods; spring in eastern, southern, central, southwestern, and Pacific states.

*Amanita calyptroderma:* White spores. Edible but don't. Eaten on West Coast but only by experts who know what they're doing.
CAP: 2–12 in. broad. Yellow to orangy, aging pale. Round, aging nearly flat. Furrowed on edge. Slimy. Smooth. Usually with large white, felty skullcaplike patch on top. Flesh white, soft.
GILLS: Creamy white or yellowish. Close. Not attached to stem.
VEIL: White, leaving yellowish thin ring.
STEM: 2–4 in. tall. Creamy. Base enclosed in rigid, white felty cup.
WHERE & WHEN: Scattered in mixed woods, grassy edges of forest; late summer, fall, into winter, along Pacific Coast.

*Amanita rubescens:* White spores. Edible but don't. Too many poisonous look-alikes in North America.
CAP: 2–6 in. broad. Dingy reddish brown with whitish to pale-red scales and warts, often clustered along edge. Round or sometimes knobbed with slightly furrowed edge. Flesh white, staining reddish, soft.
GILLS: White, stained pink to red. Crowded. Slightly attached to stem.
VEIL: Pallid, staining reddish. Fragile, leaving irregular ring.
STEM: 2–8 in. tall. Tinged dingy reddish above ring, usually with reddish stains below. Enlarging to swollen base. No cup but only reddish tissue adhering to bulb or surrounding dirt.
WHERE & WHEN: Alone or in groups under hardwoods, spring–fall, eastern North America.

*Amanita vaginata* (*Amanitopsis vaginata*): White spores. Edible but don't. Easily confused with poisonous species whose warts or ring have worn off.
CAP: 2–4 in. broad. Gray brown to brown. Bell-shaped, aging flat, often with small knob. No warts or veil remains. Deeply furrowed on edge. Slimy. Hairless. Flesh white, soft, thin.
GILLS: White, close, aging fairly well separated. Not attached to stem.
VEIL: Absent.
STEM: 3–8 in. tall. White, slender. Smooth or with flattened hairs over center. Enlarging to swollen base deep in soil, encased in white cup.
WHERE & WHEN: Alone to many under hardwoods, conifers; spring–fall.
*A. fulva:* Orange-capped variant. Mostly in eastern forests. Edible but don't.
*var. alba:* White cap.
*var. livida:* Gray to livid cap.
*A. inaurata* (*Amanitopsis strangulata*): No ring; brownish-black cap, fading to brownish gray; gray warts. Edible but don't.

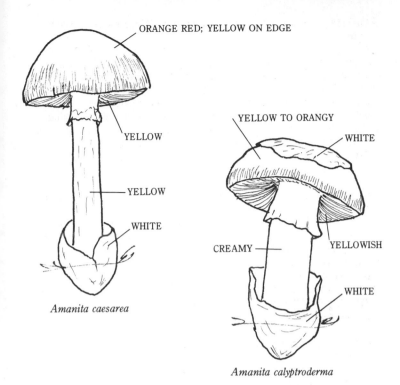

ORANGE RED; YELLOW ON EDGE

YELLOW

YELLOW

WHITE

*Amanita caesarea*

YELLOW TO ORANGY

WHITE

CREAMY

YELLOWISH

WHITE

*Amanita calyptroderma*

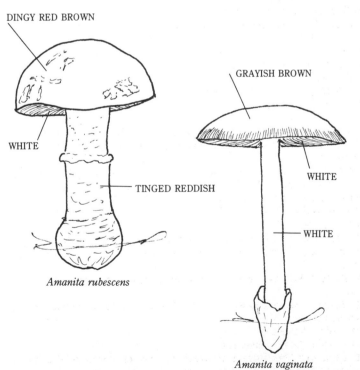

DINGY RED BROWN

WHITE

TINGED REDDISH

*Amanita rubescens*

GRAYISH BROWN

WHITE

WHITE

*Amanita vaginata*

**LEPIOTA** Four characteristics to check: (1) rough scales on cap, formed when cap expands, splitting its outer layer into irregular patches; (2) ring on stem, left behind when cap breaks away from the stem in the button stage; usually becomes movable in age; (3) smooth, bulbous base, but no cup; (4) gills not attached to the stem.

In the above characteristics, *Lepiotas* resemble the poisonous *Amanitas*, except: (1) *Lepiota* scales are an integral part of the cap and difficult to remove, while *Amanita* scales are easily rubbed off because they are not part of the cap but remains of the membrane that enclosed the entire mushroom in the button stage; (2) the *Lepiota* ring is sturdy and movable in older specimens; the *Amanita* ring is fixed and fragile; (3) both *Lepiota* and *Amanita* stems have bulbous bases, but the *Amanita* base is encased in a cuplike structure or bears the flaky, scaly, or ridged remnants of one; the *Lepiota* base is smooth with no sign of a cup. Be sure to dig up the entire mushroom base! One other difference: *Lepiota* gills turn brown on cooking; *Amanita* gills remain white.
EDIBILITY: The larger *Lepiotas* rank among the best edibles except for the green-spored *Chlorophyllum molybdites* (*Lepiota morgani*), page 36, which is very poisonous to some people. Always make a spore print before eating any large *Lepiota* to make sure it is white. The smaller *Lepiotas* are poisonous or untested, so they must not be eaten. *Lepiotas* are best cooked quickly to preserve flavor and texture. Discard the tough, stringy stems. Some cooks say to remove the scales; others say not.

• Baste caps with melted butter, salt, pepper. Broil gill sides up for a moment. Turn gill sides down, broil for another moment.
• Cut cap into long strips and sauté briefly in butter.
• Put pat of butter inside each cap; bake in covered, buttered pan.
• Dip caps in beaten egg, then in rolled, seasoned dry bread crumbs; fry.
• Stuff young bell-shaped caps with meat or vegetable stuffing. Bake.
• Chop or slice caps and use in poultry stuffing or meat loaf.

*Lepiota procera* (*Leucoagaricus procerus*); parasol *Lepiota*, tall *Lepiota*: White spores. Edible, choice.
CAP: 3–12+ in. Grayish-brown to reddish-brown surface breaks into scales as cap expands, exposing white flesh beneath, except center, which remains brown and smooth. Egg-shaped in youth, expanding into a parasol with low knob at center. Flesh white, soft, thick.
GILLS: White, becoming pinkish to brownish with minutely hairy edges. Close together, not attached to stem but with clear space between stem and gills.
VEIL: White, thick, soft. Leaving ragged, thick ring, movable when old.
STEM: 5–10 in. tall. Grayish brown. Felty, breaking into irregular scaly marking with white flesh showing in cracks. Enlarging gradually down to bulbous base, covered with white threads (mycelium). Hollow.
WHERE & WHEN: Single to scattered in open grassy areas, gardens, meadows, open woods; summer, fall, eastern half of North America.
LOOK-ALIKES: Poisonous *Chlorophyllum molybdites*'s stem is smooth, shorter and stouter than *L. procera*'s stem, which is tall, thin, rough, mottled.
*L. brunnea:* Very similar but with stouter, grooved stem; dingier color; thicker, upturned scales on cap. Edible.

# LEPIOTA

GENUS CHARACTERISTICS
- White spores
- Small to very large
- Cap dry, scaly
- Gills not attached to stem
- Ring sometimes movable, may disappear
- No cup, but base may be enlarged
- On ground

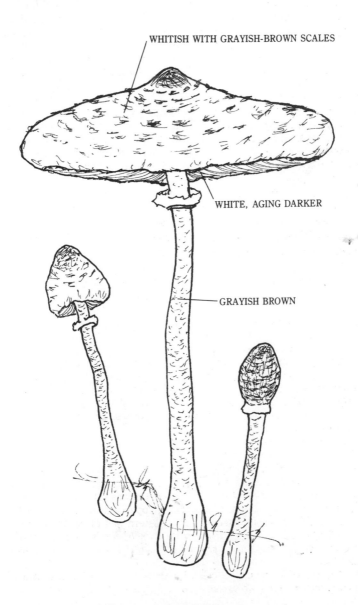

WHITISH WITH GRAYISH-BROWN SCALES

WHITE, AGING DARKER

GRAYISH BROWN

*Lepiota procera*

*Lepiota rachodes* (*Leucoagaricus rachodes, Leucocoprinus rachodes, Macrolepiota rachodes*); shaggy *Lepiota*: White spores. Edible. Look for coarsely scaly cap; large, thick ring; large, bulbous base; red staining of flesh.

CAP: 2½–6 (8) in. broad. Brownish to reddish gray, breaking up into upturned scales (shaggier than *L. procera*), exposing dingy, white flesh underneath. Nearly spherical, becoming rounded, finally flat with low center knob that remains smooth and brown. Flesh whitish, bruising orangy to red.

GILLS: White, bruising yellowish to pinkish. Not attached. Close.

VEIL: White, leaving two-layered hairy, cottony ring, movable in age.

STEM: Grayish white, bruising red brown. Gradually enlarging to bulbous base.

WHERE & WHEN: Single to groups in grassy places; summer, fall.

LOOK-ALIKES: Very hard to distinguish from poisonous *Chlorophyllum molybdites,* especially young buttons. Be sure to make spore print.

*Lepiota americana:* Creamy spores. Edible, cooked; poisonous, raw. Entire mushroom tends to redden when handled, in cooking, in age.

CAP: 1–4+ in. broad. Dull reddish brown, breaking into large scales except on center knob, exposing whitish flesh beneath. Egg-shaped, becoming conic to rounded. Edge more or less ribbed. Flesh white, reddening when bruised.

GILLS: White, bruising red. Not attached to stem. Close together.

VEIL: White, membranous. Leaving large membranous ring, often disappearing.

STEM: 2–5 in. long. White, bruising reddish, varying from stout to slender. Usually broadest above base, tapering both up and down.

WHERE & WHEN: Alone or in clusters in grassy areas; summer, fall.

*Lepiota barssii:* White spores. Edible.

CAP: 4–9 in. broad. Whitish to grayish to brownish with many small close-pressed scales. Dry. Rounded, aging flat to upturned. Flesh white, aging grayish.

GILLS: White. Not attached to stem. Close together.

VEIL: White, membranous. Leaving large white ring.

STEM: 4–9 in. tall. White, silky, not larger at base.

WHERE & WHEN: In groups in meadows, straw piles, manure heaps; summer, fall.

*Lepiota acutesquamosa* (*L. friesii*); sharp-scaled *Lepiota*: White to pale-cream spores. Edible. Recognized by its rusty-brown color, spiny scales.

CAP: 2–5 in. broad. Pale brownish to rusty brown, covered with darker, sometimes black-tipped, erect, pointed warts or scales that gradually fall off, leaving scarlike patches with paler flesh between. Rounded, expanding to almost flat, sometimes with low knob. Flesh white, soft.

GILLS: White, aging creamy to brownish. Minutely saw-toothed edges. Not attached to stem. Very crowded.

VEIL: White, somewhat cottony. Leaving white membranous ring hanging loosely around stem, with brownish scales on lower surface. Sometimes disappearing.

STEM: 2–5 in. tall. Dingy, covered with cottony fibers and a few scales. Bulbous at base, sometimes tapering slightly to top.

WHERE & WHEN: In groups on ground or on decayed wood in woods, gardens, greenhouses, on sawdust; summer, fall.

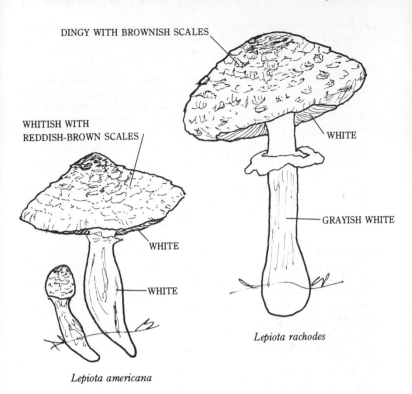

DINGY WITH BROWNISH SCALES

WHITISH WITH
REDDISH-BROWN SCALES

WHITE

WHITE

WHITE

GRAYISH WHITE

*Lepiota americana*

*Lepiota rachodes*

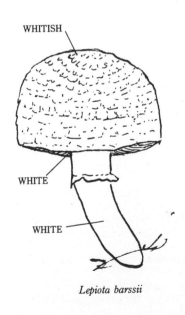

WHITISH

WHITE

WHITE

*Lepiota barssii*

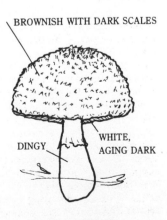

BROWNISH WITH DARK SCALES

DINGY

WHITE,
AGING DARK

*Lepiota acutesquamosa*

*Lepiota cepaestipes:* White to pale-cream spores. Edible, good. Look for whitish mealy caps, growing in graceful clusters.
CAP: 1–3 in. broad. Whitish, aging slightly pinkish; center sometimes tinged brownish; powdery with soft mealy scales, whitish to brownish. Conic to bell-shaped. Edge ribbed. Flesh white, soft.
GILLS: Whitish. Crowded together. Not attached to stem.
VEIL: White, hairy. Leaving thin, white ring. Movable. Disappearing.
STEM: 2–5 in. long. White, turning yellowish when handled. Varying from smooth and hairless to mealy with downy hairs. Enlarged at base into small bulb, arising from dense mass of white, hairlike threads (mycelium). Often curved and drooping.
WHERE & WHEN: Large graceful clusters on decomposing matter—sawdust, compost, rotting wood; spring–fall, eastern North America.

*Lepiota helveola:* White spores. Deadly poisonous, containing amanitin toxins.
CAP: ¾–2½ in. broad. Brownish, fragmenting into scales, revealing paler flesh beneath, except over center, which remains brown and smooth. Becoming reddish ocher after gathering. Rounded, then broadening, splitting along the edge, often becoming upturned; often with center knob. Flesh white to pinkish, becoming rosy when exposed to air.
GILLS: Whitish, aging creamy. Close together. Not attached to stem.
VEIL: White, fragile. Leaving slight white ring, often disappearing.
STEM: Color of cap. With fine soft hairs, slightly streaked at base. Hollow.
WHERE & WHEN: Scattered in grassy areas; summer, fall.

*Lepiota cristata:* White spores. Rated as edible in old books, but now known to be poisonous.
CAP: ½–2 in. broad. Dull reddish to reddish brown at first, breaking into small reddish-brown scales in concentric circles, finer toward edge, exposing white flesh below, except center remains reddish brown, smooth. Oval, aging nearly flat with center knob. Edge ribbed. Flesh white, thin.
GILLS: White. Close together. Not attached to stem. Edges minutely wavy.
VEIL: White, fragile. Leaving small, soft, white ring, often tinged pinkish, which breaks up and disappears.
STEM: 1–2 in. long. Whitish or tinged dingy pinkish. Smooth or downy.
WHERE & WHEN: Usually in groups in grassy areas; summer, fall.

*Lepiota clypeolaria:* White spores. Poisonous.
CAP: 1–3 in. broad. Varying from yellowish to rusty brownish, breaking up into raggedy patches and erect upturned scales, exposing creamy, hairy undersurface. Center knob remains smooth, dark. Scaliness disappears in age. Edge ribbed, fringed with veil remnants, often heavy. Dry. Egg-shaped, becoming rounded, aging nearly flat with low center knob. Flesh white, soft.
GILLS: White, covered with whitish to buff woolly hairs. Not attached to stem. Close together.
VEIL: White, cottony strands. Leaving raggedy, soft, white, indefinite hairy ring, disappearing in age.
STEM: 1½–4 in. tall. Whitish, covered with cottony, cap-color fibrils that tend to disappear. Enlarging slightly toward base. Hollow.
WHERE & WHEN: Single to numerous or in groups in open woods (mostly conifers) or fields; late summer, fall.

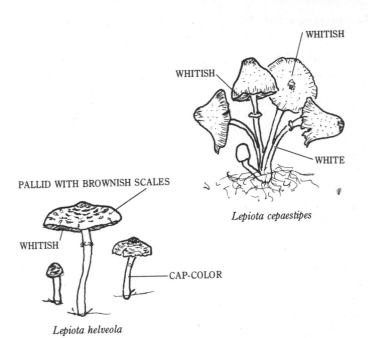

WHITISH

WHITISH

WHITE

*Lepiota cepaestipes*

PALLID WITH BROWNISH SCALES

WHITISH

CAP-COLOR

*Lepiota helveola*

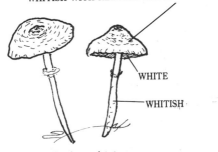

WHITISH WITH REDDISH-BROWN SCALES

WHITE

WHITISH

*Lepiota cristata*

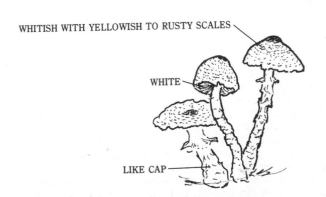

WHITISH WITH YELLOWISH TO RUSTY SCALES

WHITE

LIKE CAP

*Lepiota clypeolaria*

The following two species were formerly in *Lepiota* but have been reclassified into genera of their own.

**LEUCOAGARICUS**   Like *Lepiota* but with smooth cap and stem. (Some mycologists rank several other *Lepiotas* in this genus too.)

***Leucoagaricus naucina*** (*Lepiota naucina, L. naucinoides*); white *Lepiota*, smooth *Lepiota*: White spores. Unlike *Lepiota* with their shaggy, spotted caps, this species is white and smooth with the texture of a kid glove. Edible with caution since causes gastric upsets in some people. Never eat the gray form, sometimes densely covered with minute gray scales, but resembling the white form in all other ways.
CAP: 2–4+ in. broad. Dull white or gray, sometimes tinged yellowish or smoky at center, aging tannish. Egg-shaped at first, then rounded, aging nearly flat with low center knob. Dry, smooth, unpolished, hairless or occasionally minutely scaly. Flesh white, soft, thick.
GILLS: White, aging pinkish to grayish wine. Close together. Not attached to stem; rounded near stem.
VEIL: White, cottony, rolls back on itself to form stiff, collarlike ring with double-fringed edge. Sometimes partially disappearing.
STEM: 2–5 in. long. Cap-color. Smooth, hairless, gradually enlarging to bulbous base. No cup.
WHERE & WHEN: Solitary or scattered in groups in open grassy areas; late summer, fall.
LOOK-ALIKES: Beware mistaking poisonous white *Amanitas* for *L. naucina*. The latter has smooth cap, no cuplike structure at stem base. *Amanitas* usually have warts on their caps or ribbed cap edge, and evidence of a cup or wrapper encasing stem base. Dig up entire base to make sure it has no outer covering. And be sure you can identify the *Amanitas* before attempting *L. naucina*.

*Green Spores*

**CHLOROPHYLLUM**   Looks like and often mistaken for one of the large *Lepiotas*, except *Chlorophyllum* has greenish spores while *Lepiotas* are white spored.

***Chlorophyllum molybdites*** (*Lepiota molybdites, L. morgani*): This is the only mushroom with green spores; let them warn you that it is violently poisonous to some people, even in small quantities.
CAP: 3–11+ in. across. Buff to cinnamon at first, breaking up into patchy scales, revealing white flesh underneath. Egg-shaped when young, then remaining rounded without the center knob typical of most *Lepiotas*, sometimes becoming depressed in center. Fleshy, soft. Dry. Flesh white, aging pinkish.
GILLS: White when young, becoming dull green as spores mature. Close together. Not attached to stem.
VEIL: White, cottony. Leaving thick, white, firm ring, discoloring brownish on underside. Fringed. Often movable.
STEM: 4–10 in. high. White to grayish with brownish stains over base. Gradually enlarging to bulbous base. Firm, smooth.
WHERE & WHEN: Singly or scattered on ground in open grassy areas, open woods, sometimes in large fairy rings or arcs; spring–fall.
LOOK-ALIKES: Easily mistaken for *Lepiota procera, L. rachodes, L. brunnea*, especially in button stage. Be sure to make spore print before eating any large *Lepiota*; if it's green, you have *C. molybdites*, which can be dangerously poisonous to some people.

## LEUCOAGARICUS

GENUS CHARACTERISTICS
· Like Lepiota but with smooth cap, stem

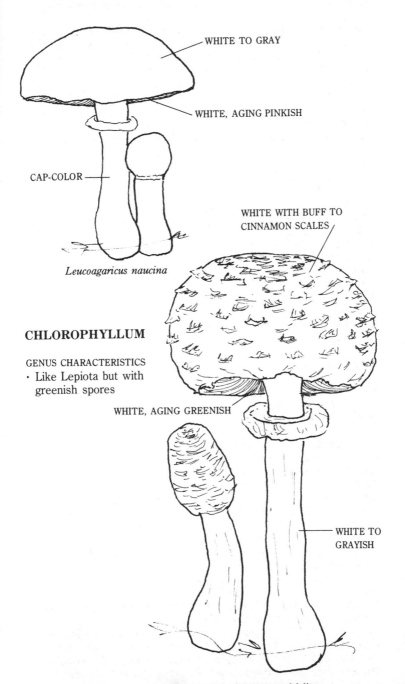

WHITE TO GRAY

WHITE, AGING PINKISH

CAP-COLOR

*Leucoagaricus naucina*

WHITE WITH BUFF TO
CINNAMON SCALES

## CHLOROPHYLLUM

GENUS CHARACTERISTICS
· Like Lepiota but with
  greenish spores

WHITE, AGING GREENISH

WHITE TO
GRAYISH

*Chlorophyllum molybdites*

**COLLYBIA AND FLAMMULINA** These frequently encountered mushrooms have soft, rounded caps with smooth, often moist surface, inrolled edge in youth, often aging flattened to upturned. Gills are attached to the stem or notched where they join it; never extend down it. Stems are brittle or fibrous and gristly, often with very soft center, of different structure from cap, but confluent with it. No ring or veil. Grow singly to clustered on humus, leaf mold, needles, rotted wood. Sometimes hard to distinguish from white-spored *Marasmius* and *Mycena*, except *Marasmius* have leathery caps that revive after drying if remoistened, although a few *Collybias* tend to do so also. *Mycenas* have fragile, small, conic to rounded caps that do not expand, lie straight against stem in youth.

EDIBILITY: Relatively bland except for well-flavored *Flammulina velutipes*. Discard tough, fibrous stems; cook quickly by sautéing or broiling; or add to soups, stews; or dip in beaten egg, bread crumbs, fry.

*Collybia dryophila;* oak-loving *dryophila*: White spores. Edible, except Orson K. Miller, Jr., reports it is poisonous to some.
CAP: 1–3 in. broad. Varying widely from yellowish to brownish to reddish brown, usually light band around edge, fading in age. Rounded, then flattening in age with upturned wavy edge, center often depressed. Moist but not slimy when wet; drying silky. Smooth. Hairless. Flesh white, thin.
GILLS: Whitish, aging buff. Crowded together. Usually rounded at stem, barely touching stem.
STEM: 1–4 in. tall. Cap-color or paler. Slightly flattened. Sometimes with swollen base, with matted strands of white threads (mycelium).
WHERE & WHEN: Several or in groups in leaf mold, deep humus, usually under hardwoods, conifers; spring–fall.

*Collybia butyracea;* buttery *Collybia*: Pale-buff spores. Edible. Similar to *C. dryophila,* except has buff spores, more irregular.
CAP: ½–3 in. broad. Bay brown in youth, fading to dingy pinkish buff. "Buttery" sheen and feeling. Rounded, expanding in age with center knob, upturned, irregular edge. Watery, soft in wet weather. Flesh white, thick.
GILLS: White. Uneven edges. Close together. Notched where they join stem.
STEM: 1–3 in. tall. Whitish or paler than cap. Slightly grooved. Hairless, except slightly downy toward base.
WHERE & WHEN: Single to scattered to many under conifers, particularly pine; summer, fall; wet winter weather in South.

*Collybia radicata* (*Oudemansiella radicata, Mucidula radicata*); rooting *Collybia*: White spores. Edible.
CAP: 1–6 in. broad. Whitish to smoky to brown, darker and wrinkled in center. Rounded, aging nearly flat often with low knob. Smooth. Hairless. Slimy when wet. Flesh white, thin.
GILLS: Pure white. Shiny. Uneven lengths, touching and not touching stem. Somewhat far apart.
STEM: 2–10 in. or more aboveground with long, tapering underground root, 6–8+ in. deep. White at top, cap-color below. Twisted, grooved.
WHERE & WHEN: Alone or scattered in hardwoods; late spring–fall.
*C. longipes:* Similar but smaller with dry, velvety, dark-brown cap, pallid stem with dark-brown scales, slender taproot; on rotted wood. Edible.

## COLLYBIA AND FLAMMULINA

GENERA CHARACTERISTICS
· White to buff spores
· Cap soft, smooth, moist
· Cap edge inrolled in youth
· Gills attached or notched at stem
· Stem brittle to fibrous
· On humus, needles, rotted wood

WHITISH, AGING BUFF

YELLOWISH TO BROWNISH

CAP-COLOR OR PALER

PALE EDGE

*Collybia dryophila*

BROWN, AGING PINKISH BUFF

WHITE

WHITISH

*Collybia butyracea*

WHITISH TO SMOKY TO BROWN

WHITE

WHITE

*Collybia radicata*

Sept. '89
Leuvenumse bos

Porseleinzwam

*Collybia maculata;* rust-spotted *Collybia*: Edible, poor. Creamy spores.
CAP: ¾–4 in. broad. Whitish, becoming spotted with orangy-yellow to reddish-brown stains; sometimes aging entirely orange yellow to rusty. Rounded, becoming expanded with wavy edge. Felty. Flesh white, firm.
GILLS: Whitish with reddish-brown stains. Notched where they join stem or almost not touching. Crowded together.
STEM: 2–4 in. tall. White, spotted like cap. Fibrous, slightly grooved, thickening at center. Hairy base, extending into soil.
WHERE & WHEN: In groups, rings or clusters on ground in woods, especially pines; summer, fall.

*Collybia confluens* (*Marasmius confluens*): White spores. Edible.
CAP: 1–2 in. broad. Reddish brown to pale brown when moist, drying buff, grayish, or whitish. Rounded, aging flat to slightly depressed with wavy edge. Sometimes minutely scaly at center. Shrivels in dry weather but tends to revive when moistened, like *Marasmius*.
GILLS: Whitish. Almost not attached to stem. Crowded together.
STEM: 2–4 in. tall. Reddish brown covered with frosty bloomlike hairs. Tough, fibrous. Hollow in age. Web of white threads (mycelium) at base.
WHERE & WHEN: Many to clustered, among fallen leaves; summer, fall.

*Collybia acervata;* tufted *Collybia*: White spores. Edible, poor.
CAP: ½–2 in. broad. Brown to reddish brown, fading as it dries, finally nearly whitish overall. Rounded, aging flat to upturned, edge slightly ribbed when wet, wavy. Smooth. Moist but not slimy when wet. Flesh white, sometimes tinged reddish brown, thin.
GILLS: White, aging pale reddish brown. Notched where they join stem. Close together.
STEM: 2–4 in. tall. Shiny brown at top, purplish brown below. Dry. Hollow. Bases fused, covered with white threads (mycelium).
WHERE & WHEN: In dense clusters of 50 or more in deep humus, rotting or buried wood, particularly conifers; summer.
*C. abundans* and *C. familia:* Similar, both densely clustered, but lighter color than *C. acervata*. *C. abundans* is pale gray brown with darker center, not changing color; whitish stem; cap depressed in center. *C. familia* is buff brown when moist, drying creamy with grayish to pallid stem; cap center seldom depressed. Both edible.

*Flammulina velutipes* (*Collybia velutipes*); velvet foot, velvet stem, winter mushroom: White spores. Edible, good. Look for slimy cap, velvety-brown stem, growing in clusters, often in cold weather.
CAP: 1–3 in. broad. Yellowish to orangy to reddish brown, paler toward edge. Rounded, aging nearly flat with upturned or wavy, ribbed edge. Slimy, shining. Flesh white to yellowish, thick, thinning at edge.
GILLS: Whitish to yellowish. Edges minutely hairy. Fairly well separated. Notched where they join stem.
STEM: 1–4 in. tall. Yellowish tan at top, dense velvety brown to blackish brown below. Tough. Curved. Slightly narrowed at base. Many fused together.
WHERE & WHEN: Usually in dense clusters, on dead and living trees or on ground containing decaying wood; in cool weather, surviving hard frosts; spring, cool summers, fall, winter thaws.

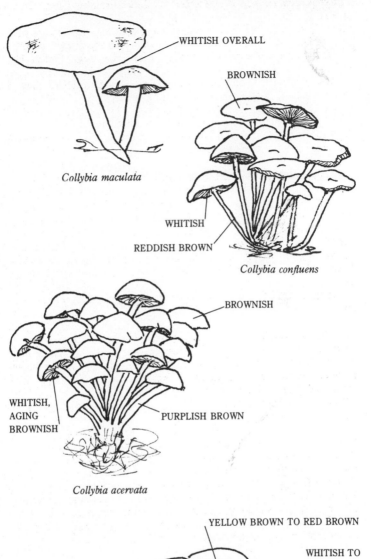

WHITISH OVERALL

BROWNISH

*Collybia maculata*

WHITISH

REDDISH BROWN

*Collybia confluens*

BROWNISH

WHITISH,
AGING
BROWNISH

PURPLISH BROWN

*Collybia acervata*

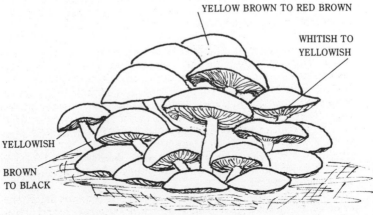

YELLOW BROWN TO RED BROWN

WHITISH TO
YELLOWISH

YELLOWISH

BROWN
TO BLACK

*Flammulina velutipes*

**MARASMIUS**  Small, rather tough, leathery mushrooms; revive after drying when placed in water or in rain. Stems thin, pliant. Gills attached to stem or notched where they join it, sometimes almost appearing free from stem. Grow in grass, leaves, needles.

EDIBILITY: Most species are too small and fragile to interest the pothunter, but *M. oreades* is a favorite. Discard tough stems, cook slowly for 20 minutes with butter and a little liquid or add to stews, soups, vegetables, sauces, gravies. A good substitute for *Armillaria ponderosa* in Oriental cooking. Excellent dried for winter use.

*Marasmius oreades;* fairy-ring mushroom, Scotch bonnets: White to buff spores. Edible. Look for "bonnet"-shaped cap, tough stem with whitish down.

CAP: 1–2 in. broad. Creamy to reddish tan when moist, fading to whitish when dry. Rounded, aging bell-shaped to flat. Domelike knob at center, irregular edge like a hat brim. Edge somewhat ribbed in age. Dry. Smooth. Hairless. Flesh white or pale tan, thin. Dried caps revive in water.

GILLS: Creamy white to buff, paler than cap. Well separated, long and short lengths intermixed, notched where they join stem, nearly free of stem.

STEM: 1–3 in. tall. Buff at top, darker brown at bottom, covered with white down near base. Slender, tough.

WHERE & WHEN: In groups, fairy rings on lawns, pastures, golf courses; spring–fall. Avoid any that have been sprayed by weed-killers, etc.

LOOK-ALIKES: Beware similar grass-inhabiting mushrooms with pink spores (*Entoloma*), black spores (*Panaeolus*), brown spores (*Galerina*), rusty spores (*Hebeloma*), white spores (small *Clitocybes*).

*Marasmius scorodonius:* White spores. Edible, smells and tastes of garlic when crushed. Use to flavor bland species or to season roasts, gravies.

CAP: ¼–¾ in. broad. Tan, tinged reddish at first, with white edge, aging whitish overall. Rounded, aging flat with wavy edge. Wrinkled. Flesh whitish, thin.

GILLS: Whitish to creamy. Attached to stem. Widely spaced.

STEM: 1–2 in. long. White at top, brownish to black below. Smooth.

WHERE & WHEN: In groups on debris under trees; summer, fall.

# MARASMIUS

GENUS CHARACTERISTICS
· White to buff spores
· Cap dry, leathery
· Dried cap revives when moistened
· Cap edge incurved in youth
· Gills attached or notched at stem
· Stem tough, pliable
· In grass, leaves, needles

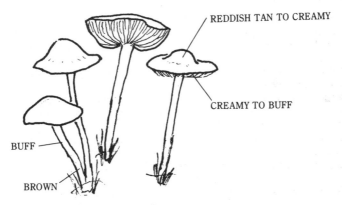

REDDISH TAN TO CREAMY

CREAMY TO BUFF

BUFF

BROWN

*Marasmius oreades*

REDDISH TAN, AGING WHITISH

WHITE TO CREAMY

WHITE

BROWNISH TO BLACK

*Marasmius scorodonius*

**TRICHOLOMA** A large genus of difficult-to-identify species with no outstanding characteristics. They are medium to large with (1) rounded caps that may flatten in age, (2) fleshy stems not easily separable from cap, (3) nonwaxy gills that are attached to the stem, usually notched where they join it, (4) white spores, (5) no ring or cup, (6) growing on ground, often abundant in conifers in the fall (species growing on wood are *Tricholomopsis*). If gills extend down stem, check *Clitocybe*. If gills are waxy when rubbed, check *Hygrophorus*. If there is a ring on the stem or cup at the base, check *Amanita*. If stem is brittle and gristly, breaking with a snap, check *Melanoleuca*.

EDIBILITY: This is a potentially dangerous genus because it has a few poisonous species that look very appetizing and tempting to the pot-hunter. The rule, as outlined by Alexander H. Smith, is to avoid any gray- to white-gilled mushroom with gray, bluish-gray, or dark brownish-gray hairy cap. The edible species are good sautéed, creamed, in soup, or in any *Agaricus* recipe—but be positive of your identification!

*Tricholoma flavovirens* (*T. equestre*): White spores. Edible, good.
CAP: 2–4 in. broad. Pale to canary yellow, sometimes tinged greenish. Often dotted with reddish-brown scales over center; young caps may be dotted overall. Rounded with inrolled margin, aging nearly flat to slightly upturned. Slimy. Smooth. Flesh white, except yellow just beneath cap surface, firm.
GILLS: Yellow. Close together. Notched where they join stem.
STEM: 1–4 in. tall. Whitish to pale yellowish. Dry. Solid. Usually hairless. Often curved. Sometimes enlarged at base.
WHERE & WHEN: Alone to scattered or in clumps on mossy or sandy ground under mixed conifers-hardwoods, or in coastal sand dunes; late summer, fall to frost, eastern North America.
LOOK-ALIKES: *Amanita phalloides*, the death cap, has been tragically mistaken for *T. flavovirens*.
*T. sulphureum:* Similar but sulphur-yellow cap, gills, and stem, strong disagreeable odor of coal-tar gas. Poisonous.

*Tricholoma portentosum:* White spores. Edible (remove slimy coating).
CAP: 2–5 in. broad. Gray with brownish or purplish tint, nearly black in center. Streaked with black fibers. Slimy. Smooth. Flesh white.
GILLS: White, aging grayish to yellowish. Not close. Notched at stem.
STEM: 2–5 in. tall. White. Slightly ribbed with clusters of fibers.
WHERE & WHEN: Scattered or in groups or rings under conifers; fall.

*Tricholoma populinum:* White spores. Edible.
CAP: 3–6 in. broad. Pale dingy reddish brown, sometimes with whitish edge. Rounded, becoming upturned and wavy. Slimy, often covered with sand. Smooth. Flesh white, thick.
GILLS: White, staining wine red. Close together. Notched at stem.
STEM: 3–4 in. tall. Whitish, staining cap-color. Smooth.
WHERE & WHEN: In large mass or rings under poplars and cottonwoods—do not eat similar mushrooms under any other tree; fall, Midwest, West.
LOOK-ALIKES: *T. pessundatum,* similar but growing under conifers and hardwoods with strong, unpleasant odor. Poisonous.

# TRICHOLOMA

GENUS CHARACTERISTICS
· White spores
· Cap medium to large, rounded, may flatten in age
· Gills usually notched at junction with stem
· Stem fleshy, stout
· On ground

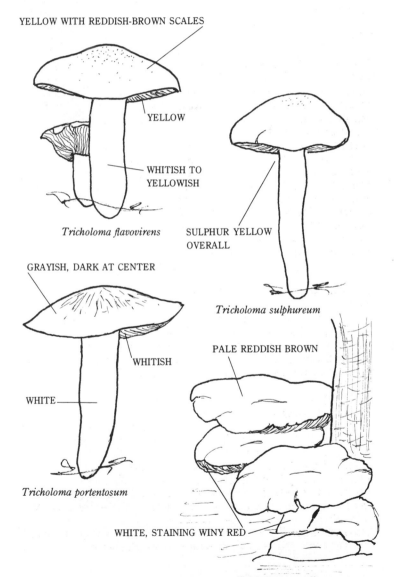

YELLOW WITH REDDISH-BROWN SCALES

YELLOW

WHITISH TO YELLOWISH

*Tricholoma flavovirens*

SULPHUR YELLOW OVERALL

*Tricholoma sulphureum*

GRAYISH, DARK AT CENTER

WHITISH

WHITE

*Tricholoma portentosum*

PALE REDDISH BROWN

WHITE, STAINING WINY RED

*Tricholoma populinum*

*Tricholoma pardinum:* White spores. Dangerously poisonous.
CAP: 3–5 (10) in. broad. Whitish with grayish hairy scales. Rounded with a low broad knob, becoming expanded. Dry. Flesh white, firm.
GILLS: Whitish. Rather close. Notched at junction with stem.
STEM: 2–4 in. tall. White. Dry. Smooth. Hairless. Solid. Sometimes enlarged at base.
WHERE & WHEN: Single to many, often in large numbers in conifers and hardwoods-conifers; fall, central and western U.S., Canada.

*Tricholoma pessundatum* (*var. montanum*): White spores. Poisonous. Strong odor of linseed oil.
CAP: 2–4 in. broad. Dark reddish brown, paler on edge. Rounded, becoming expanded. Slimy when wet, shiny when dry. Smooth. Hairless. Flesh white, thick, firm.
GILLS: White, staining reddish brown. Crowded. Notched at junction with stem.
STEM: 1½–3 in. tall. White, staining reddish brown when handled. Hairless or with a few fibrils. Sometimes slightly bulbous. About as long as cap is wide or shorter.
WHERE & WHEN: Many on ground under conifers, hardwoods; fall.

*Tricholoma saponaceum:* White spores. Poisonous. Disagreeable taste and soapy odor.
CAP: 2–4 in. broad. Gray green at center, paler around edge. Rounded with inrolled edge, becoming expanded. Dry. Smooth. Flesh white, staining pinkish, thick, firm.
GILLS: Whitish, often tinged greenish. Far apart. Deeply notched at stem.
STEM: 2–4 in. tall. White or flushed cap-color. Smooth. Bluntly tapered at base. Flesh white in upper part, pale pink in base.
WHERE & WHEN: Alone to many on ground in conifers or conifers-hardwoods; spring and fall.

*Tricholoma venenata:* White spores. Poisonous.
CAP: 1½–3 in. broad. White, aging or bruising light brownish. Minutely scaly, especially at center. Rounded, then expanding. Flesh white, tinged yellowish tan.
GILLS: White, becoming brownish when bruised. Somewhat far apart. Notched at junction with stem.
STEM: White, 2–4 in. tall, becoming brownish when bruised. Small bulb at base.
WHERE & WHEN: Scattered to many in hardwoods; fall.

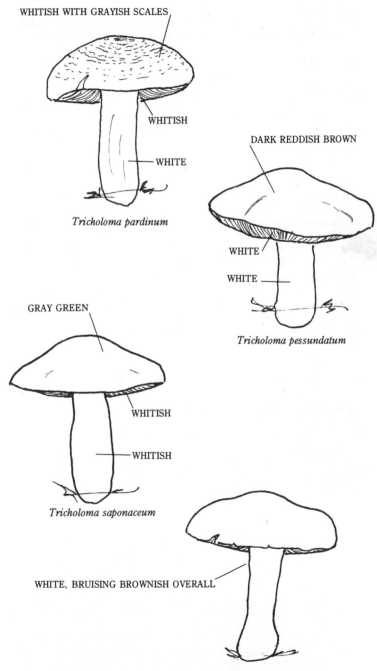

WHITISH WITH GRAYISH SCALES

WHITISH

WHITE

*Tricholoma pardinum*

DARK REDDISH BROWN

WHITE

WHITE

*Tricholoma pessundatum*

GRAY GREEN

WHITISH

WHITISH

*Tricholoma saponaceum*

WHITE, BRUISING BROWNISH OVERALL

*Tricholoma venenata*

**TRICHOLOMOPSIS** These are like *Tricholomas* but grow on wood. Rounded caps, expanding in age, usually somewhat yellowish and hairy. Fleshy stem. Gills attached to the stem, usually notched where they join it. White spores.

EDIBILITY: None known to be toxic. None rated as choice eating; only mild flavor, fair quality. Usually best to discard stems. Dot caps with butter, broil gill side up, season with lemon juice, salt, pepper. Or cut into small pieces and use in stews or with other mushrooms in a potpourri where they will absorb other flavors and lend bulk to the whole.

*Tricholomopsis rutilans* (*Tricholoma rutilans*): White spores. Edible.

CAP: 1–4 (6) in. broad. At first entirely covered with brick- to purplish-red hairs that later separate into pointed scales, revealing yellow flesh underneath. Rounded with incurved edge, aging flat, sometimes with low knob. Dry. Flesh pale yellow, thick, firm.

GILLS: Yellow. Crowded. Attached to stem in youth, becoming notched where they join stem.

STEM: 1½–4 in. tall. Cap-color, dotted with hairy scales like cap, except pale yellow with no fibers at top. Dry. Often curved. Yellow within, staining yellow when bruised.

WHERE & WHEN: Alone or scattered, attached to conifer logs and stumps; summer, fall in West.

*Tricholomopsis decora* (*Tricholoma decorum, Clitocybe decora*): White spores. Edible.

CAP: 2–3 in. broad. Yellow to brownish yellow with gray or brown fibrous scales, dense at center, scattered toward edge. Rounded with inrolled edge, becoming expanded, finally flat or depressed at center. Moist, becoming dry. Flesh yellow, firm.

GILLS: Yellow. Close together. Attached to stem, sometimes extending slightly down it.

STEM: 1½–2½ in. tall. Yellow, often with scattered scales similar to cap. Becoming hollow. Sometimes off-center.

WHERE & WHEN: Single or in small clusters on decaying conifer wood; late summer, fall in West.

LOOK-ALIKES: Closely related to *Tricholomopsis rutilans* but with blackish scales instead of reddish.

*Tricholomopsis platyphylla* (*Collybia platyphylla*): White spores. Edible.

CAP: 2–8 in. broad. Varies from whitish gray to beige to blackish brown, sometimes darker at center. Streaked with darker fibrous hairs or scales. Rounded with inrolled edge, becoming flat, sometimes upturned and wavy in age. Fragile, frequently splitting along cap edge. Slimy when wet. Flesh white to gray, thin, pliant.

GILLS: White to whitish gray. Far apart, of unequal lengths. Notched where they join stem.

STEM: 3–5 in. tall. White to grayish white, same as gills. Pithy or hollow with tough, gristly outer rind. Smooth. Hairless or with flat hairs. Bluntly rounded at base.

WHERE & WHEN: Alone or scattered on well-decayed logs, stumps, roots, or boards of hardwoods and conifers; spring–fall.

# TRICHOLOMOPSIS

GENUS CHARACTERISTICS
· White spores
· Cap rounded to flattened, often yellowish, hairy
· Gills usually notched at stem
· Stem fleshy
· On wood

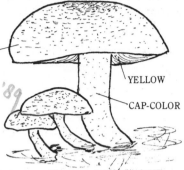

YELLOW WITH PURPLISH-RED HAIRS

*Bos achter 't*
*Witte zand 9-28-'89*

YELLOW

CAP-COLOR

*Tricholomopsis rutilans*

*koningsmantel*
*Purpergele ridder-*
*zwam*

YELLOWISH WITH GRAY OR BROWN SCALES

YELLOW

YELLOW

*Tricholomopsis decora*

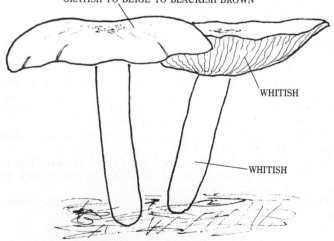

GRAYISH TO BEIGE TO BLACKISH BROWN

WHITISH

WHITISH

*Tricholomopsis platyphylla*

**MELANOLEUCA**   Recognized by their characteristic stiff stature; tall, thin, rather gristly stem; and rounded, knobbed cap that broadens in age but retains the center knob. Stem and gills are pale but never chalky white. Stem usually has brownish to blackish fibers. Gills are close together and attached to stem or notched where they join it. No ring or cup. Spores are white. Grow on the ground in fields and woods. Most were formerly classified in *Tricholoma,* and they do look like stiff, slender members of that genus.

EDIBILITY: No poisonous species are known and several are good all-purpose edibles with excellent flavor and texture, although none are commonly eaten. Discard fibrous stems.

*Melanoleuca melaleuca* (*Tricholoma melaleucum*); changeable *Tricholoma*: White spores. Edible, good. Considerable color variation, depending on water content.
CAP: 1–3 in. broad. Smoky brown when moist, drying much paler, almost tan. Broadly rounded, aging flat and upturned with darker center knob, sometimes with wavy edge. Smooth. Hairless. Moist to dry. Flesh whitish, thin.
GILLS: White. Close together. Notched where they join stem.
STEM: 1–5 in. tall. White with brownish fibers, more numerous in age. Sometimes slightly swollen at base. Flesh brownish in age.
WHERE & WHEN: Single to scattered in pastures, open woods; summer, fall in West; fall in East.

*Melanoleuca alboflavida* (*Tricholoma albiflavidum, Collybia albiflavida*): White spores. Edible, good. Paler and larger than *M. melaleuca.*
CAP: 2–5 in. broad. Whitish to creamy yellow, darker at center. Broadly rounded, expanding to almost flat with center sometimes depressed. Edge incurved, remaining so for some time. Smooth. Moist. Hairless. Flesh white.
GILLS: White to dingy. Crowded. Attached to stem.
STEM: 3–7 in. tall. Whitish or tinged cap-color. Straight, giving plant a stiff, rigid appearance. Conspicuously furrowed. Fibrous within, with a gristly outer rind. Base bulbous.
WHERE & WHEN: Alone or small groups in moist, mixed woods; summer, fall.

*Melanoleuca grammopodia* (*Tricholoma grammopodium*): White spores. Edible. Some cooks parboil with lid off to disperse unpleasant odor.
CAP: 3–6 in. broad. Grayish brown to reddish brown when moist. Fading to almost white when dry. Rounded with large central knob and incurved edge at first, aging flat, finally depressed, but retaining large central knob and thin, incurved edge. Smooth, glossy. Flesh whitish, thick.
GILLS: Whitish to cream. Close together. Extend down stem slightly.
STEM: 3–4 in. tall. Whitish, streaked entire length with dark fibers. Sometimes slightly twisted. Slightly bulbous base covered with white down.
WHERE & WHEN: In large groups or rings, in pastures, gardens, grassy woods; summer, fall.
*M. brevipes* (*Tricholoma brevipes*): Similar but smaller, same color or darker, growing in woods. Edible.

# MELANOLEUCA

GENUS CHARACTERISTICS
- White spores
- Stiff stature
- Cap wide, rounded with knob
- Gills pale, attached to stem
- Stem pale, tall, thin
- On ground

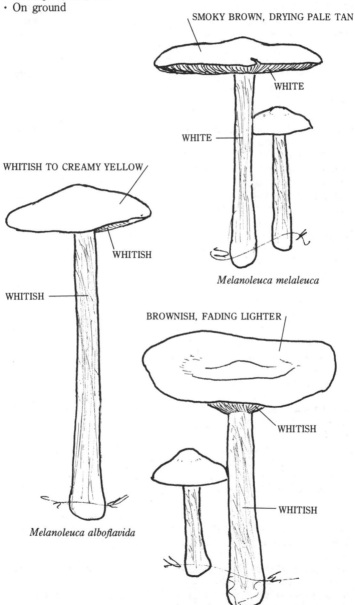

SMOKY BROWN, DRYING PALE TAN

WHITE

WHITE

*Melanoleuca melaleuca*

WHITISH TO CREAMY YELLOW

WHITISH

WHITISH

*Melanoleuca alboflavida*

BROWNISH, FADING LIGHTER

WHITISH

WHITISH

*Melanoleuca grammopodia*

**RUSSULA**  Once you learn the silhouette, you'll recognize these medium to large mushrooms easily. Look for the broad, rounded cap that flattens in age, often developing a wide saucerlike depression. Gills and stem are attached, usually white, very precise and neat in appearance. The stem is short, thick, looking and breaking like a piece of chalk. The entire mushroom is brittle, shattering when dropped or thrown against a tree. Cap and stem are continuous so do not separate easily. Russulas come in many colors—red, orange, yellow, purple, green, black, white—sometimes all on one cap. The color varies greatly, depending on whether the mushroom is in sun or shade, wet or dry, young or old. The spore color ranges from white to buff to yellow and is an important clue. Another is how far the cap skin can be peeled up the cap. They grow on soil.

EDIBILITY: Many are bitter, peppery, while others are mild and nut-like. Some say the peppery taste disappears in long cooking, but others report nausea and discomfort after eating these acrid species. Use caution with any *Russula* since they can be indigestible. It is essential that only fresh, young caps be eaten; the flavor deteriorates if any part is wilted, dried, decayed, or wormy. Long, slow stewing for 30 to 40 minutes or more is required for most species; a few tender ones will cook in 5 minutes. They can be used in casseroles, stuffing, soup, or baked, broiled, fried crisp in butter, grilled over open fire. Season with onions, garlic, bacon, lemon. *R. virescens* can be sliced raw in salads. Only the best-tasting species in this large genus are described here.

*Russula lutea:* Yellow spores. Edible. Mild taste. Cooks quickly.
CAP: 1–3 in. broad. Bright yellow, unchanging. Rounded, becoming flat to slightly depressed with grooved edge in age. Smooth, hairless. Slimy. Fragile. Flesh white, brittle. Skin totally separable from cap.
GILLS: Creamy, becoming cap-color. Barely attached to stem. Fairly far apart.
STEM: 1–2 in. tall. White, dry, smooth, hairless.
WHERE & WHEN: Alone to scattered or in groups under hardwoods, especially birch; summer, early fall.

*Russula aurata:* Pale yellow spores. Edible. Mild taste. Cooks quickly.
CAP: 2–3 in. broad. Orange to scarlet with golden patches, darker at center. Spherical, becoming rounded, finally depressed in center. Slimy, soon becoming dry, smooth to coarsely velvety. Skin separable about halfway up cap. Flesh off-white, firm, aging brittle.
GILLS: Pale cream, becoming yellow. Edges chrome yellow. Notched at stem.
STEM: 2–3 in. long. White, stained chrome yellow, especially at base.
WHERE & WHEN: Alone in mixed woods; summer, fall.

*Russula decolorans:* Yellow spores (in mass). Edible. Mild taste.
CAP: 2–5 in. broad. Orange red, fading to yellowish. Round, aging flattened-depressed. Edge slightly grooved. Slightly slimy. Skin peels from edge. Flesh white, firm, turning ashy gray in age or when cut.
GILLS: White to creamy, aging gray. Crowded. Notched where they join stem.
STEM: 2–4 in. tall. White, aging or bruising ashy. Finely lined.
WHERE & WHEN: Alone or scattered in conifers, mixed woods; summer, fall.
*R. claroflava* (*R. flava*): Similar but yellow cap, gills, spores. Edible.

*Onderbenks + Witteland*
*Russula fellea - brittle*
*yellow cap - has ridges,*
*edge. Stems white,*
*gills white.*
*Taste a little*
*sharp*
*End Sept. '85*

# RUSSULA

## GENUS CHARACTERISTICS

· White to cream to yellow spores
· Medium to large, often brightly colored
· Brittle, shatter easily
· Cap rounded to saucer-shaped
· Gills attached to stem
· Stem looks and breaks like piece of chalk
· On soil

YELLOW

CREAMY, AGING CAP-COLOR

WHITE

*Russula lutea*

ORANGE TO SCARLET
WITH GOLDEN PATCHES

CREAM, AGING YELLOW

WHITE

*Russula aurata*

ORANGE RED, FADING TO YELLOW

WHITISH

WHITE

*Russula decolorans*

***Russula emetica:*** White spores. Poisonous. Tastes instantly peppery.
CAP: 2–4 in. broad. Scarlet, fading in age or damp weather, sometimes with yellowish blotches. Rounded, becoming depressed. Slimy. Smooth, hairless. Edge deeply ribbed, upturned in age. Skin peels entirely off cap, leaving red stain. Flesh white, very soft, fragile, pink just under cap surface.
GILLS: White. Barely touch stem. Close together. Sometimes forked.
STEM: 1–4 in. tall. Dull white. Often ridged. Fragile. Hollow in age. Usually longer than cap width.
WHERE & WHEN: Scattered or in small groups on ground, deep moss, on or near rotting conifers; late summer, early fall.
***R. mariae:*** Similar but smaller, purplish-red cap, minutely velvety, less brittle, skin usually peeling only partway up cap. Stem flushed reddish over middle, not exceeding cap width. Creamy-white spores. Mild taste. Edible with care: many red Russulas are untested.
***R. fragilis:*** Similar but smaller, not pink under cap skin. Poisonous.

***Russula paludosa:*** Yellow spores. Edible. Mildly peppery. Slight fishy smell.
CAP: 3–5 in. broad. Shiny brick red, flushed with purple or yellow. Rounded to depressed to nearly flat. Edge slightly ribbed. Slimy, smooth, hairless. Flesh white to ivory, soft, thick.
GILLS: White to creamy yellow. Fairly well separated. Extending down stem at first, becoming attached or notched at stem.
STEM: 1½–4 in. tall. Dull white, becoming tinged cap-color. Dry, smooth, with low longitudinal ridges. Rusty flesh. Longer than cap width.
WHERE & WHEN: Alone to scattered in wet or mossy places under hardwoods-conifers; summer, fall, northern North America.

***Russula vesca:*** White spores. Edible, good. Mild taste.
CAP: 2–3 in. broad. Brownish red to pinkish buff, darker in center, drying to dull olive toward edge. Slightly slimy. Hemispherical, then rounded with center depression, deepening to funnel shape in age. Cap skin retracting from edge, showing white flesh and gills underneath. Edge slightly grooved. Skin separable halfway up cap. Flesh whitish or tinged cap-color directly under cap surface.
GILLS: White to cream, spotted rusty brown when old. Close to crowded. Unequal and forked lengths intermixed. Attached to stem.
STEM: 1½–3 in. tall. White, staining yellowish to rusty brown at base. Hairless. Slightly wrinkled. Tapering at base.
WHERE & WHEN: Alone or scattered in mixed woods, especially oaks and conifers, under trees in pastures, in thin woods or at woods' edge.

***Russula lepida:*** Creamy white spores. Edible. Mild taste.
CAP: 1–4 in. broad. Dark red, inclining to maroon brown, fading to yellowish or whitish, retaining red spots. Rounded, then depressed. Dry, dull, unpolished. Powdery as with a fine dust. Becoming cracked, scaly. Edge even, not grooved. Skin difficult to separate from cap. Flesh white.
GILLS: White, sometimes pink or red on edges. Rounded where they join stem. Crowded. Connected by veins.
STEM: Up to 3 in. tall. White, usually stained pink.
WHERE & WHEN: In mixed woods, especially oak, beech; summer, fall.

SCARLET

WHITE

WHITE

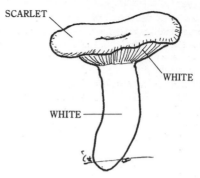

*Russula emetica*

RED, FLUSHED PURPLE, YELLOW

WHITISH

WHITE, TINGED CAP-COLOR

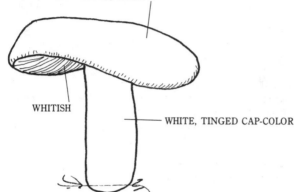

*Russula paludosa*

BROWNISH RED TO PINKISH BUFF

WHITE

WHITISH

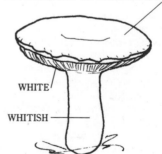
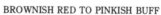

*Russula vesca*

DARK RED

WHITE

WHITE

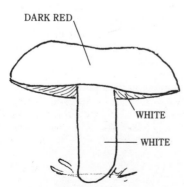

*Russula lepida*

*Russula alutacea:* Yellow spores. Edible. Mild taste when young.
CAP: 2–4 (8) in. broad. Purple red with olive or yellowish splotches, fading to whitish. Bell-shaped then rounded, expanding with slightly depressed center. Edge grooved. Skin separable almost halfway up cap. Flesh white.
GILLS: Yellowish. Edges sometimes reddish near cap edge. Notched where they join stem. Somewhat far apart.
STEM: 1–2 in. tall. White, usually flushed red or purple, especially at top. Wrinkled lengthwise.
WHERE & WHEN: Scattered in woods; summer, fall.

*Russula aeruginea:* Pale yellow spores. Edible. Mild taste.
CAP: 1½–3 in. broad. Green, sometimes tinged olive, darker at center, sometimes rusty-speckled. Rounded, expanding, becoming slightly depressed. Slightly slimy when wet, minutely velvety when dry. Skin separable to about halfway up cap. Flesh white or greenish.
GILLS: White aging creamy yellow, soon spotted brownish. Barely attached to stem. Slightly far apart.
STEM: 1½–2 in. tall. White, usually discoloring pale tan.
WHERE & WHEN: Alone or many in conifers and hardwoods, especially pine, aspen, birch; summer, fall.

*Russula virescens:* White spores. Edible. Mild taste.
CAP: 2–5 in. broad. Grayish green, developing flaky greenish or yellow patches where skin cracks, showing white flesh in between. Rusty-brown spots in age. Nearly round, becoming flattened to somewhat depressed. Always dry, unpolished to velvety. Surface soon breaking into many small, irregular patches. Edge not grooved or only slightly. Flesh white except greenish directly under skin.
GILLS: White, aging creamy. Very brittle. Close together. Sometimes forked and unequal lengths intermixed.
STEM: 1–3 in. tall. White, spotted brown where bruised. Shorter than cap diameter.
WHERE & WHEN: Alone to scattered under hardwoods or mixed conifers-hardwoods. Open grassy clearings, edges of woods, or open woods; summer.
LOOK-ALIKES: *R. aeruginea* is darker green, smooth, rather slimy in wet weather.

*Russula olivacea:* Yellow spores. Edible. Mild taste.
CAP: 3–8 (14) in. broad. Olive, mixed with dark red. Soon slightly paler at edge. Rounded, becoming flattened and slightly depressed. Hairless, becoming minutely velvety. Skin not separable from flesh. Edge not grooved. Flesh white, aging dirty yellow.
GILLS: Yellow with lemon-yellow edges, aging darker. Rather far apart. Rounded where they touch stem.
STEM: 2–3 in. tall. Dingy white, flushed purplish pink at top, velvety.
WHERE & WHEN: Alone to many in seepage areas, along streams, in conifers, mixed woods; summer, fall.

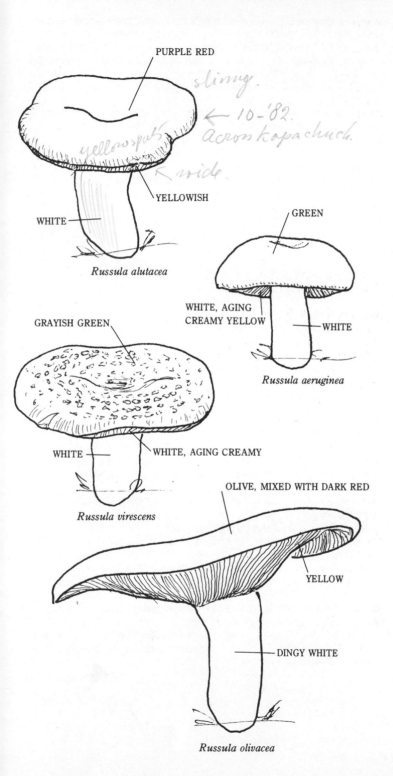

PURPLE RED

slimy.
← 10-'82.
Acronkapachuch.
R wide.
yellowspots

YELLOWISH

WHITE

*Russula alutacea*

GREEN

WHITE, AGING
CREAMY YELLOW

WHITE

*Russula aeruginea*

GRAYISH GREEN

WHITE — WHITE, AGING CREAMY

*Russula virescens*

OLIVE, MIXED WITH DARK RED

YELLOW

DINGY WHITE

*Russula olivacea*

*Russula xerampelina* (*R. atropurpurea*): Yellow spores. Edible. Mild taste. Fishy or seafood odor in age, disappears in cooking.
CAP: 2–6+ in. broad. Purplish, sometimes tinged brownish. Paler or even olive at edge. Rounded, becoming depressed with grooved, up-turned edge. Slimy, aging dry, slightly velvety. Skin separable halfway up cap. Flesh white, firm, pinkish under surface.
GILLS: Creamy yellow to orange yellow, bruising yellowish then brown. Close together. Notched where they join stem.
STEM: 3–5 in. tall. White with reddish or purplish streaks. Base bruising yellow brown. Wrinkled, grooved. Slightly club-shaped at base.
WHERE & WHEN: Scattered in mixed woods or conifers; summer, fall.

*Russula cyanoxantha:* White spores. Edible. Mild taste.
CAP: 2–3+ in. broad. Violet, sometimes tinged bluish green, with yellowish center. Rounded, expanding and becoming depressed. Edge slightly ribbed, extending beyond gills. Slimy in damp weather. Skin separable about one-third up cap. Flesh white, except reddish just beneath skin.
GILLS: White. Rounded where they join stem. Greasy to touch. Slightly crowded. Long, short, and forked gills intermixed.
STEM: 2–3 in. tall. White, occasionally flushed purplish. Smooth, hairless.
WHERE & WHEN: Scattered in hardwoods, especially beech; summer, fall.

*Russula densifolia:* White spores. Poisonous to some. Peppery taste.
CAP: 2–4 in. broad. Dingy white, becoming smoky gray, finally blackish. Rounded, then becoming shallow funnel-shaped with inrolled edge. Slimy in wet weather, becoming dry. Flesh whitish, bruising red, then black.
GILLS: Whitish, bruising dingy red to black. Close to crowded. Unequal lengths intermixed. Partially attached to stem.
STEM: 1–3 in. tall. Whitish streaked with reddish-brown stains. Smooth, hairless.
WHERE & WHEN: Alone or in groups, mainly under conifers, also hardwoods or mixed woods; summer, fall.
*R. albonigra:* Similar but stains directly black. Poisonous.
*R. nigricans:* Similar but with gills far apart. Poisonous to some.

*Russula brevipes:* Creamy spores. Edible. Slightly peppery taste.
CAP: 4–14 in. broad. White, staining dingy yellow to brownish. Rounded, becoming deeply depressed in center with rounded edge. Dry, minutely woolly. Edge not grooved. Flesh white, thick.
GILLS: White, aging pale cream, sometimes stained brownish. Extend down stem. Close together. Sometimes forked with veins in between.
STEM: 1 3 (6) in. tall. White, sometimes with brown stains. Dry, smooth, hairless.
WHERE & WHEN: Scattered under conifers or mixed woods; summer, fall.
*var. acrior:* Gills tinged bluish green. Occasionally narrow blue-green band at top of stem. Edible.
*R. delica:* Similar with longer stem, distant gills, white spores. Edible.
LOOK-ALIKES: Resemble *Lactarius,* but do not have milky juice.

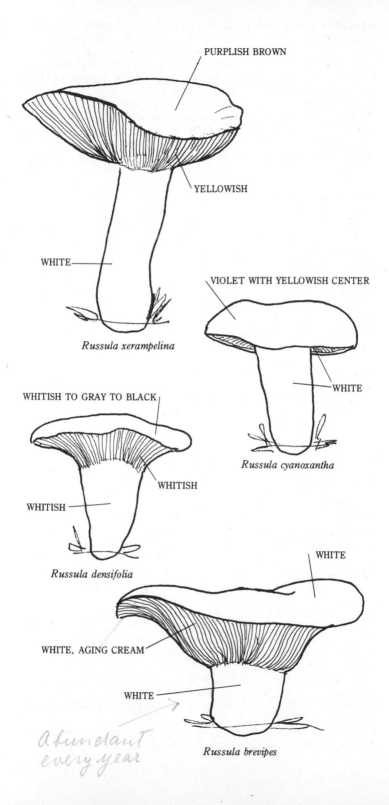

PURPLISH BROWN

YELLOWISH

WHITE

*Russula xerampelina*

VIOLET WITH YELLOWISH CENTER

WHITE

*Russula cyanoxantha*

WHITISH TO GRAY TO BLACK

WHITISH

WHITISH

*Russula densifolia*

WHITE

WHITE, AGING CREAM

WHITE

*abundant
every year*

*Russula brevipes*

**LACTARIUS**   "Milky caps," so called because they exude a milky-white or colored liquid (latex) when cut across gills or top of stem with a sharp knife or razor blade. Latex is best seen in young, fresh specimens; may be lacking in older ones or in dry weather. It has different colors in different species; sometimes changes color when exposed to air. Mild tasting in some species, peppery or bitter in others—check by merely touching latex with tongue. Most species are squat with thick, short stem and rounded cap, aging shallow funnel-shaped, often with arched edge. They have a rather stiff stature and feel sturdy and firm, but are quite fragile. The gills are usually close together, extending slightly down stem. Sometimes the cap has concentric bands of color, one fading into the other. An important clue is whether cap and/or stem are slimy, sticky, or dry. Grow on soil under trees, often in moist areas. Spores are white, buff, or yellowish.
EDIBILITY: A handful of easily recognized edibles and a host of acrid species that can cause gastroenteritis. The rule is to avoid those whose white latex turns yellow, pink, or lilac upon exposure to air. Those with unchanging white latex or white changing to brown include both edible and poisonous species. Discard stems and spongy, wormy caps. All are coarsely textured, so most cooks recommend blanching in salted water before using in a recipe. A few species cook quickly, however.
· Long, slow baking, covered, is favored. Slice, layer in greased baking pan, top with butter, bread crumbs, bake 30–40 minutes at 350°. Or omit crumbs, cover with cream or condensed milk, season with chopped herbs, butter, bake 1 hour. Or bake caps with pat of butter in each. Classic recipe for *L. volemus* is to bake with bacon strips.
· Pickle in vinegar or marinate in oil, lemon, and/or vinegar. Serve as hors d'oeuvres with mayonnaise or sauce remoulade. Or slice into salad, such as Caesar or green bean; sprinkle with Parmesan cheese.
· Add to casseroles, stuffings. Or dip in egg, flour, deep fry. Or add to sautéed onions, with sour cream, lemon juice, chopped chives.

*Lactarius volemus:* White spores. Edible. Fishy odor. Mild taste.
CAP: 2–3 (4½) in. broad. Buff brown to orange brown. Rounded, soon becoming depressed. Dry. Smooth, sometimes minutely cracked. Hairless. Flesh whitish, slowly bruising dark brown. Latex white, changing slowly to brownish, plentiful.
GILLS: Cap-color or lighter, bruising brownish. Close. Run down stem.
STEM: 2–3 in. tall. Cap-color or lighter, often stained darker.
WHERE & WHEN: Scattered to groups in moist hardwoods, or mixed hardwoods-conifers; summer, eastern North America.
*L. corrugis:* Sister species but with yellowish-cinnamon, velvety cap, very wrinkled, especially near edge; yellowish gills. Edible.

*Lactarius vellereus:* White spores. Poisonous. Very bitter.
CAP: 2–5 in. broad. Whitish. Rounded with inrolled edge, becoming depressed, almost funnel-shaped. Dry. Velvety. Flesh white, staining brownish; firm. Latex white, slowly changing to brownish.
GILLS: White, aging cream, bruising brown. Rather far apart. Run down stem.
STEM: ½–2½ in. tall. Whitish. Minutely velvety. Dry.
WHERE & WHEN: Scattered under hardwoods-conifers summer, fall, in East.

# LACTARIUS

GENUS CHARACTERISTICS
· White to yellowish spores
· Caps rounded to funnel-shaped
· Gills usually extend down stem slightly
· Gills exude milky or colored juice when cut
· Stem short, thick
· On soil under trees

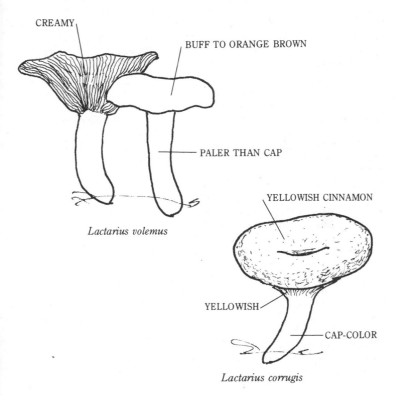

CREAMY

BUFF TO ORANGE BROWN

PALER THAN CAP

*Lactarius volemus*

YELLOWISH CINNAMON

YELLOWISH

CAP-COLOR

*Lactarius corrugis*

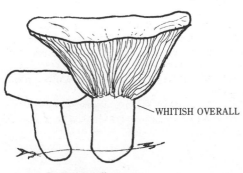

WHITISH OVERALL

*Lactarius vellereus*

*Lactarius hygrophoroides:* White spores. Edible. Mild taste.
CAP: 1–3 in. broad. Yellowish to yellowish brown to tawny reddish. Rounded with inrolled edge, aging somewhat funnel-shaped. Dry. Velvety. Flesh pallid, unchanging, brittle. Latex white, unchanging, plentiful.
GILLS: White, aging creamy. Far apart. Run slightly down stem.
STEM: 1–2 in. tall. Cap-color, often bright yellow at base. Hairless.
WHERE & WHEN: Scattered under hardwoods; summer, fall, eastern North America.
LOOK-ALIKES: Widely spaced gills like *Hygrophorus* but the white latex tells you it is a *Lactarius*. Other *Lactarii* with widely spaced gills are unpalatable or untested.

*Lactarius deliciosus:* Pale-yellowish spores. Edible. Mild taste. Several variants, all edible but not always meriting the name *deliciosus*.
CAP: 2–6 (12) in. broad. Carrot color with concentric bands of darker orange, mottled dingy green. Rounded with inrolled edge, becoming almost funnel-shaped. Sticky to slimy in wet weather. Flesh pallid to pale orange, staining green. Latex carrot-colored, leaving green stains on flesh.
GILLS: Bright orange, bruising green. Close. Extend down stem.
STEM: 1–3 in. tall. Paler than cap, turning green when handled or in age. Dry. Nearly hairless. Narrowing at base.
WHERE & WHEN: Alone to several under conifers—moist areas, boggy places, along streams; late summer, fall.
*L. thyinos:* Similar but carrot color overall, no color bands, scant saffron-color latex, flesh slowly staining green. Stem as well as cap sticky. Gills far apart, extending well down stem. In eastern North America in cold springy cedar swamps. Edible.

*Lactarius sanguifluus:* Pale-yellow spores. Edible, better than *L. deliciosus*. Mild taste.
CAP: 2½–5 in. broad. Carrot-colored, usually darker in center with paler concentric bands of color, staining green in age. Rounded with inrolled edge, then depressed in center. Slightly slimy. Flesh orangy, becoming muddy bloodred where cut. Latex dark bloodred, scanty.
GILLS: Dull purplish red, bruising green. Close together. Run down stem.
STEM: ¾–2 in. tall. Pale orange. Dry. Hollow. Narrow at base.
WHERE & WHEN: Scattered or in groups under conifers in West; summer, fall.
*L. subpurpureus:* Similar but smaller, more pink, under eastern conifers; fall. Edible, bitter taste disappearing in cooking.

*Lactarius indigo:* Yellowish spores. Edible. Mild taste. The only all-blue mushroom, bruising green. Cooks quickly.
CAP: 2–6 in. broad. Blue with concentric bands of darker blue fading to silvery gray, staining green. Rounded, then flat, becoming depressed to funnel-shaped. Edge inrolled, becoming arched and elevated. Slimy, then becoming only slightly sticky. Smooth. Hairless. Flesh indigo, staining green, firm. Latex deep indigo, slowly changing to dark green.
GILLS: Indigo, bruising green. Close. Extend down stem.
STEM: Cap-color. Dry. Becoming hollow.
WHERE & WHEN: Scattered or in groups under conifers-hardwoods; summer, fall, after heavy rains, most common in Southeast.
*L. paradoxus:* Similar but grayish-indigo cap, pale-orange gills, blue flesh, red latex; eastern North America. Edible.

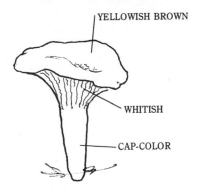

YELLOWISH BROWN

WHITISH

CAP-COLOR

*Lactarius hygrophoroides*

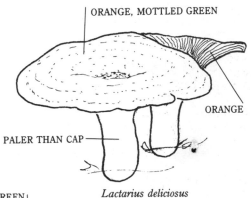

ORANGE, MOTTLED GREEN

ORANGE

PALER THAN CAP

*Lactarius deliciosus*

ORANGE, STAINING GREEN

PURPLISH RED

PALE ORANGE

*Lactarius sanguifluus*

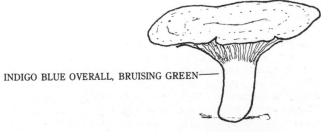

INDIGO BLUE OVERALL, BRUISING GREEN

*Lactarius indigo*

***Lactarius camphoratus:*** White spores. Edible. Mild taste. Strong fragrance likened to sweet clover or curry powder. Too strong for some people unless mixed with milder species or dried, used as seasoning.
CAP: ½–1½ in. broad. Dark brownish red. Rounded with inrolled edge, expanding, becoming depressed with small knob. Dry. Hairless. Sometimes slightly wrinkled. Flesh cap-color, thin. Latex white, unchanging.
GILLS: Whitish, aging red brown. Close together. Run down stem.
STEM: ½–2 in. tall. Cap-color or paler. Dry, smooth, powdery.
WHERE & WHEN: Scattered or in groups on ground or very rotten wood, usually with conifers; summer, fall.
***L. rufus:*** Very similar but larger; mild taste slowly becoming very hot. Poisonous. Beware any acrid-tasting, brownish-red species.
***L. subdulcis:*** Similar but paler, slight odor, mildly peppery. Edible.

***Lactarius torminosus:*** White spores. Poisonous. Very peppery.
CAP: 2–4 in. broad. Creamy white with delicate pink center, often with concentric pinkish bands. Broadly rounded, aging nearly funnel-shaped. Edge remains inrolled. Sticky to slimy. Hairless at center; edge covered with dense whitish to pinkish hairs. Flesh white to pinkish, unchanging. Latex white, unchanging.
GILLS: White, developing pinkish tinge. Close. Run down stem.
STEM: 1–3 in. tall. White to pinkish; yellow-spotted. Dry. Smooth. Hairless or powdery. Hollow in age.
WHERE & WHEN: Scattered under birch; summer, fall.

***Lactarius representaneus:*** White spores. Poisonous. Peppery taste.
CAP: 3–6 (8) in. broad. Pale yellow with orangy-buff hairs. Orange in center. Rounded with inrolled edge, aging flat, then depressed. Slimy. Hairless to powdery over center, densely woolly elsewhere with long hairs fringing edge. Flesh white, staining lilac. Latex white, gradually changing to lilac, staining flesh lilac.
GILLS: Pale yellowish, staining lilac. Close. Run down stem.
STEM: 2–3 in. tall. Pale yellowish, covered with depressed, shiny orange spots. Slightly larger at base. Hollow or pithy.
WHERE & WHEN: Scattered under conifers; late summer, fall.
***L. uvidus:*** Also with white latex changing to lilac, but with slimy, smooth, hairless cap, brownish gray tinged lilac. White gills and stem. Poisonous.
CAUTION: None of the lilac-staining *Lactarii* should be eaten.

***Lactarius scrobiculatus:*** White spores. Poisonous. Peppery.
CAP: 2–6 in. broad. Yellow, often darker over center with darker concentric bands of color. Broadly rounded with inrolled edge, aging depressed with flat edge. Sticky to slimy. Hairless in center but with matted hairs extending beyond edge in youth. Flesh white, staining yellow. Latex white, changing to sulphur yellow. Scanty.
GILLS: Whitish to yellowish, staining dark yellow. Close. Run down stem.
STEM: 1–2½ in. tall. Cap-color with depressed brighter spots. Dry. Hairless.
WHERE & WHEN: Scattered under conifers; late summer, fall.
***L. chrysorheus:*** Also with white latex changing to yellow; yellow spores; sticky, hairless, pinkish-buff cap with darker concentric rings; white gills; dry off-white stem. In northern, western U.S. Poisonous.
CAUTION: Avoid species with white latex changing to yellow.

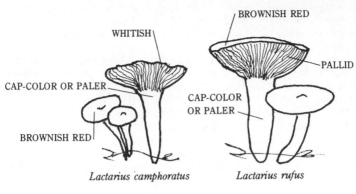

WHITISH

BROWNISH RED

CAP-COLOR OR PALER

BROWNISH RED

PALLID

CAP-COLOR OR PALER

*Lactarius camphoratus*

*Lactarius rufus*

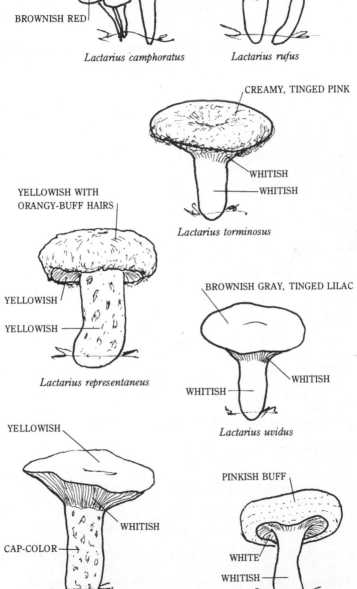

CREAMY, TINGED PINK

WHITISH

WHITISH

*Lactarius torminosus*

YELLOWISH WITH ORANGY-BUFF HAIRS

YELLOWISH

YELLOWISH

*Lactarius representaneus*

BROWNISH GRAY, TINGED LILAC

WHITISH

WHITISH

*Lactarius uvidus*

YELLOWISH

WHITISH

CAP-COLOR

*Lactarius scrobiculatus*

PINKISH BUFF

WHITE

WHITISH

*Lactarius chrysorheus*

**HYGROPHORUS**  Small but seldom inconspicuous mushrooms because of their bright colors—red, orange, yellow, white, gray, brown—peeking through the fallen leaves and grass. Caps range from sharply conic to flat, often very slimy. Gills are the giveaway: they have a waxy, translucent look and when rubbed hard enough to crush them slightly, will feel waxy and leave a waxy layer on your fingers. They are thick and usually far apart, attached to the stem or extending down it. Each gill is wedge-shaped—broadest where gills attach to the cap, tapering to a point on the edge. The entire mushroom is very fragile, often disintegrating by the time you get it home. They grow on ground or duff, often in late fall when few other mushrooms are around. Spores are white.

EDIBILITY: A few species are delicious, a few unpalatable, the majority bland; one, *H. conicus,* is suspected to be poisonous raw. Some sauté quickly, others need slow stewing for at least 20 minutes. Good in pâtés, casseroles, croquettes, meat loaf, rice, pasta sauce, any standard mushroom recipe. Remove slime from cap if excessive with debris sticking to it. Many species are similar and hard to distinguish. The best-tasting ones are described here.

*Hygrophorus pratensis:* White spores. Edible.
CAP: 2–4 in. broad. Orange or orange buff. Bell-shaped, then rounded, sometimes with broad knob, often splitting in center. Edge incurved in youth. Moist, drying dull, somewhat scurfy. Flesh tinged cap-color, thick.
GILLS: Cap-color or paler. Far apart. Run down stem.
STEM: 2–3 in. tall. Cap-color or paler. Stout. Dry. Downy white at top in youth. Finely ribbed.
WHERE & WHEN: Scattered in woods, grassy places; spring, fall.

*Hygrophorus coccineus:* White spores. Edible.
CAP: 1–2 in. broad. Bright bloodred, sometimes tinged orangy, often fading to whitish. Conic with blunt top, aging rounded to upturned with low knob. Moist to tacky. Flesh reddish to orange, soft.
GILLS: Yellowish orange to orange red. Far apart. Attached to stem.
STEM: 1–3 in. tall. Red to orange red with yellow base. Moist. Smooth. Often flattened and fluted. Hairless.
WHERE & WHEN: Scattered in wet grassy areas, mixed woods; summer, fall.
*H. puniceus:* Similar but larger; slimy cap, stem; white base. Edible.
*H. conicus:* Orange to red cap, stem, bruising blackish; yellowish gills. Poisonous raw.

*Hygrophorus miniatus:* White spores. Edible.
CAP: ⅓–1½ in. broad. Scarlet, fading to orange to yellowish. Round, aging almost flat with depressed center. Moist. Smooth, becoming minutely roughened when dry. Flesh cap-color.
GILLS: Paler red than cap, aging yellow. Far apart. Attached to stem.
STEM: 1–2 in. tall. Cap-color. Smooth.
WHERE & WHEN: Small groups, moist soil, decayed wood in conifers; summer, fall.
*H. cantharellus:* Similar but with longer, more slender stem; gills farther apart, extending farther down stem. Edible.

# HYGROPHORUS

GENUS CHARACTERISTICS
- White spores
- Small, often brightly colored
- Cap conic to flat, often slimy
- Gills waxy looking and feeling, far apart, extend down stem, wedge-shaped in cross section
- On ground or duff

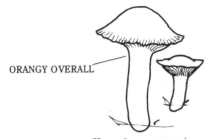

ORANGY OVERALL

*Hygrophorus pratensis*

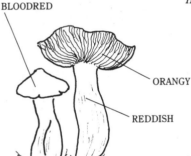

BLOODRED

ORANGY

REDDISH

*Hygrophorus coccineus*

SCARLET

PALER THAN CAP

CAP-COLOR

*Hygrophorus miniatus*

*Hygrophorus ceraceus:* White spores. Edible.
CAP: 1 in. broad. Waxy yellow, not changing. Rounded to flat. Grooved edge. Slimy. Flesh yellow, fragile.
GILLS: Yellow. Far apart. Run down stem.
STEM: 1–2 in. tall. Cap-color. Smooth. Hollow. Fragile.
WHERE & WHEN: Scattered, open grassy places in woods; summer, fall.

*Hygrophorus hypothejus:* White spores. Edible, good dried as a crisp nibble.
CAP: 1–3 in. broad. Yellow with light-brown, slimy covering. Round, expanding to almost flat. Flesh yellow.
GILLS: White, aging yellow. Far apart. Run slightly down stem.
STEM: 3–6 in. long. White to yellowish. Less slimy than cap, with slimy ring, soon disappearing.
WHERE & WHEN: Groups under newly fallen leaves in woods; late fall.

*Hygrophorus gliocyclus:* White spores. Edible.
CAP: 2–6 in. broad. White to ivory, often with yellowish center. Round, then flat to shallowly depressed. Slimy. Smooth. Flesh white, firm.
GILLS: Whitish, not spotting. Extend down stem. Far apart.
STEM: Whitish, flushed yellowish. Slimy ring at stem top. Satiny above ring; slimy, dingy cream below.
WHERE & WHEN: Scattered under conifers; fall, sometimes spring.
*H. flavodiscus:* Similar but cap dries orange buff. Gills flushed pink at first. Frequently found with *H. fuligineus.* Edible.

*Hygrophorus niveus:* White spores. Edible.
CAP: 1–2 in. broad. White to ivory. Rounded, then flattening. Edge ribbed. Moist but not very sticky. Flesh white.
GILLS: Cap-color. Far apart. Extending down stem.
STEM: 1–3 in. tall. Cap-color. Dry. Tapering downward.
WHERE & WHEN: Scattered in grass, pastures, clearings; summer, fall.
*H. borealis:* Similar but with very slimy cap. Edible.
*H. eburneus:* Similar but larger; slimy cap, stem; under trees. Edible.

*Hygrophorus sordidus:* White spores. Edible.
CAP: 3–6 in. broad. White, rarely tinged yellowish. Rounded to expanded to flat. Edge incurved at first with remnants of downy veil. Slimy when wet, usually with leaves and debris sticking to it. Hairless. Flesh white, soft.
GILLS: White, aging slightly yellowish. Far apart. Extend down stem.
STEM: 2–4 in. tall. White. Dry. Hairless but minutely mealy at top.
WHERE & WHEN: Many on ground among leaves under hardwoods; fall, eastern North America.
*H. subalpinus:* Similar with narrow, flaring ring, bulbous stem; in spring near melting snowbanks under western conifers, rarely in late fall. Edible.
*H. ponderatus:* Similar southern winter species with slimy stem, under conifers. Edible.

YELLOW OVERALL

*Hygrophorus ceraceus*

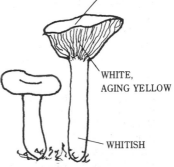

YELLOW WITH BROWNISH SLIME

WHITE,
AGING YELLOW

WHITISH

*Hygrophorus hypothejus*

WHITISH OVERALL

*Hygrophorus gliocyclus*

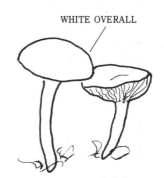

WHITE OVERALL

*Hygrophorus niveus*

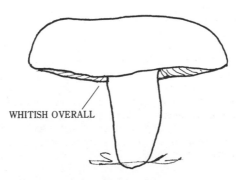

WHITISH OVERALL

*Hygrophorus sordidus*

*Hygrophorus agathosmus:* White spores. Edible. Odor of bitter almonds.
CAP: 1½–3 in. broad. Ashy gray. Rounded, aging flat. Edge inrolled. Slimy. Smooth. Hairless. Flesh white to grayish, soft.
GILLS: White, aging dingy gray. Far apart. Attached to stem.
STEM: 1½–3 in. tall. Whitish to grayish. Dry. Smooth. Hairless.
WHERE & WHEN: Scattered under mixed conifers; summer, fall.

*Hygrophorus camarophyllus:* White spores. Edible.
CAP: 1½–5 in. broad. Smoky gray, finely lined. Rounded to nearly flat, sometimes slightly depressed. Moist to sticky when wet. Flesh white.
GILLS: White tinged grayish. Waxy. Close. Run slightly down stem.
STEM: 1–5 in. tall. White at top, cap-color below. Silky, hairy, except hairless at base.
WHERE & WHEN: In groups under pine, spruce; in spring near melting snowbanks; elsewhere summer, fall.

*Hygrophorus fuligineus:* White spores in mass. Edible.
CAP: 1½–4 in. broad. Brownish black, darker in center, very slimy. Round, then expanding. Flesh off-white, turning dark.
GILLS: White to ivory. Fairly far apart. Extending down stem.
STEM: 1½–4 in. tall. Paler than cap. Slimy.
WHERE & WHEN: In groups in woods under newly fallen leaves; fall.

*Hygrophorus russula:* White spores in mass. Edible.
CAP: 2–6 in. broad. Pinkish with pallid edge at first, center spotted purplish, aging more purplish overall. Sometimes bruising yellow. Rounded, aging nearly flat with irregular, upturned edge. Dry, except slightly sticky when young and moist. Smooth. Flesh white to pinkish, thick, firm.
GILLS: Pinkish, soon developing purplish-red spots. Very close together, unlike other *Hygrophori*. Extending slightly down stem.
STEM: 1–3 in. tall. Pallid, soon staining like cap. Dry.
WHERE & WHEN: Scattered or groups, under hardwoods, conifers; summer, fall.
*H. erubescens:* Very similar but gills far apart. Edible.
*H. purpurascens:* Similar but with veil, fibrous ring; in West. Edible.

**LYOPHYLLUM**   Gills in most species stain yellow to blue to black. Or if not staining (as species described here), caps are white, gray, gray brown to black; stems are rather thick; cap changes color in drying. Rounded caps, incurved at first, aging flat. Soapy feeling. Gills attached to stem or extend slightly down it. White spores. Grow on ground.

*Lyophyllum decastes* (*Clitocybe multiceps, Tricholoma aggregatum*): White spores. Edible. Be sure they haven't been sprayed with pesticides, etc.
CAP: 1½–4½ in. broad. Creamy to tan to dark gray. Rounded, aging flat, often irregular. Edge incurved at first. Soapy feeling. Hairless. Flesh white, not staining, firm.
GILLS: White, aging pallid. Close. Attached to or run down stem.
STEM: 1–5 in. tall. White, sometimes stained brownish at base. Smooth. Hairless or with a few minute fibers. Moist to dry.
WHERE & WHEN: In dense clusters on ground in grass, along roadsides, vacant lots, among piles of organic debris; early spring, fall.

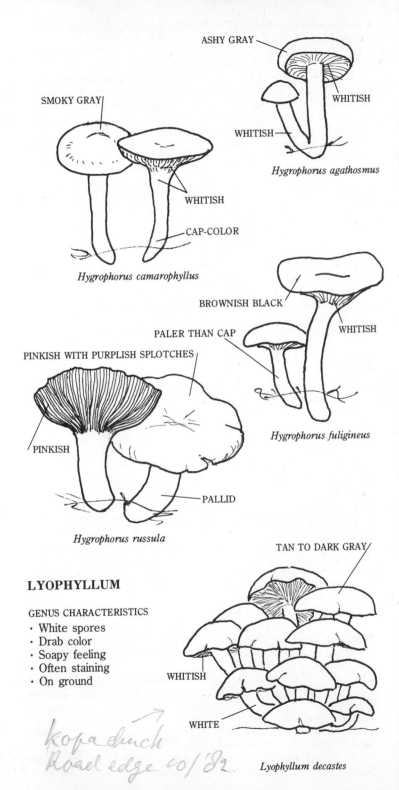

ASHY GRAY

WHITISH

WHITISH

*Hygrophorus agathosmus*

SMOKY GRAY

WHITISH

CAP-COLOR

*Hygrophorus camarophyllus*

BROWNISH BLACK

WHITISH

PALER THAN CAP

*Hygrophorus fuligineus*

PINKISH WITH PURPLISH SPLOTCHES

PINKISH

PALLID

*Hygrophorus russula*

## LYOPHYLLUM

GENUS CHARACTERISTICS
- White spores
- Drab color
- Soapy feeling
- Often staining
- On ground

TAN TO DARK GRAY

WHITISH

WHITE

*Lyophyllum decastes*

kopa dinch
Road edge 40/'82

**CLITOCYBE**  A large, complex genus of small to large mushrooms. Sometimes called "funnel fungi" because the gills usually extend down the stem and the cap becomes depressed, often funnel-shaped, at maturity. The cap edge is inrolled at first. The cap is fleshy at the center, thinner at the edge. The stem is externally fibrous, spongy within, frequently hollow, continuous with and of same substance as the cap; not easily separable from it. The gills are never free from the stem, but always attached to it. Spores are white to buff. Similar, very small, delicate, waxlike, funnel-shaped fungus is *Omphalina*.
EDIBILITY: Most are inedible or untested with only a few edible, highly flavored species and a few poisonous. Discard stems if too fibrous. Sautéing is usually best, or dip in egg, bread crumbs and fry; or stew and use the juices to make a white sauce. If coarse, chop fine. Some are too strongly flavored to eat alone but good as seasoning.

*Clitocybe gibba* (*C. infundibuliformis*): White spores. Edible (discard stem). Look for pinkish-tan, deeply depressed cap.
CAP: 2–3½ in. broad. Pinkish tan, fading to nearly white. Flat, soon becoming slightly depressed, finally funnel-shaped. Edge inrolled at first, often irregular, sometimes ribbed. Moist. Finely silky. Flesh white, thin.
GILLS: White, aging pale buff. Extend down stem. Crowded. Forked.
STEM: 1–3 in. tall. Cap-color or paler. Dry. Spongy within. Hairless except for dense white threads (mycelium) over base.
WHERE & WHEN: Alone to scattered, attached to decaying leaves and refuse under trees of all kinds; summer, fall.
*C. flaccida:* Similar except rusty-brown cap and stem, whitish to yellowish gills. Edible, tart, good in relish, catsup, for pickling.
*C. maxima:* Similar color, shape, except much larger, growing up to 1 foot across. Edible, fair.
*C. geotropa:* Similar medium-size species, up to 6 in. broad, buff to pinkish-tan cap and stem, paler gills, with mint fragrance. Edible.

*Clitocybe nebularis:* Pale-yellow spores. Edible; indigestible for some.
CAP: 3–6 in. broad. Grayish to pale brownish gray, darker at center, usually covered with white powdery bloom. Rounded, then becoming flat with shallow depression, often a pointed knob. Edge incurved at first, later becoming wavy. Dry. Slightly hairy. Flesh white, tough, thick. Sometimes with mushroom parasite, *Volvariella surrecta*, growing from cap.
GILLS: Whitish to yellowish, extending only slightly down stem. Crowded.
STEM: 2–4 in. tall. Like gills or flushed with cap-color. With scattered buff-brown hairs. Curved. Sometimes off-center. Base often enlarged.
WHERE & WHEN: Alone or several or groups in humus and soil in mixed conifer and hardwood forests; late summer, fall.
*C. robusta* (*C. alba*): Similar but with 3–4-in. white cap, whitish gills, white to buff stem, 1–2 in. tall, without buff-brown hairs on stem. Among leaves in woods. Edible.

# CLITOCYBE

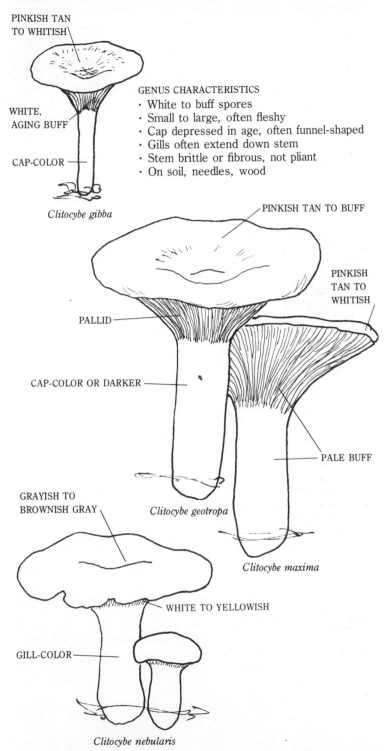

PINKISH TAN
TO WHITISH

WHITE,
AGING BUFF

CAP-COLOR

*Clitocybe gibba*

GENUS CHARACTERISTICS
· White to buff spores
· Small to large, often fleshy
· Cap depressed in age, often funnel-shaped
· Gills often extend down stem
· Stem brittle or fibrous, not pliant
· On soil, needles, wood

PINKISH TAN TO BUFF

PINKISH
TAN TO
WHITISH

PALLID

CAP-COLOR OR DARKER

PALE BUFF

*Clitocybe geotropa*

*Clitocybe maxima*

GRAYISH TO
BROWNISH GRAY

WHITE TO YELLOWISH

GILL-COLOR

*Clitocybe nebularis*

**Clitocybe odora** (*C. connexa, C. viridis*): Pinkish-cream spores. Edible. Strong anise fragrance in youth. Too aromatic to be eaten alone; add 1 or 2 caps to soups, stews or combine with bland mushrooms. Or dry, grind, use as flavoring.
CAP: 1–4 in. broad. Bluish green to dull green in moist weather, drying whitish. Covered with whitish cast when young. Rounded, aging broadly rounded or with irregular, upturned edge. Streaked with hairs. Moist. Flesh greenish white to white to pallid, thin, soft.
GILLS: Whitish, aging pale buff or tinged bluish green. Attached to stem or extending partially down it. Close together.
STEM: 1–3 in. tall. Whitish to buff to bluish green. Moist. Enlarged at base. Downy above, base covered with white threads (mycelium).
WHERE & WHEN: Scattered in fir needles, often attached to leaves and debris, under hardwoods or mixed hardwoods-conifers, or on edge of woods; late summer, fall.
*var. pacifica:* Dull-green cap, stem, gills; gills attached to stem; yellowish spores; growing under conifers. Edible.
**C. olida** (*Hygrophoropsis*): Similar but smaller, dull orange. Edible.
**C. suaveolens:** Similar with same strong fragrance but white to off-white, with white spores, growing in conifers. Edible.

**Clitocybe clavipes:** White spores. Edible (some people say not with alcohol).
CAP: 1–3 in. broad. Drab grayish brown, sometimes tinged olive; paler at edge. Rounded, becoming flat with slightly depressed center, often with low pointed knob. Extreme edge tending to remain incurved for some time. Moist, becoming water-soaked in wet weather. Flesh whitish, thick.
GILLS: White, aging yellowish. Extend down stem. Close together, forked.
STEM: 1–2½ in. tall. Whitish to grayish with grayish hairs, often tinged olive. Enlarging over lower two-thirds into club-shaped base. Somewhat spongy within, often waterlogged.
WHERE & WHEN: Alone to scattered to abundant, usually under conifers, especially pine, or in mixed woods; summer, fall.

**Clitocybe aurantiaca** (*Cantharellus aurantiacus, Hygrophoropsis aurantiaca*); false chanterelle: White spores. Edible for some; reported poisonous by others, possibly because mistaken for poisonous *Omphalotus olearius*.
CAP: 1–4 in. broad. Very variable in color from yellowish or orangy (sometimes toned dark brown or even blackish) to occasionally pale cream or whitish. Rounded, aging flat to shallowly depressed. Edge often lobed at first, aging upturned. Dry. Soft, suedelike to velvety. Flesh cap-color, soft.
GILLS: Orangy to yellow to cream to nearly white. Extend down stem. Crowded, narrow, repeatedly forked, suggesting a *Cantharellus*.
STEM: 1–3 in. tall. Cap-color or paler. Finely velvety. Dry, enlarging downward. Often off-center, curved, twisted. Spongy within, often hollow.
WHERE & WHEN: Alone to scattered to many on ground or rotted wood or standing dead wood, under hardwoods and conifers; late summer, fall, northern U.S. and adjacent Canada.
LOOK-ALIKES: Resembles *Cantharellus* but has true gills, while *Cantharellus* has only blunt veins. Resembles *Omphalotus olearius* but the latter is larger, grows in large clusters with bases fused together.

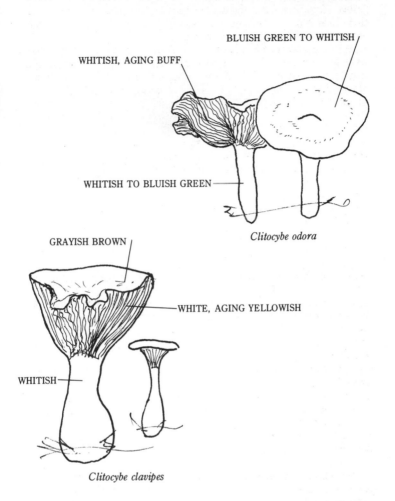

BLUISH GREEN TO WHITISH

WHITISH, AGING BUFF

WHITISH TO BLUISH GREEN

*Clitocybe odora*

GRAYISH BROWN

WHITE, AGING YELLOWISH

WHITISH

*Clitocybe clavipes*

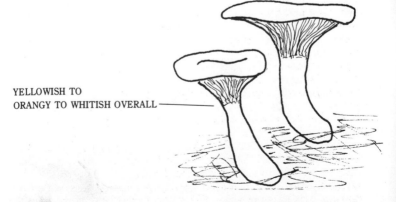

YELLOWISH TO
ORANGY TO WHITISH OVERALL

*Clitocybe aurantiaca*

*Clitocybe dealbata* (*C. sudorifica*): White spores. Poisonous.
CAP: ½–2 in. broad. Grayish white when moist, drying whitish. Rounded, aging flat or with depressed center. Edge incurved in youth, nearly even in age. Smooth. Hairless. Flesh grayish white, thin.
GILLS: Grayish white to buff. Extend down stem. Close together.
STEM: 1–3 in. tall. Cap-color. Short, tough, hairless to minutely downy. Sometimes curved, slightly larger at top.
WHERE & WHEN: Alone to scattered to many, occasionally in rings, in grass, lawns, or on leaves in open woods; late summer, fall.
*C. rivulosa:* Similar but more pinkish. Poisonous.
*C. cerussata:* Similar but larger, 1–3 in. whitish arched cap, often with round scalloped edge, in dense clusters. Poisonous.
LOOK-ALIKES: Beware these small whitish *Clitocybes* growing in grass, often side by side with edible species. They can be mistakenly gathered with *Marasmius oreades, Clitopilus prunulus, Agaricus campestris.*

LACCARIA  Most distinctive characteristic of these small mushrooms is their widely spaced, somewhat waxy-looking gills, purplish to flesh-colored, attached to the stem or extending slightly down it. The stem is fibrous, longer than cap width. Caps are rounded, aging nearly flat to upturned. Spores are white to pale lilac. Sometimes confused with *Hygrophorus* or *Lactarius.*
EDIBILITY: Edible but rather bland. Discard tough, stringy stems. Caps best simmered with more strongly flavored ingredients. Good with eggs after simmering in chicken broth with chopped ham; spike with sherry or Marsala.

*Laccaria laccata* (*Clitocybe laccata*): White spores. Edible.
CAP: ½–3 in. broad. Wide color variation depending on water content, fading from mahogany to cinnamon to orangy tan to pinkish. Returns to original color when remoistened. Rounded, aging flat or upturned, often depressed in center. Edge sometimes ruffled and uneven. Smooth when moist, aging slightly roughened with mealy texture. Flesh cap-color, soft.
GILLS: Cap-color or paler pink, somewhat waxy looking. Well separated, irregular. Powdered with white spores in age. Extend slightly down stem.
STEM: 2–4 in. tall. Cap-color or dingy flesh-colored, often shaded whitish or purplish at base. Scurfy with scattered loose scales. Fibrous.
WHERE & WHEN: Single to many in moist habitats in woods; spring–fall.
*L. ochropurpurea* (*Clitocybe ochropurpurea*): Similar but with pale-lilac spores; purple well-separated gills with pallid cap (purplish when moist), sometimes cracking. Stem cap-color. Eastern North America. Edible.
*L. amethystina* (*Clitocybe amethystina*): Similar but beautiful violet-purple overall, drying pale grayish or whitish. Pale-lilac spores. Edible.

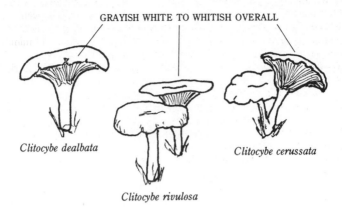

GRAYISH WHITE TO WHITISH OVERALL

*Clitocybe dealbata*

*Clitocybe rivulosa*

*Clitocybe cerussata*

## LACCARIA

GENUS CHARACTERISTICS
· White to pale-lilac spores
· Purplish to flesh color
· Gills far apart, waxy looking, attached to stem
· Stem fibrous
· Variable habitat

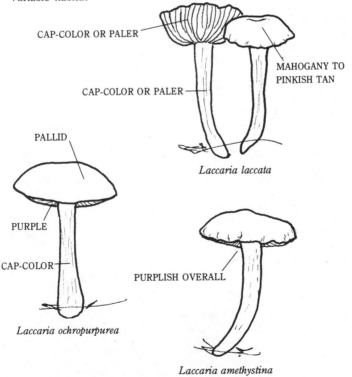

CAP-COLOR OR PALER

MAHOGANY TO PINKISH TAN

CAP-COLOR OR PALER

*Laccaria laccata*

PALLID

PURPLE

CAP-COLOR

*Laccaria ochropurpurea*

PURPLISH OVERALL

*Laccaria amethystina*

**ARMILLARIA AND ARMILLARIELLA** These genera are so similar some regard them as one, *Armillaria.* The cap surface is minutely hairy to scaly. All but one species (*Armillariella tabescens*) have a ring on the stem. There is never a cup at the stem base. The cap and stem are difficult to separate since the gills are attached to the stem (in *Armillariella* they extend slightly down the stem). The spores are white, except they are creamy yellow in one form of *Armillariella mellea. Armillaria* grow on the ground alone or in tufts of 2 or 3. *Armillariella* grow in clusters on wood or from buried wood.

They are easy to separate from other white-spored genera that have rings: remember that *Amanita* and *Lepiota* gills are not attached to the stem (and *Amanita* has a cup at the stem base). In *Cystoderma,* the cap and lower stem are conspicuously grainy. In *Catathelasma,* the ring is double and the gills extend down the stem. In *Lentinus,* the gill edges are serrated and the flesh is tough.

EDIBILITY: This is a good group of edibles, adaptable to a wide variety of recipes. There are no known poisonous species, although a few are tough and tasteless. Use only young, fresh, firm specimens; discard any that are turning soggy or discolored. Thinly slice stems on diagonal since they are not as tender as caps; discard stems if tough and stringy.

· *Armillariella mellea* and *A. tabescens* are strongly flavored and good in soups, stews, mushroom loaf, or sautéed in butter and served with meat or scrambled eggs. They can be highly seasoned. Most people eat only the young caps of *A. mellea.* It is found frequently in large quantities, literally by the bushelful, but any oversupply can be preserved by canning, freezing, drying, pickling.

· *Armillaria ponderosa* and *A. caligata* are closely related to the Japanese matsutake mushroom, widely used in Japan, and are excellent in Oriental recipes—stir-fry dishes, sukiyaki, tempura, chicken yakitori, shabu-shabu. Their flavors are well complemented by Japanese soy sauce, mirin wine, ginger. For example: Slice, dip in soy sauce (or marinate in soy sauce and mirin), brush with oil, broil. Or, slice thin, wrap in foil with sliced fish fillets or seafood, thinly sliced green vegetables (blanched), bit of wine or stock, salt, pepper. Bake at 400° for 20 minutes. Serve with lemon and soy sauce. They are also delicious added to soups, rice, stuffings, or shish kebab. Or slice and bake moistened with white wine, chicken broth, lots of melted butter, chopped fresh herbs, salt, pepper.

# ARMILLARIA AND ARMILLARIELLA

ARMILLARIA CHARACTERISTICS
· White spores
· Cap hairy to scaly
· Gills attached to stem
· Ring on stem
· Alone or in tufts of 2 to 3 on ground

ARMILLARIELLA CHARACTERISTICS
· Same as above except:
· One species does not have ring
· Gills extend slightly down stem
· In clusters on wood or buried wood

*Armillaria*

*Armillariella*

*Armillaria ponderosa;* pine mushroom, white matsutake: White spores. Edible, good. Distinctive spicy, sweet odor, somewhat like cinnamon.

CAP: 3–8 (15) in. broad. White, gradually becoming covered with cinnamon-brown threads and patches in age. Thick, fleshy, broadly rounded, becoming flat in age. Sticky to moist. Narrow, white, inrolled, flaplike edge. Flesh white, firm.

GILLS: White, gradually staining cinnamon. Crowded. Notched where they join stem.

VEIL: White, membranous. Leaving skirtlike, flaring ring; white on upper surface, spotted cinnamon on underside.

STEM: 2½–7 in. tall. White and smooth above ring; covered with cinnamon scales and hairs below ring in age. Sticky when wet. Thick, tapering toward base. Often curved.

WHERE & WHEN: Single to scattered under mixed conifers, especially pines, huckleberries, rhododendrons; fall.

*Armillaria caligata* (*Tricholoma caligatum*): White spores. Edible, choice. Recognized by its red-brown scales, hairy lower stem, prominent ring.

CAP: 2–6 in. broad. Winy-brown to dark-cinnamon fibrils covering whitish to pinkish undersurface. Rounded, aging almost flat, sometimes slightly depressed. Dry. Flesh white, firm.

GILLS: White to grayish, aging brown. Crowded. Attached to stem.

VEIL: Dull white, soft, membranous. Leaving conspicuous flaring ring with hairy covering on lower surface, similar to cap and stem, turning dingy brownish.

STEM: 1½–3½ in. long. Whitish and smooth above ring; brownish and scaly like cap below ring. Dry. Sometimes larger at center.

WHERE & WHEN: Single to numerous under mixed hardwoods and conifers; late fall, eastern North America and along Pacific Coast.

*Armillaria zelleri* (*Tricholoma zelleri*): White spores. Edible but very poor quality.

CAP: 2–10 (12) in. broad. Orangy brown or mottled orange and olive brown. White on inrolled edge, often fringed with veil remnants. Covered with gelatinous layer in youth, soon drying out and breaking into small scales. Bell-shaped, becoming rounded with center knob to nearly flat in age. Flesh white, bruising orangy brown.

GILLS: Off-white to tan, often brown-spotted in age. Attached to stem. Crowded.

VEIL: White, membranous. Leaving ring that stands out from stem at first, then hangs down.

STEM: 1½–5 in. long. White with downy hairs above ring. Colored layer of cap continues below ring. Tapering to pointed base with blunt end.

WHERE & WHEN: Scattered to many or in large fairy rings or arcs under conifers, rhododendrons, in moss, lichen beds; fall, Pacific Northwest, East, Midwest.

LOOK-ALIKES: *Tricholoma aurantium* has similar coloration but its fragile transparent veil breaks early, usually leaving no ring. Inedible.

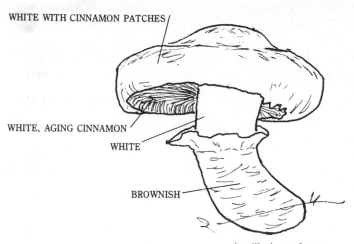

WHITE WITH CINNAMON PATCHES

WHITE, AGING CINNAMON

WHITE

BROWNISH

*Armillaria ponderosa*

WHITE WITH REDDISH-BROWN SCALES

WHITE, AGING BROWN

WHITE

BROWNISH

*Armillaria caligata*

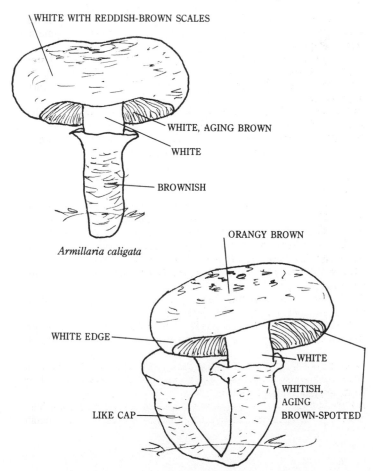

ORANGY BROWN

WHITE EDGE

WHITE

WHITISH, AGING BROWN-SPOTTED

LIKE CAP

*Armillaria zelleri*

*Armillariella mellea* (*Armillaria mellea*); honey mushroom, shoe-
string mushroom: White to creamy-yellow spores. Young caps are
edible, choice. Unpleasant odor and taste disappear in cooking. Great
variations in color and shape, but can always be identified because it
is the only white-spored mushroom with a ring growing on wood in
clusters.

CAP: 2–6 in. broad. Varies from honey yellow to tannish to rusty to
dark brown, darker at center. Hemispheric at first, becoming rounded
to upturned, sometimes with a knob. Inrolled edge in youth, finely
ribbed in age. Minutely scaly with a tuft of fine erect hairs over center.
Sticky to slimy in wet weather. Often dusted with white spores falling
from other caps in the same cluster. Flesh white, discoloring to brownish in age.

GILLS: White to dingy cream, staining rusty to dingy brown in age.
Often powdered with white spores. Attached or extending slightly
down stem. Fairly close together to somewhat far apart.

VEIL: White to buff to yellow, with clusters of hairs. Leaving a cottony
to membranous whitish ring, often tinged brownish.

STEM: 2–8 in. long. Dingy white with downy hairs above ring. Dingy
becoming rusty-stained below ring. Slender, sometimes enlarging toward base or top. Often with shoestringlike roots, blackish in age,
under tree bark. Both roots and wood are luminous in the dark.

WHERE & WHEN: In small to large clusters on living and dead conifers or hardwoods or on soil from buried wood. In large clumps at
base of tree, then swarming up the tree as decayed places appear,
often from same log each year, sometimes by the hundreds; late summer, fall. Alexander H. Smith reports the form growing in lower Great
Lake and southern states is yellower, nearly hairless, with stem narrowing downward to a point, with creamy-yellowish spores, growing
in large clusters, usually from buried wood. A darker, more scaly form
grows in northern and forested mountainous areas, appearing later in
the fall, usually not from buried wood but aboveground portions; stem
not narrowing downward.

*Armillariella tabescens* (*Clitocybe monadelpha, C. tabescens*): White
spores. Edible, good. Differs from *A. mellea* in that it has a dry cap,
no veil or ring.

CAP: 1–4 in. broad. Honey yellow aging pinkish brown to orangy
brown. Rounded, aging flat to depressed. Dry. Minutely hairy with
dense erect hairs in center. Flesh white, staining brown in age; brown
at stem base.

GILLS: Whitish, aging yellowish then brownish. Extend slightly down
stem. Somewhat far apart.

VEIL: Absent.

STEM: 2–8 in. long. Silky white near top, gradually darkening toward
base. Often tapering toward base. Dry. Of same consistency as cap.
Sometimes with rootlike strands permeating wood.

WHERE & WHEN: In large clusters at base of living and dead trees,
on roots, stumps, or on ground from buried wood; summer, fall.

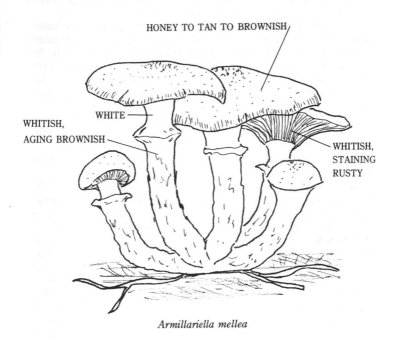

HONEY TO TAN TO BROWNISH

WHITE

WHITISH,
AGING BROWNISH

WHITISH,
STAINING
RUSTY

*Armillariella mellea*

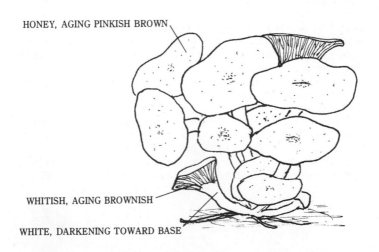

HONEY, AGING PINKISH BROWN

WHITISH, AGING BROWNISH

WHITE, DARKENING TOWARD BASE

*Armillariella tabescens*

**CATATHELASMA**   These large, fleshy mushrooms can be identified by two characteristics: they have a double veil and their gills extend down the stem. The inner veil extends from the inner edge of the cap to the stem just below the gills, while the outer veil extends from the outer cap edge and covers the entire stem. The inner veil is delicate and rather hairy, while the outer veil is membranous and more sturdy. When they break, they leave a double ring that flares upward at first. They grow on the ground in forested areas, singly or several together.
EDIBILITY: Two species are known to be edible, although of poor quality. They are best pickled and preserved in oil. If you like their flavor, they can be sautéed in butter or used in other dishes.
LOOK-ALIKES: These species were formerly classified in *Armillaria* but differ in having the double veil and gills extending down the stem. The careless might confuse them with *Amanita,* which should be carefully checked.

*Catathelasma imperialis* (*Armillaria imperialis, Biannularia imperialis*): White spores. Edible but poor quality.
CAP: 6–18 in. broad. Dingy yellow brown, sometimes tinged olive, aging dark brown. Rounded, aging flat. Sticky when wet, soon becoming dry. Somewhat cracked in center. Edge tightly inrolled in youth. Flesh white, firm, very thick. The young buttons are very hard, sometimes 6 in. thick.
GILLS: Buff to olivish. Extending down stem. Close together.
VEIL: Double. Pinkish-buff to brownish membranous outer veil envelops stem and extends to outer cap edge. Inner veil extends from inner cap edge to stem, covering gills. It is more delicate, softer, with clusters of hair. Leaving persistent double ring that flares upward at first.
STEM: 4½–7 in. long. Thick at top, narrowing to point at base. White above ring, colored like cap below ring.
WHERE & WHEN: Single to several in western conifer forests, particularly in Pacific Northwest; summer, fall.

*Catathelasma ventricosa* (*Armillaria ventricosa*): White spores. Edible but of poor quality.
CAP: 4–14 in. broad. Whitish to ashy gray. Rounded, becoming broadly rounded in age. Dry. Smooth, hairless, shining. Flesh white, firm.
GILLS: Whitish, aging pinkish buff. Extend down stem. Crowded.
VEIL: Double. Pallid, membranous outer veil attached to upper cap edge. More fragile inner veil attached to inner cap edge. Leaving double ring.
STEM: 2½–6 in. long. Dry, white above ring; dull yellow below ring. Enlarged midway, tapering to narrow, rooting base.
WHERE & WHEN: Alone or several in mixed woods, under pines, rhododendron; late summer, fall, eastern North America.

# CATATHELASMA

GENUS CHARACTERISTICS
· White spores
· Large, fleshy, dingy
· Double veil and ring
· Gills extend down stem
· On ground under trees

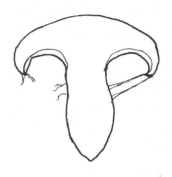

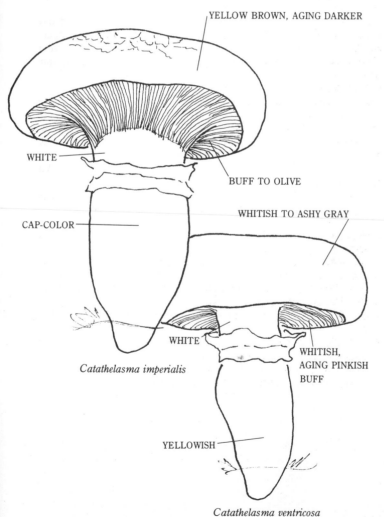

YELLOW BROWN, AGING DARKER

WHITE

BUFF TO OLIVE

CAP-COLOR

WHITISH TO ASHY GRAY

WHITE

*Catathelasma imperialis*

WHITISH, AGING PINKISH BUFF

YELLOWISH

*Catathelasma ventricosa*

**CYSTODERMA**  These small, pretty, fragile mushrooms have a grainy-mealy coating on cap and stem (which distinguishes them from *Armillaria*). They have a veil in youth that tears away from the stem, remaining attached to the cap edge, often leaving little or no ring, or in some species a flaring, prominent one. Gills are attached to the stem, separating *Cystoderma* from *Lepiota*, which has gills free from the stem. They often grow in great numbers on ground or on well-decayed wood.
EDIBILITY: Most are too small but the following are worth collecting.

*Cystoderma cinnabarinum* (*Armillaria cinnabarina*): White spores. Edible.
CAP: 1–3 in. broad. Pallid, covered with bright cinnamon-red to orange-brown grainy particles, darker at center. Oval, becoming rounded to flat. Edge incurved at first, later fringed with veil fragments. Flesh whitish, stained rusty under cap surface.
GILLS: White to creamy. Close together. Attached to stem at first, then separating from it.
VEIL: Fragile, grainy, leaving fragments fringing cap edge and a thin ring that soon disappears.
STEM: 1–2¼ in. long. Grainy and colored like cap below ring; pale and smooth above.
WHERE & WHEN: Single or in small groups on ground or on well-decayed conifer wood under conifers, hardwoods; late summer, fall.
*C. granulosum* (*Lepiota granulosa*): Similar but smaller, about 2 in. broad; yellowish brown to cinnamon; no ring; scaly stem; grows often with moss under hardwoods, conifers; summer, fall. Edible.

**LENTINUS**  Of hard, tough consistency, growing on wood, attached by a short stem. Gills have sawtooth edges, especially in age. Spores are white. A closely related genus, *Lentinellus*, differs in its stem being off-center or absent.
EDIBILITY: Most are too tough, but fresh, young caps of the two described here are edible. Parboil, cook long and slowly. Or dry, then grate to flavor gravies, soups, other foods.

*Lentinus lepideus:* White to buff spores. Young caps edible.
CAP: 2–6 in. broad. Whitish to dingy yellow, breaking into small, coarse brown scales, often disappearing. Hemispheric, becoming rounded, aging nearly flat to depressed. Edge incurved at first, aging straight. Slimy when young, soon becoming dry. Flesh white, tough.
GILLS: White, aging yellowish, bruising rusty brown. Edges irregular, saw-toothed. Close to slightly distant. Notched where they join stem.
VEIL: Buff. Membranous, leaving ridgelike ring that may disappear.
STEM: 1–4 in. tall. White, minutely hairy above ring; white, aging reddish brown, scaly below ring. Often slightly off-center, curved, tapering to base. Hard. Flesh white, aging yellow to rusty at base.
WHERE & WHEN: Single to several on logs, stumps of conifers, especially larch; on hardwoods; on oak, pine lumber, rail ties, posts; spring, fall.
*L. ponderosus:* Similar but larger (up to 15 in. broad), without a ring. Cap more pinkish buff. In Pacific Northwest. Young caps edible.

# CYSTODERMA

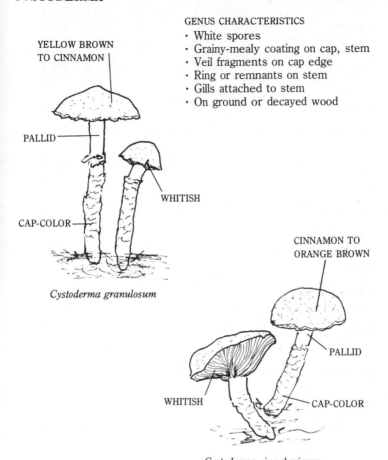

GENUS CHARACTERISTICS
· White spores
· Grainy-mealy coating on cap, stem
· Veil fragments on cap edge
· Ring or remnants on stem
· Gills attached to stem
· On ground or decayed wood

YELLOW BROWN
TO CINNAMON

PALLID

WHITISH

CAP-COLOR

*Cystoderma granulosum*

CINNAMON TO
ORANGE BROWN

PALLID

WHITISH

CAP-COLOR

*Cystoderma cinnabarinum*

# LENTINUS

GENUS CHARACTERISTICS
· White spores
· Cap tough, leathery
· Gills with sawtooth edges
· Stem short
· May have ring
· On wood

YELLOWISH WITH BROWN SCALES

WHITE,
AGING YELLOW

WHITE

*Lentinus lepideus*

**PLEUROTUS**   These soft, fleshy (never woody) mushrooms, with off-center stems or none at all, grow on wood or buried wood, usually in large overlapping masses, often high in the tree. Their spores are white to buff to lilac-tinted, which separates them from similar genera with off-center or no stems, growing on wood: *Crepidotus* has brown spores; *Phyllotopsis,* pink; *Gymnopilus,* yellowish brown. Their gill edges are smooth, not saw-toothed as in *Lentinus* and *Lentinellus.* Small, shiny, black beetles are usually darting about in their gills, good indicators that you have found a *Pleurotus.*

EDIBILITY: Some are tough or bitter but a few are eagerly sought for the table, particularly the oyster mushroom, *P. ostreatus.* Gather young, tender caps, cut away the tough part where it joins the wood. Submerge caps in salted water until the beetles abandon ship, so you can skim them off. Drain. Long, slow cooking is required. *P. ulmarius* requires parboiling before adding to your recipe.

· The classic recipe for *P. ostreatus:* Use small caps whole or cut up large caps, dip in beaten egg, roll in cracker crumbs, fry in butter or deep fat. Drain on absorbent paper. Toss parsley sprigs into the hot pan until they are crisp and green. Serve together.

· Bake thin strips with lemony cream sauce or cheese sauce or Madeira sauce.

· Slice, precook slowly in butter, covered, for 5–10 minutes, add to cream soups, fried rice, rice pilaf, sukiyaki, stew, casseroles, oyster-mushroom stew, for final cooking.

· Cut up and pickle. Use as hors d'oeuvre, relish, salad.

*Pleurotus ostreatus* (*P. sapidus, P. columbinus*): White to buff to grayish-lilac spores. Edible, choice. The "oyster-mushroom complex" includes several forms, varying slightly in cap and spore color.
CAP: 1–6 in. broad. White to oyster gray to tan, aging umber brown in cold weather. Shaped like a fan or oyster shell. Edge inrolled, often wavy or lobed. Smooth. Moist. Flesh white, firm.
GILLS: Whitish to grayish, far apart, veined, extending to base.
STEM: Up to ½ in. long or none at all. Downy white with dense white hairs around base. Attached to side of cap.
WHERE & WHEN: Single, or usually in clusters, overlapping one above the other, on hardwoods and conifers (aspen, willow, beech, maple, cottonwood, alder, pine), branches, logs, stumps, trunks; spring, cool and wet summers, fall, early winter.

*Pleurotus porrigens* (*Pleurocybella porrigens, Pleurotus albolanatus*); angel's wings: White spores. Edible but bland; a good extender. Very thin, pliant (other species not pliant), very narrow, crowded gills.
CAP: 2–4 in. broad. Glistening snow-white, aging pale cream. Fan-shaped or like clam shell. Edge inrolled at first. Pliant. Dry. Minutely hairy. Cottony toward base. Flesh white, very thin.
GILLS: White, aging pale cream. Thin. Crowded together. Extend to base.
STEM: Absent.
WHERE & WHEN: Clustered on conifer logs, stumps, especially hemlock; late summer, fall.

# PLEUROTUS

GENUS CHARACTERISTICS
· White to buff to lilac spores
· Cap soft, fleshy, not woody, dull-colored
· Gill edges smooth
· Stem usually off-center or absent
· Clustered on wood or buried wood

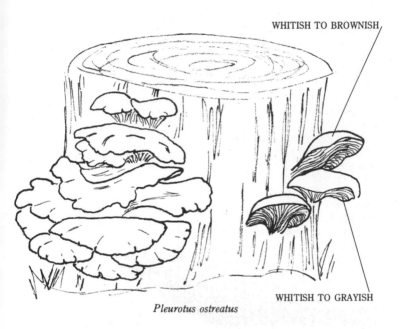

WHITISH TO BROWNISH

WHITISH TO GRAYISH

*Pleurotus ostreatus*

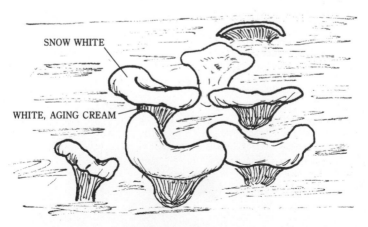

SNOW WHITE

WHITE, AGING CREAM

*Pleurotus porrigens*

*Pleurotus ulmarius* (*Lyophyllum ulmarium*): Buff to white spores. Edible, tough; parboiling, long cooking required.

CAP: 2–5 in. broad. White to buff, aging tan to brown, sometimes tinged yellow or reddish brown. Rounded, aging flat with shallow center depression. Edge inrolled, splitting. Covered with fine scales; frequently cracking. Flesh white, hard.

GILLS: White to cream. Fairly far apart. Attached or notched at stem.

STEM: 2–5 in. long. Whitish, aging yellowish pink. Minutely hairy at top. Cottony below. Sometimes with swollen base. Curving out and up from tree.

WHERE & WHEN: Single to several on hardwoods, especially elm, usually living trees, from wounds, knotholes, branch stubs, often high in tree; fall, early winter. Mostly eastern North America.

*Pleurotus elongatipes* (*Tricholoma unifactum*): Edible. Buff spores.

CAP: 1–6 in. broad. Creamy, often tinged pink, mottled with darker water spots over center. Rounded, aging nearly flat. Moist. Hairless. Flesh whitish to pinkish buff, firm.

GILLS: Buff, often tinged pinkish. Veined. Far apart. Notched where they join stem.

STEM: 2–9 in. tall. White. Hairless, except stiff white hairs at base. Curved or bent, sometimes enlarged at base. Soft, cottony center.

WHERE & WHEN: Single to dense groups at base of hardwood trees, or on logs, limbs, shrubs, fallen dead wood; late summer, fall.

**OMPHALOTUS** Recognized by distinctive bright orange color. Grows in clusters at base of stumps or from buried roots.

*Omphalotus olearius* (*Clitocybe illudens*); jack-o'-lantern, false chanterelle: Yellowish-white spores. Poisonous.

CAP: 3–6 in. broad. Orangy yellow to bright orange. Rounded, aging flat, often depressed in center with or without shallow knob. Edge inrolled in youth, becoming even in age. Streaked with flat hairs. Flesh white to orange-tinted, thin, firm.

GILLS: Yellowish orange. Sharp-edged. Crowded together. Extend down stem. Luminescent when fresh if you look at them in the dark for several minutes.

STEM: 3–8 in. tall. Cap-color or paler. Darker at base. Downy to somewhat scaly in age. Many fused together. Sometimes off-center. Curving gracefully upward. Tapering to a narrow base.

WHERE & WHEN: Large, dense clusters at base of hardwood stumps or on ground from buried roots; late summer, fall, eastern North America.

LOOK-ALIKES: Sometimes mistaken for edible *Cantharellus*. However, *O. olearius*'s gills are crowded, sharp-edged, unforked, while *Cantharellus* does not have true gills, but merely blunt veins, far apart and forked.

*O. subilludens:* Similar species found in South. Poisonous.

*O. illudens:* Similar Pacific Coast species. Poisonous.

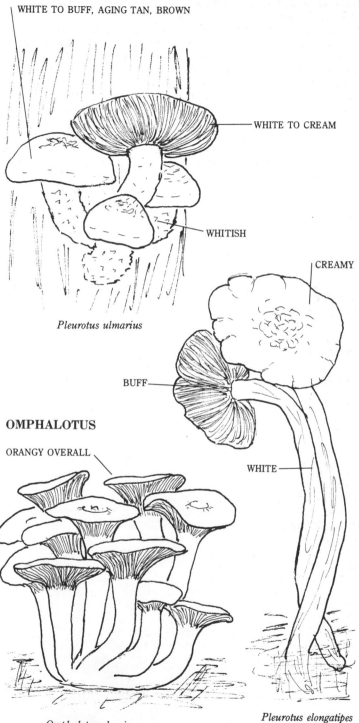

WHITE TO BUFF, AGING TAN, BROWN

WHITE TO CREAM

WHITISH

CREAMY

*Pleurotus ulmarius*

BUFF

**OMPHALOTUS**

ORANGY OVERALL

WHITE

*Omphalotus olearius*

*Pleurotus elongatipes*

**VOLVARIELLA**  This distinctive genus is infrequently encountered, always a thrill to find. The young mushroom button is completely
enclosed within a membranous cover that ruptures as the stem begins
to elongate, remaining around the stem base like a loose sack or cup.
There is never a ring on the stem. The cap is fleshy, soft, bell-shaped
at first, becoming rounded, sometimes nearly flat in age, easily separated from the stem. The gills are not attached to the stem and age
pink to salmon, the color of the spores—a quick way to separate them
from *Amanita,* which has white gills and spores.

EDIBILITY: There are no poisonous species but many are too small
to be treated as edibles—you may even find a tiny, perfectly formed
species, *V. surrecta (V. loveiana)* growing as a parasite on the cap of
another mushroom, usually *Clitocybe nebularis.* The larger species,
described here, may be used as all-purpose edibles. Stems may be
sliced thinly and cooked along with the caps.

*Volvariella bombycina* (*Volvaria bombycina*); the silky *Volvaria*:
Pink to salmon spores. Edible. Sometimes quite large, weighing 1 lb.
CAP: 2–8 in. broad. White to yellowish with white edge fringed with
fine hairs. Egg-shaped to bell-shaped, becoming rounded in age. Dry.
Covered with silky fibers, becoming rather scaly in age. Flesh white,
soft, thick over cap center, thinning toward edge. Cap extends beyond
gills.
GILLS: White, then pink to rosy; not attached to stem; edges finely
toothed.
STEM: 2–8 in. long. White, silky, shining. Dry. Enlarging at base.
CUP: Dull whitish, discoloring to dingy yellowish. Deep, thick, envelops stem base like a large, loose bag.
WHERE & WHEN: Single to several in crotches, hollows, knotholes
of tree trunks or on logs, sticks, stumps; summer and fall. May reappear in same place for several years.

*Volvariella speciosa* (*Volvaria speciosa*): Pink spores. Edible.
CAP: 2–4 (6) in. wide. Whitish to grayish, tinged darker over center.
Egg-shaped then bell-shaped, becoming rounded to almost flat with
broad knob at center. Slimy when wet; shiny when dry. Flesh white,
thick, soft.
GILLS: White, aging rosy. Not attached to stem. Crowded. Edges
finely toothed.
STEM: 2–4 (8) in. tall. Whitish. Solid. Minutely hairy at first, becoming
smooth. Swollen at base.
CUP: White, large, lobed with ragged edge.
WHERE & WHEN: Rich soil, rotting grass, straw, compost heaps,
corn fields; occasionally in woodlands, but usually cultivated areas;
summer.
*V. volvacea:* Pink spores. Edible. 2–3-in. broad cap, grayish yellow
streaked with blackish fibrils. Bell-shaped, becoming rounded. Flesh
white, soft, thick at center, very thin elsewhere. Rosy gills. Stem
2–4 in. long, white, solid. Whitish to grayish lobed cup. Grows in rich
soil, compost, in greenhouses; summer.
*V. taylori:* Dark-rose spores. Edible. 1–2-in. white, conical to
rounded cap. Edge is lobed and finely cracked. Rosy gills. 1–3-in.
stem, pallid, thick, solid, slightly bulbous at base. Date-brown cup,
small, lobed. Grows on decayed hardwoods; summer.

# VOLVARIELLA

GENUS CHARACTERISTICS
- Pink to salmon spores
- Cap silky, bell-shaped to rounded
- Gills whitish, aging pink to salmon
- Gills not attached to stem
- No ring on stem
- Sacklike cup at stem base
- On wood, debris, rich ground

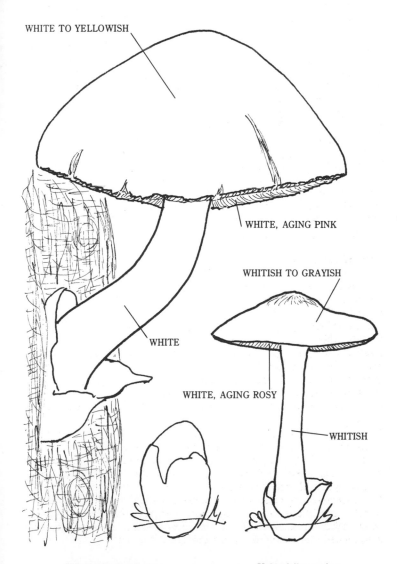

WHITE TO YELLOWISH

WHITE, AGING PINK

WHITISH TO GRAYISH

WHITE

WHITE, AGING ROSY

WHITISH

*Volvariella bombycina*          *Volvariella speciosa*

**PLUTEUS**   Look for these clues: Soft, fleshy, rounded caps that flatten with age; gills not attached to the stem; cap and stem easily and cleanly detached (all it takes is a slight twist of the stem to pull it off, leaving a smooth, rounded hole in cap); no ring on stem and no cup at stem base; found on wood—old logs, stumps, sawdust. Be sure you don't have an *Entoloma,* which also has pink spores and gills but with gills attached to stem.

EDIBILITY: There are no poisonous species but most are too small to be of interest as food. Some people rank the larger ones, described here, as good eating; others think they're mediocre. They are best sautéed in butter or broiled. The stems are tougher than the caps and require longer cooking. The soft flesh deteriorates rapidly, so refrigeration and prompt cooking are necessary.

*Pluteus cervinus;* deer or fawn mushroom: Dull salmon-pink spores. Edible. Great variation in color and size; probably a complex of many varieties.
CAP: 2–5½ in. broad. Varies from whitish to dingy tan to grayish brown, aging lighter. Sometimes streaked with darker fibrils over center. Conic at first, becoming rounded to flat in age, sometimes with broad knob at center. Often slightly wrinkled. Dull when dry, shining when wet. Flesh white, soft, thin on edge, thicker toward center. Often curved.
GILLS: White, aging salmon pink. Not attached to stem—end ⅛ in. from stem. Close together. In age, lose rigidity and collapse against each other.
STEM: 2–6 in. long. White, tinged dingy. Smooth to slightly hairy. Dry, solid. Enlarging toward base.
WHERE & WHEN: Single to several on decaying hardwoods and conifers, sawdust, buried wood; spring–fall. One of the earliest spring fungi.
*P. magnus:* Very similar to *P. cervinus* but with deep-brown, almost black, cap with pale edge, thicker stem. Edible.
*P. pellitus:* All-white species, 1–2-in. cap. Edible.
*P. albipes:* White stem; grayish, yellowish, or brown cap. Edible.

*Pluteus granularis:* Pale-pink spores. Edible.
CAP: 1–2 in. broad. Yellow to brown, sprinkled with minute blackish granules, giving a smoky, velvety hue; center often darker. Rounded, then becoming flat with slight knob at center.
GILLS: Whitish, aging pinkish. Not attached to stem. Crowded.
STEM: 2–3 in. long. Pallid to brownish, usually paler at top. Velvety.
WHERE & WHEN: Single to several, decaying wood, fallen trees; summer, fall.

*Pluteus umbrosus:* Pale-pink spores. Edible.
CAP: 2–4 in. broad. Smoky to blackish brown. Bell-shaped, becoming rounded to nearly flat. Wrinkled with downy center.
GILLS: Whitish, then pinkish with minutely toothed brownish to blackish edges. Not attached to stem.
STEM: 1–3 in. long. Colored like or paler than cap; slightly hairy. Solid. Larger toward base.
WHERE & WHEN: Single to several, decaying wood, often in swamps, along streams; summer, fall.

# PLUTEUS

GENUS CHARACTERISTICS
· Pink to salmon spores
· Cap soft, fleshy, rounded, aging flat
· Cap edge incurved in youth
· Gills whitish, age pink to salmon
· Gills do not touch stem
· Cap and stem easily separated
· No ring on stem
· No cup at base
· On wood, sawdust

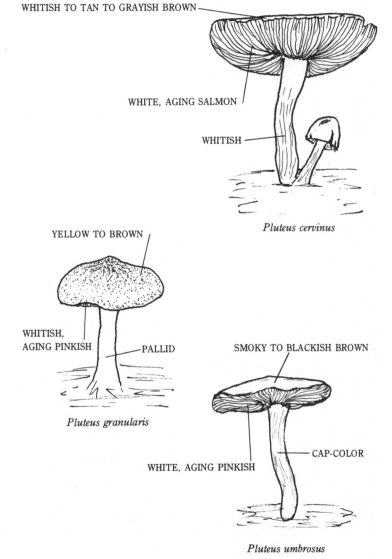

WHITISH TO TAN TO GRAYISH BROWN

WHITE, AGING SALMON

WHITISH

*Pluteus cervinus*

YELLOW TO BROWN

WHITISH,
AGING PINKISH

PALLID

*Pluteus granularis*

SMOKY TO BLACKISH BROWN

CAP-COLOR

WHITE, AGING PINKISH

*Pluteus umbrosus*

**ENTOLOMA**   These are the salmon-spored mushrooms that can cause trouble. Some are poisonous, the edibility of most of them is untested, many are difficult to tell apart. Thus it is recommended that no *Entoloma* be eaten except for the very distinctive *E. abortivum*. It is a large genus with considerable variation in the species. The soft, fleshy caps sometimes are conic and pointed, but more often are rounded, sometimes becoming flat, upturned, and wavy, often lopsided. The edge is inrolled in youth, often cracking in age. The cap surface often has a polished sheen. The gills are whitish at first, staying white quite a while before becoming pinkish with spores. They are attached to the stem or are notched at the junction of stem and gills. The stem is longer than the cap is wide, often brittle, ridged, or grooved, rather fleshy, sometimes twisted. They grow on the ground.

*Entoloma abortivum* (*Clitopilus abortivus, Rhodophyllus abortivus*): Salmon-pink spores. Edible. So named because frequently it does not develop normally but is malformed into irregular, whitish, ball-shaped masses, lacking cap and gills. Usually both forms are found together, but sometimes the abortive form is found alone. Both forms are edible, but never eat the normal form unless the malformed is alongside to guarantee correct identification. Good sautéed in butter.
CAP: 2–5 in. broad. Gray or grayish brown, rounded with inrolled edge at first, becoming flat or slightly depressed at center. Edge sometimes wavy. Silky when young, smooth when old. Flesh white, fragile.
GILLS: Grayish, aging pale dusty rose. Crowded. Extend down stem slightly.
STEM: 1½–4 in. tall. Cap-color or paler. Solid, downy.
WHERE & WHEN: Singly or in groups, normal and malformed side by side, on ground or much-decayed or buried wood under hardwoods, around stumps, or in open places; summer, fall. Eastern North America.

*Entoloma sinuatum* (*E. lividum, Rhodophyllus sinuatus, R. lividus*); lead-colored lawn mushroom: Salmon-pink spores. Poisonous.
CAP: 3–6 in. broad. Dingy brown to lead-colored to whitish. Broadly bell-shaped, becoming nearly flat with slight knob. Edge inrolled at first, becoming straight and often split in age. Soapy feeling when wet, drying silky. Flesh white, thick, firm.
GILLS: Cream to grayish, aging pink. Rounded where they touch stem, fairly well-separated, wavy edges.
STEM: 1½–5 in. tall. White, tinged grayish with a few scattered scales. Shining, silky. Short, sturdy.
WHERE & WHEN: Scattered under hardwoods, conifers, or mixed woods, wet lawns, wooded pastures; summer, fall.

*Entoloma rhodopolium:* Rosy-pink spores. Poisonous.
CAP: 2–5 in. broad. Umber to smoky brown when moist, fading to pale brownish gray. Slightly slippery surface when wet; silky and shiny when dry. Slightly bell-shaped, becoming nearly flat to somewhat depressed with slight knob at center. Wavy edge. Flesh white, splits easily.
GILLS: Whitish, aging deep rose. Slightly notched at stem, rather far apart.
STEM: 1½–4 in. long. White, downy, becoming hollow. Splits easily.
WHERE & WHEN: Single or groups or clusters of 2 or 3 on ground in mixed and deciduous woods; summer, fall.

# ENTOLOMA

GENUS CHARACTERISTICS
· Salmon-pink spores
· Cap fleshy, often with polished sheen, cracked edge
· Gills attached to stem, age salmon pink
· Stem pallid, often grooved
· On ground

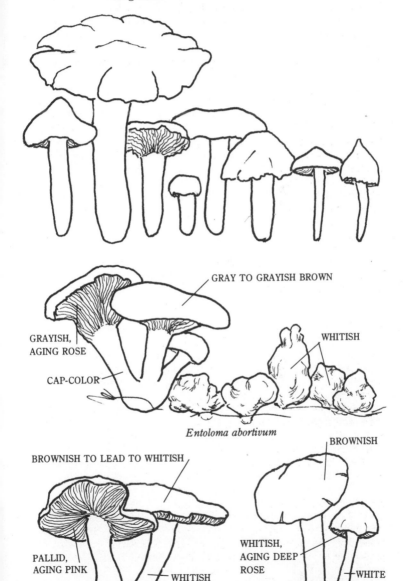

GRAY TO GRAYISH BROWN

GRAYISH, AGING ROSE

CAP-COLOR

WHITISH

*Entoloma abortivum*

BROWNISH TO LEAD TO WHITISH

PALLID, AGING PINK

WHITISH

*Entoloma sinuatum*

BROWNISH

WHITISH, AGING DEEP ROSE

WHITE

*Entoloma rhodopolium*

**LEPISTA** Variable in color and size, depending on age, habitat, weather. Often lilac, pinkish, buff, whitish. Rounded caps begin to flatten in age, then edges become upturned and wavy, giving lopsided, jaunty look. Gills are notched just before they reach stem—it looks like a knife cut a chunk out of them. Stem is stout with bulbous base, no ring or cup.

EDIBILITY: Ranked among the top 5 edibles. Their strong, pronounced, delicious flavor and good-sized meaty caps make them well suited to any recipe calling for mushrooms. Their caps tend to become waterlogged in rainy weather, so they're best picked when dry.

*Lepista nuda* (*Clitocybe nuda, Tricholoma nudum, Rhodopaxillus nudus*); woods blewit: Pinkish-buff spores. Edible, very choice. Fragrant odor.

CAP: 2–4 (5) in. broad. Lilac, but in age the blue fades out leaving dingy pinkish-brown tint, often darker over the center. Rounded in youth with inrolled edge, aging flat with uplifted wavy edge, sometimes with low knob. Moist. Smooth. Hairless. Flesh lilac, becoming pale or grayish.

GILLS: Color of cap, becoming paler, more flesh-colored in age. Crowded together. Notched just before they touch stem.

STEM: 1–3 in. long. Cap-color, often denser color at top, more rusty brown at base. Scattered white hairs on lower part. Often bulbous.

WHERE & WHEN: Single to numerous to clustered in deep leaves or needles under hardwoods and conifers, or around sawdust, compost piles, mounds of leaves or grass clippings; summer, fall.

*Lepista irina* (*Clitocybe irina, Tricholoma irinum, Rhodopaxillus irinus*): Pale pinkish-buff spores. Edible, choice; poisonous to some. Fragrant odor.

CAP: 1½–6 in. broad. Whitish to dingy gray to pale tan, darker if water-soaked, with white cottony edge. Rounded with inrolled edge, becoming flat with broad low knob. Sticky, becoming dry. Flesh white to pinkish, thick, soft.

GILLS: Whitish, aging dingy pinkish buff. Notched just before touching stem. Crowded. When cap turns up, gills appear to extend down stem.

STEM: 1–3 in. long. Dull whitish, aging dingy. Darker toward base. Hairy. May be thicker in middle. Slightly bulbous base.

WHERE & WHEN: In groups, often large rings, under conifers or mixed hardwoods; spring, late summer, fall.

*Lepista saeva* (*Clitocybe saeva, Rhodopaxillus saevus, Tricholoma personatum, L. personata*); common blewit, blue legs: Pale dingy-pink spores. Edible, good. Not as fragrant as other two species.

CAP: 2½–5½ in. broad. Grayish to buff to flesh-colored, rarely with lilac tint; fading in age, sometimes to dingy white. Hemispherical in youth, becoming rounded to flat with wavy, upturned edge. Covered with a powdery bloom at first with downy cap edge, becoming smooth. Flesh whitish, firm. Tends to look water-soaked in wet weather.

GILLS: Cap-color, never bluish, crowded, notched at the stem.

STEM: 2–4½ in. long. Pale lilac to bluish gray, covered with white or rosy fibrils. Stout, slightly bulbous base.

WHERE & WHEN: Solitary or in rings in grassy areas in open places or thin woods, along hedges; fall.

# LEPISTA

GENUS CHARACTERISTICS
· Pinkish-buff spores
· Often lilac, pinkish, buff, whitish
· Cap rounded, becoming upturned, wavy
· Gills notched at stem
· Stem stout, often bulbous
· No ring or cup
· On soil, decaying matter

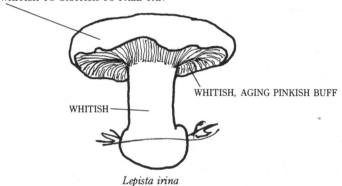

LILAC, AGING PINKISH BROWN OVERALL

*Lepista nuda*

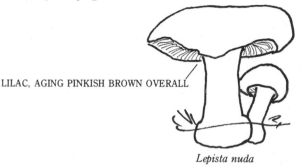

WHITISH TO GRAYISH TO PALE TAN

WHITISH, AGING PINKISH BUFF

WHITISH

*Lepista irina*

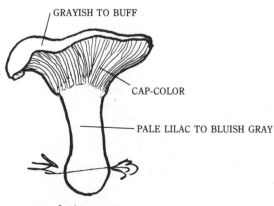

GRAYISH TO BUFF

CAP-COLOR

PALE LILAC TO BLUISH GRAY

*Lepista saeva*

**CLITOPILUS**   These are whitish to grayish mushrooms with the look and feel of kid gloves. They have pink to salmon-pink spores and grow on the ground. Their whitish gills age pinkish with maturing spores and not only are attached to the stem but extend down it. The rounded caps become flattened in age, and finally upturned or depressed, often with a wavy, irregular edge. The fleshy, solid stems sometimes are off-center. Care must be taken not to mistake them for a gray-capped, pink-spored *Entoloma* or for a white-spored, white-gilled *Clitocybe*.

EDIBILITY: There are no poisonous species. *C. prunulus* is esteemed as one of the most delicious mushrooms. *C. orcellus* is more delicately flavored. They are good creamed, stewed, sautéed in butter, added to stew, croquettes, or meat loaf.

*Clitopilus prunulus;* plum mushroom: Salmon-pink spores. Edible, choice.
CAP: 2–4 in. broad. Dull white to ashy gray with kid-glove texture. Broadly rounded, becoming flat with edges upturned and wavy in age. Dry. Flesh white, soft.
GILLS: Whitish to pale cream, aging dirty pinkish. Extending down stem. Fairly well separated. Easily separated in patches from cap.
STEM: 1½–3 in. long. Dull white. Covered with white cottony down. Sometimes off-center. Often curved.
WHERE & WHEN: Single to a few on ground in open woods, often on edges of paths, mossy banks, sandy soils; summer and fall.

*Clitopilus orcellus:* Pale-salmon spores. Edible. Some mycologists say this is not a separate species from *C. prunulus.* However, *C. orcellus* is considerably smaller, more irregular, its gills are closer together than *C. prunulus,* and it is somewhat sticky while *C. prunulus* is dry.
CAP: 1–3 in. broad. Whitish to smoky to yellowish. Rounded, aging flat. Cap edge is inrolled, often lobed and irregular. Surface is somewhat sticky. Flesh white, soft.
GILLS: White, aging pinkish buff. Extend down stem. Close together.
STEM: 1–2 in. tall. White. Silky, covered with minute hairs. Sometimes off-center.
WHERE & WHEN: Single to several in grassy areas—open fields, lawns—or open woods; summer and fall.

*Clitopilus albogriseus:* Pink spores. Edible, although very small.
CAP: ½–1 in. broad. Pale gray. Rounded, becoming flat and depressed in center. Edge rolled under.
GILLS: Grayish, becoming pinkish. Touches stem or extends down it. Close together.
STEM: ½–1 in. long. Pale gray, whitish at base, smooth.
WHERE & WHEN: Single or in groups on ground in mixed woods; summer, fall.

# CLITOPILUS

GENUS CHARACTERISTICS
· Pink to salmon spores
· Whitish to grayish with kid-glove texture
· Cap rounded, becoming flat or depressed
· Gills extend down stem
· Gills whitish, aging pale pink
· On ground

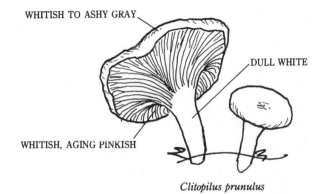

WHITISH TO ASHY GRAY

DULL WHITE

WHITISH, AGING PINKISH

*Clitopilus prunulus*

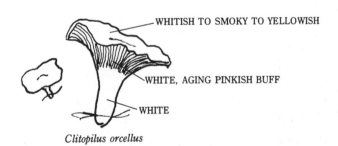

WHITISH TO SMOKY TO YELLOWISH

WHITE, AGING PINKISH BUFF

WHITE

*Clitopilus orcellus*

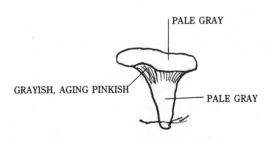

PALE GRAY

GRAYISH, AGING PINKISH

PALE GRAY

*Clitopilus albogriseus*

**GALERINA**  At least 3 deadly species; entire genus should be strictly avoided. Small with conic to rounded, smooth caps; long, thin, brittle stems. Cap edge is minutely grooved; in youth pressed tightly to stem. Gills are attached to stem. There may be a veil and ring. Rusty-brown spores. Grow in deep moss or on wood, sometimes buried, usually clustered.

*Galerina autumnalis* (*Pholiota autumnalis*): Rusty-brown spores. Deadly poisonous.
CAP: 1–2 in. broad. Dark brown when moist, drying light tan. Edge fades last so cap is often two-toned with tannish center and dark-brown edge. Slightly sticky to slimy. Rounded, sometimes with small knob. Hairless, smooth. Edge faintly ribbed. Flesh light brown, thick.
GILLS: Pale rusty brown. Attached to stem. Close together.
VEIL: Hairy. Leaving thin, bandlike, white, hairy ring; may disappear.
STEM: ½–2 in. tall. Brown streaked with white fibers. Darkening from base upward in age. Dry.
WHERE & WHEN: Alone to many in dense groups on well-decayed hardwood and conifer logs; sometimes on buried wood, thus appearing to grow on ground; early spring, late fall, warm winter weather.

*Galerina venenata:* Rusty-brown spores. Deadly poisonous.
CAP: ½–1½ in. broad. Cinnamon brown when wet, fading to dingy yellowish white. Moist. Broadly rounded, often slightly misshapen, sometimes with wavy edge, splitting in age. Flesh brownish, thick.
GILLS: Golden brown to dull cinnamon. Attached to stem. Far apart.
VEIL: Hairy, leaving hairy, bandlike ring on most specimens.
STEM: 1–1½ in. long. Brownish, thin, dry. White threads at base.
WHERE & WHEN: Scattered in grass, probably from buried wood; late fall, winter, Pacific Northwest.

*Galerina marginata* (*Pholiota marginata*): Brown spores. Deadly poisonous.
CAP: ¾–1¾ in. broad. Dark reddish brown when moist, fading to yellowish tan or orangy tan when dry. Smooth. Rounded, then flattening in age. Slightly ribbed edge. Flesh color of cap.
GILLS: Yellowish brown, becoming cap-color. Attached to stem. Far apart.
STEM: ¾–2 in. long. Cap-color or paler with frostlike bloom above fibery ring, sometimes disappearing. Base may be enlarged. Hollow.
WHERE & WHEN: In tufts and dense clusters on or near conifers, especially on rotted wood; spring–fall.

**CONOCYBE**  Recent research reveals some species contain poisonous and hallucinogenic properties; none is edible. They have bright rusty-brown spores; conic to rounded caps, not slimy; long, thin, fragile stems, may stain blue; sometimes a veil and ring; grow in grass or deep moss.

*Conocybe filaris:* Bright rusty-brown spores. Deadly poisonous in quantity.
CAP: ¼–¾ in. broad. Brownish when wet, fading to pale brownish to yellowish brown when dry. Rounded. Edge is faintly ribbed.
GILLS: Cinnamon. Attached to stem. Fairly well separated.
STEM: ¾–1½ in. long. Pallid. Thin with prominent ring that may become movable or disappear. Slightly enlarged at base.
WHERE & WHEN: On lawns, under or near conifers; summer, fall, in West.

# GALERINA

GENUS CHARACTERISTICS
· Rusty-brown spores
· Cap small, conic to rounded
· Cap edge often grooved
· Stem long, thin, brittle
· Gills attached to stem
· May have veil, ring
· In deep moss or on wood

BROWN, DRYING TAN

PALE RUSTY

BROWN

*Galerina autumnalis*

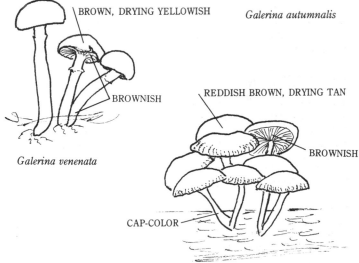

BROWN, DRYING YELLOWISH

BROWNISH

*Galerina venenata*

REDDISH BROWN, DRYING TAN

BROWNISH

CAP-COLOR

*Galerina marginata*

# CONOCYBE

GENUS CHARACTERISTICS
· Bright rusty-brown spores
· Tiny, fragile
· Cap conic to rounded
· Stem long, thin, may stain blue
· Gills attached to stem
· Sometimes veil, ring
· In grass or moss

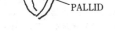

BROWNISH, FADING WHEN DRY

CINNAMON

PALLID

*Conocybe filaris*

**INOCYBE**    These are good examples of what mushroom hunters disparagingly call the "LBM"—Little Brown Mushroom—commonly found, difficult to identify by species, many poisonous, all to be avoided. Inocybes have pointed to rounded caps, usually with a knob at center, with hairy fibers streaking the cap from center to edge, often silky. The edge tends to split as the cap expands. The spores are dull brown and coat the light-colored gills in age. The gills are attached to the stem, sometimes notched at the junction of gill and stem. Often there is a hairy veil, sometimes leaving a faint hairy ring on the stem. They grow in the woods, usually on soil, occasionally on well-decayed wood.

*Inocybe fastigiata:* Dull-brown spores. Poisonous. Many similar species.
CAP: ¾–2½ in. broad. Straw to yellowish brown. Sharply conic then rounded with center knob; edge splitting in age. Streaked with hairy fibers. Flesh white, aging dingy yellow, thin.
GILLS: White, soon olive, then brownish. Close. Notched at stem.
STEM: 1–2½ in. long. White to tannish. Minutely hairy. Enlarging downward, sometimes twisted. No veil.
WHERE & WHEN: Under hardwoods, conifers, lawns beneath trees; summer, fall.

*Inocybe geophylla:* Pale-brown spores. Poisonous.
CAP: ½–1½ in. broad. White. Sharply pointed cap becoming round, then flat with center knob, upturned edge, often splitting. Silky. Flesh white.
GILLS: White to grayish, aging brownish. Notched or attached to stem. Close.
VEIL: White, webby, leaving faint hairy ring on stem.
STEM: ¾–2½ in. long. Cap-color. Silky, minutely hairy.
WHERE & WHEN: Under hardwoods, conifers, sometimes grassy areas; summer, fall.
*var. lilacina:* Lilac overall, aging to dingy cream.

*Inocybe lanuginosa:* Yellow-brown spores. Poisonous.
CAP: ½–1½ in. broad. Dark brown, bell-shaped to rounded with center knob, edge upturned in age. Coated with tufted hairs. Flesh tan.
GILLS: White, aging brown. Fairly far apart. Attached or notched.
STEM: 1–3 in. long. Pallid with dark-brown hairs. Hairy veil disappears.
WHERE & WHEN: Well-decayed wood in hardwoods, conifers; summer, fall.

*Inocybe napipes:* Dull-brown spores. Deadly poisonous.
CAP: 1½–3 in. broad. Dark brown, sometimes silvery sheen. Bell-shaped, becoming flat or upturned with large knob. Slippery (not slimy) feeling when wet, silky when dry. Flesh white, thin.
GILLS: White, aging dull grayish brown. Attached to stem.
STEM: 2–4 in. tall. Pallid at top, brownish below. Satiny. Bulb at base.
WHERE & WHEN: On ground under conifers; fall, sometimes spring.

*Inocybe pudica:* Dull-brown spores. Poisonous.
CAP: 1–2 in. broad. White, turning pink or reddish in age, sometimes only around edges. Bell-shaped. Slippery when wet. Flesh white.
GILLS: White, often becoming pinkish or red, eventually brown with spores. Notched at stem. Young specimens have hairy veil.
STEM: 1–3 in. long. White, staining like gills and cap. Silky.
WHERE & WHEN: In conifers; late summer to winter.

# INOCYBE

GENUS CHARACTERISTICS
· Dull-brown spores
· Cap pointed to rounded, knob at center, edge
  split
· Usually streaked with hairy fibers
· Gills attached or notched at stem, age dark with
  spores
· May have hairy veil, ring
· On soil in woods

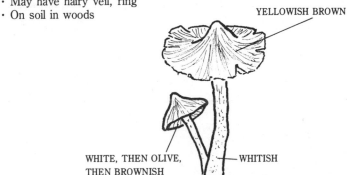

YELLOWISH BROWN

WHITE, THEN OLIVE,
THEN BROWNISH

WHITISH

*Inocybe fastigiata*

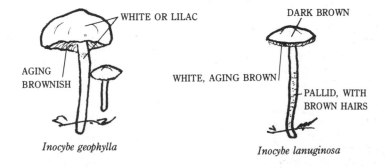

WHITE OR LILAC

AGING
BROWNISH

*Inocybe geophylla*

DARK BROWN

WHITE, AGING BROWN

PALLID, WITH
BROWN HAIRS

*Inocybe lanuginosa*

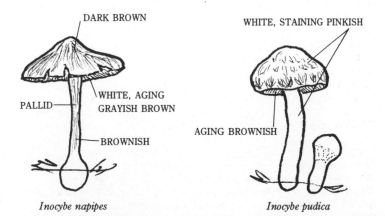

DARK BROWN

WHITE, AGING
GRAYISH BROWN

PALLID

BROWNISH

*Inocybe napipes*

WHITE, STAINING PINKISH

AGING BROWNISH

*Inocybe pudica*

**HEBELOMA** These are fleshy, appetizing-looking mushrooms that look just right for the stewpot—but they're poisonous or suspect and a good reminder that you can't judge a mushroom's edibility by its looks. They have dull-colored rounded caps with incurved edges in youth, often becoming wavy to upturned in age. The cap surface is tacky to slimy in moist weather, not too noticeable on dry days. Stems are powdery white, dry, fleshy. The gills are attached to the stem and are light-colored in youth, aging dull brown as they become coated with spores. The spores are dull yellow brown with none of the brighter rusty hue of *Inocybe* and *Cortinarius*. The stems are whitish, powdery or scaly, fleshy. There is a spiderweblike veil in youth on some species, leaving a hairy ring. All grow on soil, usually with hardwoods and conifers.

*Hebeloma crustuliniforme;* poison pie: Dull yellow-brown spores. Poisonous.
CAP: 1½–3 in. broad. Creamy, darkening to crust brown over center. Rounded, sometimes with low knob in age, usually wavy and irregular. Slimy when moist, causing grass and dirt to stick to the cap. Flesh white, aging pale brown.
GILLS: White to grayish, becoming dull brown with spores, beaded with tiny drops of moisture in damp weather. Close together. Attached to the stem.
STEM: 1–3 in. long. Dull white, sometimes tawny over base. Flecked with fine hairs at top, nearly smooth toward the bulbous base. No veil.
WHERE & WHEN: Single to several in open areas under conifers and hardwoods, old sawdust piles, sometimes in large rings; late summer, fall.

*Hebeloma sinapizans:* Tobacco-colored spores. Poisonous.
CAP: 2–5 in. broad. Creamy, darkening to cinnamon brown at center. Rounded, becoming expanded, irregular. Tacky to the touch when moist. Flesh white.
GILLS: Dingy white, aging pale cinnamon. Notched where they are attached to the stem. Minutely irregular edges.
STEM: 1–2½ in. long. White, ringed with tiny scales. Becoming hollow. No veil.
WHERE & WHEN: Single or in groups in moist ground in conifer-hardwood forests; fall.

*Hebeloma mesophaeum:* Dull yellow-brown spores. Poisonous.
CAP: ½–1½ in. broad. Brownish over center, shading to pallid around the edge. Rounded with incurved edge at first, becoming expanded with broad knob in age. Sometimes with hairy remnants of veil on edge. Slimy in moist weather. Flesh whitish, thin, firm.
GILLS: White, aging brownish. Attached to stem. Notched at junction of gill and stem.
STEM: 1½–3 in. long. Whitish, but brownish toward base. Slender. Dry. Brown flesh. Veil of fine hairs, like spiderweb, leaves hairy ring on stem and sometimes hairs on cap edge.
WHERE & WHEN: Several to numerous in grassy areas or bare ground, usually under conifers but other trees too; fall, occasionally spring, summer.

# HEBELOMA

GENUS CHARACTERISTICS
· Yellow-brown spores
· Cap dull-colored; rounded, often irregular; slimy
  to tacky
· Cap edge incurved in youth
· Gills attached to stem, age color of spores
· Sometimes spiderweblike veil, hairy ring
· Stem fleshy, dry, powdery white
· On soil

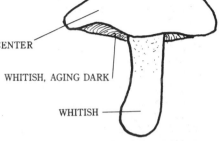

CREAMY WITH CRUST-BROWN CENTER

WHITISH, AGING DARK

WHITISH

*Hebeloma crustuliniforme*

CREAMY WITH CINNAMON CENTER

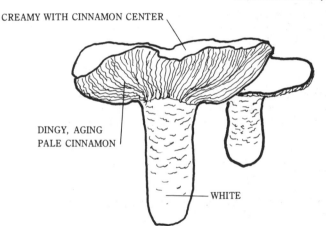

DINGY, AGING
PALE CINNAMON

WHITE

*Hebeloma sinapizans*

BROWNISH CENTER, PALLID EDGE

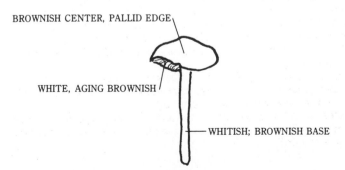

WHITE, AGING BROWNISH

WHITISH; BROWNISH BASE

*Hebeloma mesophaeum*

**AGROCYBE** These are medium to large mushrooms that are difficult to identify because they look like typical mushrooms with no striking characteristics. They have whitish to brownish caps and stems with dark-brown spores that coat the whitish gills at maturity. They usually have a ring that may disappear. They grow in grass, wood mulch, needles, leaf mold.

EDIBILITY: Some species are edible. The stems are tough and should be discarded. They are difficult to distinguish from such poisonous genera as *Hebeloma,* however, so they are not recommended for the amateur collector.

*Agrocybe praecox* (*Pholiota praecox, P. temnophylla*): Cigar-brown spores. Edible but too easily confused with poisonous *Hebeloma.*
CAP: 1–3 in. broad. Light brownish when moist; whitish when dry. Darker in center. Hemispheric, becoming rounded to nearly flat, upturned and wavy in age. Hairless. Dry. Flesh white, soft, thick.
GILLS: Creamy at first, aging brownish with spores. Attached to stem. Close together.
VEIL: White, becoming powdery with brown spores. Stretched tightly from stem to cap edge before breaking. Leaves large ring high on stem, or sometimes adheres to cap edge in ragged patches.
STEM: 2–4 in. long. White, brownish at base, often with thickened base.
WHERE & WHEN: Single to several in lawns, grassy places; spring and early summer. One of the earliest mushrooms.

*Agrocybe dura* (*Pholiota dura*): Yellowish-brown spores. Young caps are edible, but positive identification can be difficult.
CAP: 1–4 in. broad. Whitish to tawny. Broadly bell-shaped, sometimes with slight knob, becoming flattened in age. Edge usually festooned with veil remnants. Surface powdery, cracking over center and finally all over. Flesh white, thick, tough.
GILLS: White, aging brownish with spores. Close together. Rounded near stem but attached to it.
VEIL: Whitish, leaving cottony, torn ring.
STEM: 2–4 in. long. White, thickened toward top, often irregularly shaped.
WHERE & WHEN: In meadows, parks, gardens; summer.

*Agrocybe pediades* (*Naucoria pediades, N. semiorbicularis*): Rusty-brown to cigar-brown spores. Caps are edible but could be confused with poisonous *Hebeloma,* so avoidance is recommended.
CAP: ½–2½ in. broad. Creamy to dingy yellowish, aging light brownish, darker at center. Bell-shaped to rounded, rarely flat. Slimy when wet. Hairless. Flesh pallid, firm.
GILLS: Whitish to light yellowish brown, aging dark brown with spores. Attached to stem, fairly well separated.
STEM: 1½–3 in. long, whitish to light brown with scattered minute hairs. Slightly larger at base. No veil or ring.
WHERE & WHEN: Several to numerous in lawns, grassy areas; spring–fall.

# AGROCYBE

GENUS CHARACTERISTICS
· Dark-brown spores
· Cap whitish to dull brown
· Gills attached to stem, whitish, aging dark with
  spores
· Stem fleshy, whitish to brownish
· Usually a ring on stem
· In grass, wood mulch, needles

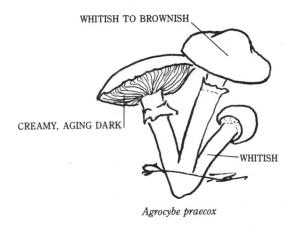

WHITISH TO BROWNISH

CREAMY, AGING DARK

WHITISH

*Agrocybe praecox*

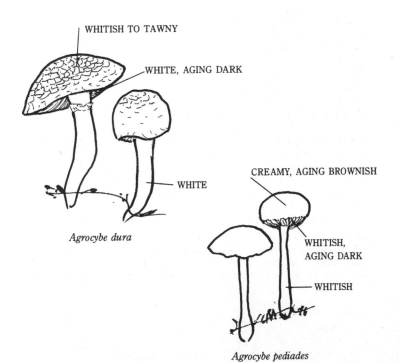

WHITISH TO TAWNY

WHITE, AGING DARK

WHITE

*Agrocybe dura*

CREAMY, AGING BROWNISH

WHITISH,
AGING DARK

WHITISH

*Agrocybe pediades*

**CORTINARIUS**   This is the largest genus of gilled mushrooms in North America—an overwhelming 800 species catalogued so far by Alexander H. Smith. It's easy to recognize the genus but often difficult to determine the species since many are closely related. The easiest way to tell a *Cortinarius* is to look at the gills of a mature specimen. If they are heavily coated with cinnamon to rusty-brown spores, you have a *Cortinarius*. Once you learn the look of those powdery gills, you'll recognize them automatically. Another way: In very young stages, the gills are covered with a gossamer, cobwebby veil. If copious, it may remain on the stem as a hairy ring or an indefinite band; if fragile and meager, it may disappear quite early. Typically, *Cortinarii* have bell-shaped to rounded caps that frequently flatten in age, often with a broad knob. The gills are attached to the stem, and cap and stem are difficult to separate. The gills may be variously colored in youth but soon turn rusty brown with maturing spores. The stem is often enlarged into a bulbous base, looking ill-proportioned and malformed. It starts out thick and squat, elongating until tall and fairly slender. This huge genus has a wide variety of beautiful colors—bright red, deep purple, delicate lilac, bluish green, all shades of yellow and brown. In age, most of them fade to brownish. They are forest mushrooms, preferring shady, moist soil, and proximity to certain trees.
**EDIBILITY:** Most of these 800 species have never been tested. A few of the very distinctive, easily recognized species can be eaten safely. A few are poisonous. Many are bitter or chemical tasting. They have dry flesh so should be cut into small pieces and well stewed in butter; moistened with a sauce, such as sour cream; or made into croquettes. The stems are usually too tough to be used.

*Cortinarius alboviolaceus:* Rusty-brown spores. Edible.
CAP: 1–2½ in. broad. Silvery white, tinged lilac. Bell-shaped, becoming rounded to nearly flat with center knob. Edge is rolled under until mature. Covered with dry, silky hairs. Flesh pale lilac, thin.
GILLS: Whitish violet, aging cinnamon brown. Attached to stem. Far apart.
VEIL: White, cobwebby, in youth only, leaving hairy ring.
STEM: 1½–3 in. long. Color of cap, except violet beneath veil and upper part, aging silvery and shining. Enlarging downward to club-shaped basal bulb. Dry, silky, minutely hairy.
WHERE & WHEN: Single to several on ground in thin stands of conifers-hardwoods; late summer, fall.

*Cortinarius violaceus:* Rusty-brown spores. Edible, good, sweet tasting.
CAP: 2–5 in. broad. Dark violet (scores of *Cortinarii* are bluish to violet, but this is the only one dark violet overall). Rough with small, dry, hairy tufts or scales. Rounded then flattening, somewhat knobbed. Metallic sheen when old. Edge fringed with hairs. Flesh grayish purple, thick, firm.
GILLS: Color of cap, maturing brownish cinnamon. Notched where they attach to stem. Fairly well separated.
VEIL: Violet, cobwebby, on very young specimens only, leaving hairy ring.
STEM: 2½–6 in. long. Dark purple, enlarging toward base, dry, hairy. Flesh violet.
WHERE & WHEN: Single to several in open woods among debris in conifer forests; fall, primarily northern U.S. and Canada.

# CORTINARIUS

GENUS CHARACTERISTICS
- Rusty-brown spores
- Cap fleshy, rounded, often knobbed
- Cobwebby veil when young
- Gills attached to stem, age rusty brown with spores
- Base often enlarged or bulbous
- On soil in woods

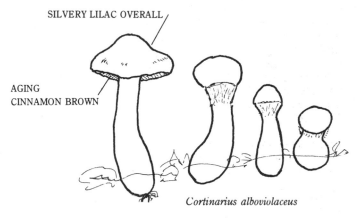

SILVERY LILAC OVERALL

AGING
CINNAMON BROWN

*Cortinarius alboviolaceus*

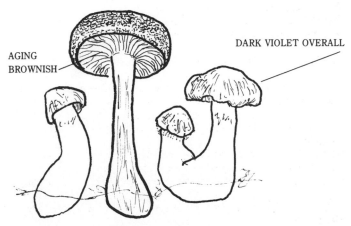

AGING
BROWNISH

DARK VIOLET OVERALL

*Cortinarius violaceus*

*Cortinarius collinitus:* Rusty-brown spores. Edible (peel off slimy surface).
CAP: 1–4 in. broad. Yellowish to orange yellow to orange brown with paler edge, often lilac-tinted. Rounded to nearly flat in age. Edge incurved in youth, becoming upturned in age. Very slimy, unpleasant to handle when moist; drying to varnishlike surface. Flesh whitish to yellowish, firm.
GILLS: Pallid to pinkish to pale violet, aging rusty brown. Attached to stem. Rather far apart.
VEIL: Pure white, hairy, under a thin slimy layer.
STEM: 2–5 in. long. Paler than cap. Top white. Yellowish brown below with dull white hairs covered by slimy patches of bluish to yellowish-brown remnants of a universal veil that enclosed the entire mushroom in youth. Sometimes bulging in center or narrowing downward.
WHERE & WHEN: In groups in thin stands of conifers, hardwoods; summer, fall.

*Cortinarius corrugatus:* Rusty-brown spores. Edible, both cap and stem. Recognized by its distinctive corrugated cap.
CAP: 2–4 in. broad. Pale tawny to reddish brown. Rounded to bell-shaped. Very wrinkled and corrugated. Sticky. Hairless. Flesh white, firm, thin.
GILLS: Purplish at first, becoming rusty with spores. Attached to stem. Close together.
STEM: 4–6 in. long. Colored like cap. Enlarging toward basal bulb. Slimy.
WHERE & WHEN: Single to clumps in moist areas under hardwoods, especially beech, maple; summer, fall, eastern North America.

*Cortinarius armillatus:* Rusty-brown spores. Edible. Recognized by the reddish bands on stem.
CAP: 2–4½ in. broad. Tawny red to brick red, lighter at cap edge. Rounded to bell-shaped, becoming flat in age. Edge incurved in youth, flattening in age, sometimes fringed with veil remnants. Moist. Flesh pallid, thick, spongy.
GILLS: Pale dingy cinnamon, aging dark rusty brown. Attached to stem. Well separated.
VEIL: Hairy to nearly membranous, leaving 2–4 bands encircling stem that turn color as they catch the falling spores.
STEM: 3–6. in. long. Dull to reddish brown, lighter above veil, circled by 2–4 orangy-red bands of veil tissue. Enlarging toward white bulbous base. Dry.
WHERE & WHEN: Single to several under mixed conifers-hardwoods, especially birch; summer, fall. Mostly eastern North America.

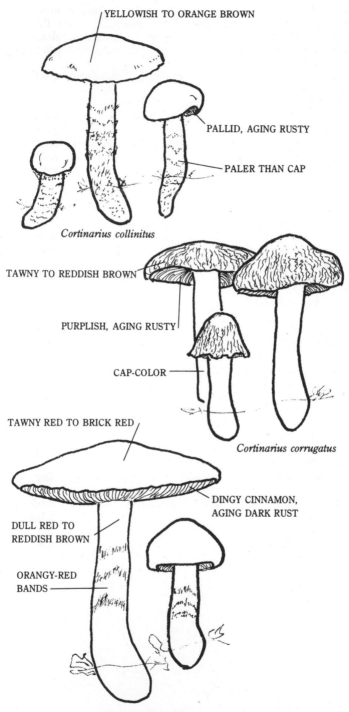

YELLOWISH TO ORANGE BROWN

PALLID, AGING RUSTY

PALER THAN CAP

*Cortinarius collinitus*

TAWNY TO REDDISH BROWN

PURPLISH, AGING RUSTY

CAP-COLOR

*Cortinarius corrugatus*

TAWNY RED TO BRICK RED

DINGY CINNAMON,
AGING DARK RUST

DULL RED TO
REDDISH BROWN

ORANGY-RED
BANDS

*Cortinarius armillatus*

*Cortinarius purpurascens:* Rusty-brown spores. Edible cooked; poisonous raw.
CAP: 4–5 in. broad. Violet brown to reddish brown, fading in dry weather; dark-spotted in humid weather and when old. Slimy. Rounded with incurved edge in youth, aging wavy and upturned. Flesh blue.
GILLS: Bluish tan, aging cinnamon, bruising purple. Notched where they attach to stem. Crowded together.
STEM: 2–3 in. tall. Pale bluish, thick, bulbous, hairy, bruising purplish blue when touched.
WHERE & WHEN: In mixed woods; fall.

*Cortinarius orellanus:* Rusty-brown spores. Deadly poisonous.
CAP: 1–3 in. broad. Brownish tinted pinkish, orange, or red. Conic with incurved edge at first, becoming round with center knob. Dry, hairy. Flesh yellowish, juicy.
GILLS: Yellowish orange. Slightly uneven edges. Attached to stem. Far apart.
STEM: 2–4 in. long. Yellowish or slightly paler than cap, darkening and enlarging toward base.
WHERE & WHEN: In mixed woods; summer, fall.

*Cortinarius traganus:* Rusty-brown spores. Poisonous. Pungent, disagreeable odor.
CAP: 1½–4 in. broad. Pale lilac overall. Shaped like an hourglass in youth with round cap atop round bulbous base, aging nearly flat with low knob, sometimes cracking overall. Dry, hairy. Flesh ocher, thick, firm.
GILLS: Pale lilac, soon turning yellow rusty brown. Attached to stem. Fairly well separated.
VEIL: White, tinted lilac, becoming streaked with rusty-brown spores. Hairy, leaving hairy ring that may disappear.
STEM: 1½–2½ in. long. Color of cap, becoming whitish and woolly at bulbous base.
WHERE & WHEN: Single to numerous in old-growth conifer woods; fall.

*Cortinarius vibratilis:* Clay-brown spores. Poisonous. Pungent odor, bitter taste that you can detect by merely touching your tongue to cap surface.
CAP: 1–3½ in. broad. Pale tan to yellowish. Slimy and darker color when moist; paler when dry. Rounded. Flesh white, soft.
GILLS: Whitish becoming cinnamon. Attached to stem. Close together.
VEIL: White, cobweblike, becoming brown with spores, leaving a hairy ring or zone on stem that disappears.
STEM: 2–5 in. long. Pure white, slimy, enlarging toward base.
WHERE & WHEN: Scattered to many in moss in conifer forests, especially hemlock; summer, fall.

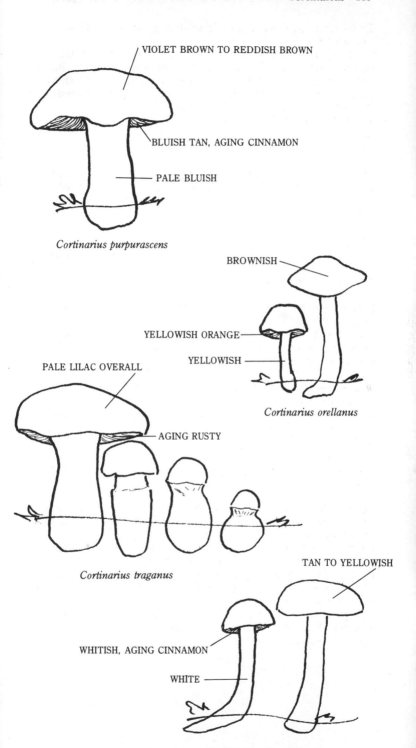

VIOLET BROWN TO REDDISH BROWN

BLUISH TAN, AGING CINNAMON

PALE BLUISH

*Cortinarius purpurascens*

BROWNISH

YELLOWISH ORANGE

YELLOWISH

*Cortinarius orellanus*

PALE LILAC OVERALL

AGING RUSTY

*Cortinarius traganus*

TAN TO YELLOWISH

WHITISH, AGING CINNAMON

WHITE

*Cortinarius vibratilis*

The following two species were formerly included in *Pholiota,* but have been reclassified into genera of their own—*Togaria* and *Rozites.* Each is the only species in its genus.

**TOGARIA**   Pale yellowish-brown spores. Golden to orangy with mealy-powdery coating. Large, flaring ring.

***Togaria aurea*** (*Phaeolepiota aurea, Pholiota aurea*): Pale yellow-brown spores. Edible (discard stems), although some people are allergic to it so take the usual precautions, page 7. Very distinctive with its golden, mealy coating.
CAP: 2–8 (14) in. broad. Golden yellow to orangy, covered with a powdery, mealy substance that rubs off easily. Spherical with incurved edge when young, becoming rounded sometimes with center knob. The edge, sometimes cracked, is fringed with ragged veil remnants. Flesh whitish yellow, thick, firm.
GILLS: Yellow brown, becoming cinnamon, but not dark rusty brown. Attached to stem, often rounded where they join stem. Close together.
VEIL: Yellow on upper surface, dark buff below, covered with same mealy substance as on cap. Membranous, leaving a large flaring ring.
STEM: 2–6 (10) in. tall. Buff, hairless above ring, covered with velvety granules below. Enlarged toward base.
WHERE & WHEN: Single to numerous under or near old-growth Douglas fir, alder, vine maple; fall.

**ROZITES**   Dingy rusty-brown spores. Tan to orange brown. Wrinkled cap, covered at first with white hoary coating. Large white, movable ring.

***Rozites caperata*** (*Pholiota caperata*); gypsy mushroom: Dingy rusty-brown spores. Edible, choice. Discard stems.
CAP: 2–5 in. broad. Tannish to orangy brown, covered at first with a thin, white hoary coating, giving frosted appearance. Wrinkled, even corrugated, seldom smooth. Never sticky. Egg-shaped at first, flattening in age. Flesh white, thick, firm.
GILLS: Pale tan, often streaked with darker- and lighter-brown bands, aging rusty. Attached to stem. Close together. Edges uneven.
VEIL: White, membranous, leaving conspicuous movable ring, sometimes disappearing in age.
STEM: 2–4½ in. long. Dingy white to pale tan, enlarging toward base. Thick, fibrous, hairless, dry.
WHERE & WHEN: Several to many on ground in conifer or mixed conifer-hardwood stands; summer, fall.

# TOGARIA

GENUS CHARACTERISTICS
· Pale yellowish-brown spores
· Cap golden to orangy, mealy-powdery coating, veil remnants fringing edge
· Gills age cinnamon brown
· Ring large, flaring
· Stem buff; granular like cap
· On soil under conifers, hardwoods

GOLDEN TO ORANGY

YELLOW BROWN, AGING CINNAMON

BUFF

*Togaria aurea*

# ROZITES

GENUS CHARACTERISTICS
· Pale rusty-brown spores
· Cap tan to orange brown, rounded to flat, wrinkled
· Gills age rusty
· Ring large, white, movable, may disappear
· Stem dingy to tan; base enlarged
· On ground under conifers, hardwoods

TANNISH TO ORANGY BROWN

PALE TAN, AGING RUSTY

WHITISH TO PALE TAN

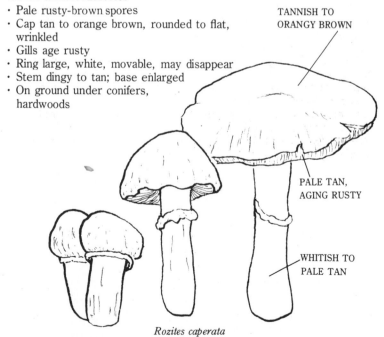

*Rozites caperata*

**PAXILLUS**   This small genus has several striking features. The cap edge is tightly rolled under, remaining so well into maturity. The gills can be easily separated in patches from the cap—just as the layer of pores may be separated from the cap in some Boletes. The gills extend down the stem and where they join the stem are often forked and interconnected to the extent that they resemble pores rather than gills. The gills usually stain brownish when bruised. The stem may be off-center or absent. The spores are yellow brown.

EDIBILITY: There has long been disagreement on the edibility of these species—some people saying they are coarse and poorly flavored while others enjoy them. *P. involutus* is now known to be dangerous. Repeated ingestion builds up an allergic sensitivity that eventually leads to serious illness, even death. People who have eaten it for years can suddenly become ill upon eating it one more time. This toxicity may vary in different regions. *P. atrotomentosus,* tough and of poor flavor, is now suspected and not recommended as an edible.

*Paxillus involutus:* Yellow-brown spores. Poisonous.
CAP: 2–5 in. broad. Dull yellowish brown, sometimes tinged olive or reddish. Often spotted or with obscure zones of color circling cap. Rounded in youth, then flattening with a large saucerlike depression in age. Edge is tightly inrolled until late age, often somewhat ribbed, coated with grayish down in youth. Dry, with matted downy surface, becoming smooth in age. Sticky when wet. Flesh dingy tan to brownish yellow, bruising brownish; thick, soft.
GILLS: Pallid, aging to greenish yellow, discoloring to dark brown to reddish brown when cut or bruised. Crowded together. Narrow. Extend down stem, often forked and cross-veined where they join stem, so they resemble pores. Easily separated from cap.
STEM: 1–3 in. tall. Color of cap, streaked or spotted darker brown. Dry, smooth. Not off-center as in *P. atrotomentosus*. Shorter than cap diameter, usually tapering downward.
WHERE & WHEN: Alone or in groups, near or sometimes on wood, under mixed hardwoods-conifers, base of stumps, in city lawns; late summer, fall.

*Paxillus atrotomentosus;* black-footed *Paxillus*: Suspected, not recommended, very poor quality. Yellowish-brown spores.
CAP: 2–5 in. broad. Yellowish brown to dark brown; tan in very dry weather. Rounded, then flat and depressed in center. Edge tightly rolled under until maturity. Dry with flattened hairs. Flesh white, thick.
GILLS: Buff to yellowish, sometimes bruising brown. Close together. Often forked and interconnected near stem. Easily separated from cap.
STEM: 2–3 in. tall. Covered with dark-brown, velvety down. Thick, usually off-center, sometimes nearly lateral in large clusters. Enlarged toward base, often with rootlike base.
WHERE & WHEN: Alone to scattered tufts of several specimens on well-decayed conifers, especially around old stumps, or from buried wood; summer, fall.

# PAXILLUS

GENUS CHARACTERISTICS
· Yellow-brown spores
· Cap yellowish to brownish; rounded, becoming depressed; edge tightly inrolled
· Gills extend down stem; porelike at base; often bruise brown; easily separated from cap
· Stem may be off-center or absent
· Near or on wood

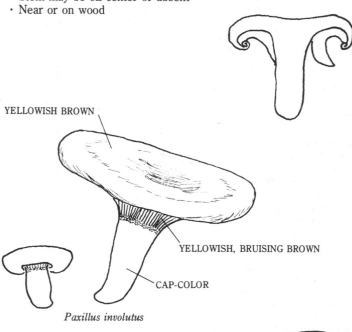

YELLOWISH BROWN

YELLOWISH, BRUISING BROWN

CAP-COLOR

*Paxillus involutus*

YELLOWISH BROWN
TO DARK BROWN

YELLOWISH

VELVETY BROWN

*Paxillus atrotomentosus*

**PHYLLOPORUS** This species has been shifted from genus to genus, finally placed in one of its own, of which it is the only species. Except for its gills, looks like a Bolete and is sometimes called a gilled Bolete.

***Phylloporus rhodoxanthus*** (*Paxillus rhodoxanthus, P. paradoxus, Gomphidius rhodoxanthus*); yellow-rose *Paxillus*: Brownish-olive spores. Caps are edible, good.
CAP: 1–3 in. broad. Variable in color, reddish to brownish to orangy cinnamon, or even yellowish olive. Soon cracking, revealing yellow flesh. Rounded, cushion-shaped, flattening in age, sometimes upturned. Dry. Velvety to the touch, aging smooth. Flesh yellowish, firm.
GILLS: Yellow, bruising bluish green or brownish. Fairly well separated. Usually thicker than those of other gilled mushrooms. Extend down stem. Sometimes forked and interconnected by cross veins somewhat resembling pores.
STEM: 1–2½ in. long. Cap-color or paler, yellow at base, dotted with small russet scales over lower two-thirds. Firm, tapering toward base, sometimes thin, sometimes stout.
WHERE & WHEN: Single to scattered on ground under conifers or in mixed conifer-hardwood stands; fall.

**GYMNOPILUS** These are rusty-orange to yellowish mushrooms, growing on wood or buried wood, their bright colors shining out in the forest. Their gills are attached to the stem, and cap and stem are not easily separated. The spores are orangy brown to red brown. None is edible. Several species, including the one described here, sometimes contain unknown toxins causing dizziness and hallucinatory confusion.

***Gymnopilus spectabilis*** (*Pholiota spectabilis, G. junonius*): Orange to rusty-orange spores. Poisonous. Very bitter. Colored like *Togaria aurea* but lacking the mealy coating.
CAP: 2–7 in. broad. Golden to apricot yellow to reddish orange. Rounded, aging nearly flat. Hairless in youth, then covered with fine brownish or reddish-brown fibrils. Flesh yellowish, firm.
GILLS: Yellowish, aging rusty. Attached to stem. Edges minutely hairy.
VEIL: Yellowish, membranous. Leaving yellow membranous ring on stem.
STEM: 3–4 in. long. Color of cap, except brownish near base. Dry. With a few scattered hairs. Sometimes swollen in middle with pointed base.
WHERE & WHEN: Single, but usually in tufts from buried wood or on stumps, logs of hardwoods and conifers; spring to early winter.

# PHYLLOPORUS

GENUS CHARACTERISTICS
· Brownish-olive spores
· Looks like Bolete except for gills
· Gills extend down stem, bruise bluish
· On ground under conifers, hardwoods

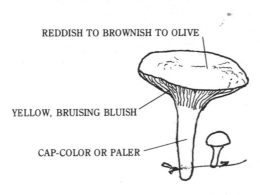

REDDISH TO BROWNISH TO OLIVE

YELLOW, BRUISING BLUISH

CAP-COLOR OR PALER

*Phylloporus rhodoxanthus*

# GYMNOPILUS

GENUS CHARACTERISTICS
· Orangy-brown to red-brown spores
· Brightly colored, orange to yellowish
· Cap rounded, flattening in age
· Gills attached or extending down stem
· Often with cobwebby veil, ring
· Stem central, yellowish
· On wood or buried wood

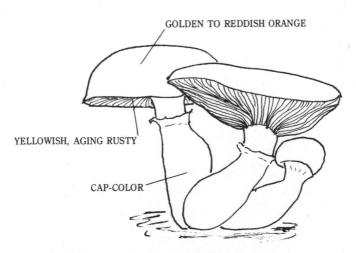

GOLDEN TO REDDISH ORANGE

YELLOWISH, AGING RUSTY

CAP-COLOR

*Gymnopilus spectabilis*

**PHOLIOTA**   Usually growing on wood or buried wood, often in large conspicuous clusters. The caps and stems are often covered with scales, although some species are smooth with no scales. The caps are small and often very slimy. The gills are attached to the stem; cap and stem are not easily separated. The spores are drab to dark brown and color the gills at maturity. The gills are covered with a veil in youth that usually leaves a membranous ring on the stem, sometimes disappearing in age. There is no cup at the stem base.

EDIBILITY: Formerly all were considered edible, but gastrointestinal poisonings have been reported, so caution is necessary. Some species are still eaten—sautéed, made into patties, in stews, or used in most mushroom recipes. Remove the slimy or scaly coating and discard the stems if they are coarse and tough. But be sure the species agrees with you and that your identification is correct. *Pholiotas* are tricky.

*Pholiota squarrosa:* Rusty-brown spores. Young specimens are edible for some people, poisonous for others. Proceed with caution.
CAP: 1–5 in. broad. Brownish yellow to greenish yellow with tawny to brownish upturned scales, concentrically arranged. Spherical with incurved edge at first, then rounded, broadening in age, often with wavy edge, hanging veil remnants. Dry surface, never sticky although often moist. Flesh pale yellowish, firm.
GILLS: Yellowish, sometimes tinged olive, becoming olive brown and finally dingy brown with spores. Attached to stem, sometimes notched where they join stem. Close together.
VEIL: Whitish, tough, membranous, leaving fleecy ring on stem, sometimes disappearing in age.
STEM: 1½–5 in. long. White above ring; covered with rough yellow-brown scales below, much like those on cap. Tapering downward. Spongy inside. Dry, never sticky.
WHERE & WHEN: In large clusters at base or on wood of conifers, hardwoods, invading decayed areas; summer, fall.
CAUTION: Some people suffer gastrointestinal upsets after eating this species although others have eaten it for years (young caps only; old ones taste awful). Be sure to follow the precautions, page 7. Eat sparingly and DON'T consume with alcohol.

*Pholiota squarrosoides:* Brown spores. Caps are edible after removing scales.
CAP: 2–5 in. broad. Creamy white covered with bristly, pointed rusty-brown scales (not as densely scaly as *P. squarrosa*), aging brownish between the scales. Conic with inrolled edge at first, aging rounded, with veil remnants hanging in points from cap. Slimy cap surface beneath scales. Flesh white, firm.
GILLS: White, aging brownish with maturing spores (not green tinge as in *P. squarrosa*). Notched where they join stem. Close together.
VEIL: Pallid, hairy, leaving cottony, raggedy ring, often disappearing.
STEM: 2–4 in. long. Whitish at top, covered with rusty-brown scales below ring. Dry, very scaly.
WHERE & WHEN: Usually in dense clusters on fallen logs, dead trunks of hardwoods—alder, maple, birch; late summer, fall.

# PHOLIOTA

GENUS CHARACTERISTICS
· Dark-brown to drab-brown spores
· Cap and stem often scaly, slimy
· Gills attached to stem, age color of spores
· Most species have ring
· Clustered on wood, decaying matter

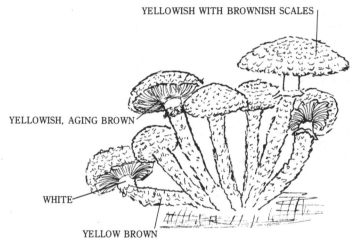

YELLOWISH WITH BROWNISH SCALES

YELLOWISH, AGING BROWN

WHITE

YELLOW BROWN

*Pholiota squarrosa*

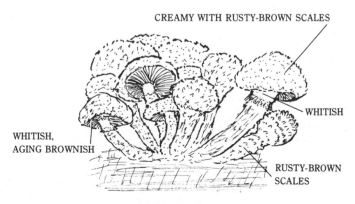

CREAMY WITH RUSTY-BROWN SCALES

WHITISH

WHITISH,
AGING BROWNISH

RUSTY-BROWN
SCALES

*Pholiota squarrosoides*

*Pholiota squarrosa-adiposa:* Dark cinnamon-brown spores. Edible after removing slimy covering and scales, but mediocre. Identified by its slimy cap, dry scaly stem, clusters on hardwood logs.

CAP: 2½–5 in. broad. Slimy yellowish tan to brownish with conspicuous rusty-brown scales. Rounded, becoming flat with edge fringed with veil remnants. Flesh yellow, thick.

GILLS: Pale yellow, aging brown. Attached to stem.

STEM: 2½–4 in. long. Dry. Yellow covered with small, dry, brown scales, much like cap, aging brownish at base. With small, yellowish ring. Becoming hollow.

WHERE & WHEN: Clustered on decaying hardwood stumps, trunks, sometimes hundreds on one log; late summer, fall.

*Pholiota terrestris:* Dark cinnamon-brown spores. Edible but mediocre. Great variation in size, color, scaliness.

CAP: 1–4 in. broad. Slimy, dingy to yellow brown, covered with darker-brown, pointed, dry scales that become slimy in wet weather. Rounded, aging flat. Soft scales may rub off, leaving smooth cap, not sticky. Flesh light brown.

GILLS: Pallid, darkening to grayish brown, finally yellowish brown. Attached to stem. Close together.

STEM: 2–6 in. long. Dry. Dingy ivory or buff, usually becoming brown at base, covered with brownish scales, similar to cap, below a fibrous band left by the veil. Slender, longer than width of cap.

WHERE & WHEN: Usually in clusters, appearing to be on ground, but actually growing from buried wood, near trees in open places—clearings in woods, along paths, old roads, lawns; spring and fall.

*Pholiota destruens:* Brown spores. Edible when young.

CAP: 3–8 in. broad. Slimy when wet. Creamy, aging light brown with scattered, large, soft, whitish to buff scales. Rounded, broadening in age, often with center knob. Sometimes cracking across top. Copious cottony pieces of veil hanging from edge. Flesh white, firm.

GILLS: Pallid, aging brownish from spores. Notched where they join stem. Close together.

VEIL: Cap-color or paler; membranous, leaving loose ring high on stem, sometimes disappearing in age.

STEM: 2–7 in. long. Lighter than cap, aging brownish. Silky above ring, covered below with woolly tufts. Enlarging toward base.

WHERE & WHEN: Single rarely, usually in clusters on limbs, cut ends of logs, dead wood of aspen, cottonwood, balsam, poplar; late fall.

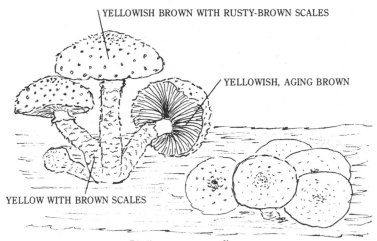

YELLOWISH BROWN WITH RUSTY-BROWN SCALES

YELLOWISH, AGING BROWN

YELLOW WITH BROWN SCALES

*Pholiota squarrosa-adiposa*

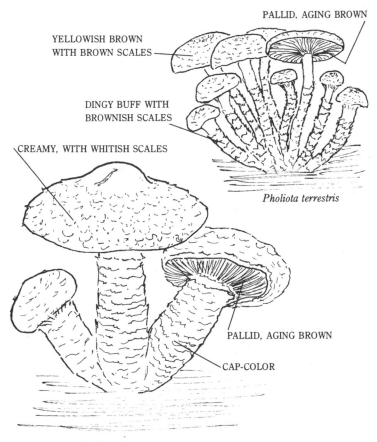

PALLID, AGING BROWN

YELLOWISH BROWN
WITH BROWN SCALES

DINGY BUFF WITH
BROWNISH SCALES

CREAMY, WITH WHITISH SCALES

*Pholiota terrestris*

PALLID, AGING BROWN

CAP-COLOR

*Pholiota destruens*

*Pholiota aurivella;* golden *Pholiota*: Brown spores. Edible if slimy covering is peeled off, but poisonous to some people.
CAP: 1½–4 (6) in. broad. Slimy, tawny to yellow orange, darker at center, with large wine-red scales that may wash off in wet weather. Hemispherical with inrolled edge at first, broadening in age, sometimes knobbed. Flesh yellow, firm.
GILLS: Light yellow, aging rusty brown. Notched where they attach to stem.
STEM: 2–3 in. tall. Yellowish brown, hairy above thin, yellowish ring; dry tawny scales below, becoming slimy in wet weather. Usually curved.
WHERE & WHEN: Single to several on living trunks and fallen logs of deciduous trees primarily, conifers occasionally; spring and fall.
LOOK-ALIKES: Not recommended in western North America because of similarity to poisonous *P. hiemalis*. Could also be confused with *P. squarrosa-adiposa*.

*Pholiota hiemalis;* winter *Pholiota*: Brown spores. Poisonous.
CAP: 1–2 in. broad. Slimy, yellow, covered with broad rusty-brown, gelatinous scales. Hemispherical with incurved edge at first, broadening in age. Flesh yellow, firm.
GILLS: Yellowish, aging brown with spores. Attached to stem.
STEM: 2–3 in. tall. Slimy, yellow with rusty-brown, gelatinous scales. Band of fibers, left by veil, near top of stem.
WHERE & WHEN: In clusters on rotting conifer logs; fall, early winter.

*Pholiota abietis:* Brown spores. Edible but not recommended to western pothunters because easily confused with *P. hiemalis*.
CAP: 1–4 in. broad. Slimy, yellow with reddish-brown center and gelatinous spots. Rounded, broadening in age with center knob. Flesh pale yellow, tough.
GILLS: Pale brownish, aging darker brown.
STEM: 2–4 in. long. Slimy, yellow with brown scaly markings. Not darkening toward base. No ring, but merely a band of fibers.
WHERE & WHEN: Clustered on dead conifer logs or stumps; fall.

*Pholiota mutabilis* (*Kuehneromyces mutabilis*); changeable *Pholiota*: Rusty-brown spores. Young caps are edible but easily mistaken for poisonous *Galerina*, so not recommended for inexperienced collectors. Strong flavor, good in soups, stews.
CAP: 2–3 in. broad. Color changes depending on weather: deep cinnamon when moist, fading to yellowish brown when dry. Center fades first with edge remaining darker. Smooth, looks and feels greasy. Rounded becoming expanded, sometimes knobbed or depressed in center. Edge thin, transparent. Flesh whitish, thin.
GILLS: Yellowish, aging cinnamon. Attached to stem. Close together.
STEM: 2–3 in. tall. Pallid above ring; rust to brown and covered with fine, dark scales below ring. Thin, usually curved, becoming hollow. With membranous, slightly scaly ring.
WHERE & WHEN: In large dense clusters on conifers and broad-leaved trees, often covering top of log; spring–fall.
LOOK-ALIKES: Easily mistaken for poisonous *Galerina autumnalis*, which has thin, bandlike ring, lacks the scales on stem, and does not ordinarily grow in large clusters.

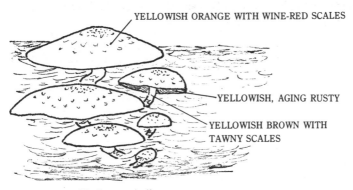

YELLOWISH ORANGE WITH WINE-RED SCALES

YELLOWISH, AGING RUSTY

YELLOWISH BROWN WITH
TAWNY SCALES

*Pholiota aurivella*

YELLOW WITH RUSTY-BROWN SCALES

YELLOWISH, AGING BROWN

LIKE CAP

*Pholiota hiemalis*

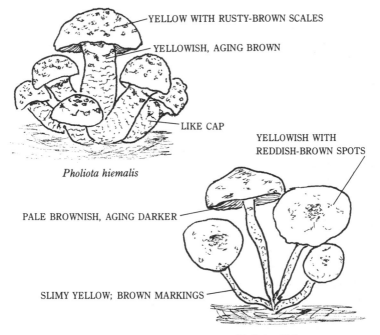

YELLOWISH WITH
REDDISH-BROWN SPOTS

PALE BROWNISH, AGING DARKER

SLIMY YELLOW; BROWN MARKINGS

*Pholiota abietis*

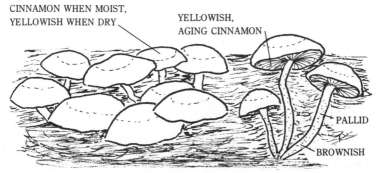

CINNAMON WHEN MOIST,
YELLOWISH WHEN DRY

YELLOWISH,
AGING CINNAMON

PALLID

BROWNISH

*Pholiota mutabilis*

**AGARICUS**   The mushroom sold in supermarkets is an *Agaricus* and a good example of the genus. It is an easy genus to recognize, even for a beginner, but some of the species are difficult to differentiate from each other, even for the professional mycologist. Identifying characteristics: chocolate-brown spores, large to medium size, white to brown to gray-brown rounded caps that may become flattened in age; pinkish gills that age chocolate brown with spores; gills that are not attached to the stem; gills at first enclosed by a veil that breaks leaving a ring on the stem, sometimes very conspicuous; cap and stem easily and cleanly detached; no cup at the stem base (this is important to note to separate *Agaricus* from *Amanita*). The species can be divided roughly into 3 groups: those that stain yellowish when bruised or cut, those that bruise reddish, and those that remain unchanged.

EDIBILITY: *Agaricus* includes many choice edibles, and *A. campestris* is one of the world's most famous mushrooms. A few species cause gastrointestinal distress in some people. When trying a new species for the first time, be sure to follow the precautions, page 7. *Agaricus* are excellent in any dish calling for mushrooms—in omelets, stuffings, soup, mushroom loaf, rice casserole, creamed on toast, or with chicken livers, pickled, sautéed, broiled. Their large meaty caps are perfect for stuffing with a wide variety of combinations.

• Slice *A. campestris* and use raw in tossed or chef's salad. Or marinate in dressing for 1 hour before adding to salad.

• Dip *Agaricus* slices in beaten egg, then in bread crumbs mixed with finely grated cheese. Fry in hot oil for a few minutes.

• Coat slices with flour seasoned with cayenne, garlic, salt. Deep-fat-fry 2 minutes. Drain on absorbent paper.

• Lightly brown slices in butter. Add spoonfuls of Marsala or sherry, allowing each to evaporate quickly. Stir in unsweetened whipping cream and cook 10 minutes. Serve on toast. Good with poached eggs.

• Fry diced bacon, add mushrooms, and brown. Add white wine and chicken stock. Simmer. Transfer bacon and mushrooms to serving dish. Thicken juices with cornstarch; season with salt, pepper; pour over mushrooms.

• Sauté with floured fish seasoned with salt, pepper, garlic. Serve with melted clarified butter.

• Stuff fish with a mixture of sautéed sliced mushrooms and chopped onion; soft bread crumbs; chopped, seeded, peeled cucumbers.

• Top fried or baked eggplant slices with sautéed mushroom caps filled with crumbled fried bacon and chopped parsley.

• Bake sautéed mushroom slices, chopped scallions, parsley in alternate layers with chopped oysters and sour cream. Season with nutmeg, salt, pepper. Top with mushroom mixture and sour cream. Bake 25 minutes at 350°.

• To prepare caps for stuffing, dip in butter or brown lightly or use raw.

• Stuff with browned bread crumbs, minced mushroom stems, chopped walnuts. Broil 2 minutes.

• Stuff with creamed clams, seasoned with minced onions and crumbled fried bacon. Sprinkle with bread crumbs, cayenne. Broil 3 minutes.

• Stuff with deviled crab or add to deviled crab. Bake 15 minutes at 350°.

• Stuff with mashed avocado, garlic, salt, ground cumin seed.

# AGARICUS

GENUS CHARACTERISTICS
· Chocolate to blackish-brown spores
· Cap white to brown to gray brown
· Ring on stem
· Gills not attached to stem; pinkish, aging
  chocolate brown to blackish brown
· No cup at base
· On ground

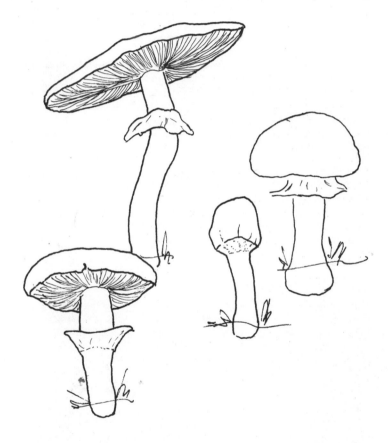

***Agaricus campestris*** (*Psalliota campestris*); pink bottom, field, or meadow mushroom: Purplish-brown spores. Edible, excellent. Everybody's favorite. Don't confuse with *Stropharia coronilla*.
CAP: 1½–4 (6) in. broad. Creamy white, often becoming light brownish in age. Rounded, aging nearly flat. Dry, silky smooth, sometimes with small hairy scales. Flesh white, firm, sometimes tinted brownish red; usually does not change color but sometimes stains slightly pink. Edge of cap extends slightly beyond gills.
GILLS: Bright pink, aging purplish brown with spores. Not attached to stem. Crowded close together.
VEIL: White, fragile, no patches on underside, leaving thin, ragged ring on stem, often soon obliterated.
STEM: 1–2½ in. long. White, sometimes discoloring to dingy rose. Dry. Smooth above ring; hairy below.
WHERE & WHEN: Common in grassy areas—lawns, parks, meadows, golf courses, even above timberline, always in open; summer, fall.

***Agaricus rodmani*** (*A. bitorquis, A. edulis, Psalliota rodmani*): Chocolate-brown spores. Edible, one of most flavorful. Similar to *A. campestris* but larger, squatter, with double ring, on hard-packed soils.
CAP: 2–6 (10) in. wide. Dull white, maturing yellowish to yellowish brown or even grayish. Rounded, aging nearly flat. Smooth, sometimes with hairs; surface finely cracked in age. Edge inrolled in youth. Flesh white; usually not changing color, but sometimes bruising pinkish.
GILLS: White before veil breaks, then pale pink aging deep chocolate brown. Not attached to stem. Close together.
VEIL: White, woolly, leaving double ring that sticks straight out from center of stem in youth.
STEM: ¾–3 in. long. White, hairless, solid, short, narrowing at base.
WHERE & WHEN: In lawns, hard-packed soil, barnyards, parks, pathways; spring–fall.

***Agaricus diminutivus*** (*Psalliota diminutiva*): Chocolate spores. Edible.
CAP: 1–1½ in. broad. Whitish or yellowish; center brownish or reddish brown with scattered, thin, brownish scales. Sometimes entire cap is reddish. Rounded, then flat to depressed in center. Thin, fragile.
GILLS: Brownish pink, aging blackish brown. Not attached to stem.
RING: White, thin, slightly downy on undersurface.
STEM: 1–2 in. long. Pallid, smooth.
WHERE & WHEN: Associated with *A. silvaticus*, in woods, leaves, moss; fall.

***Agaricus nivescens;*** snowy cap: Chocolate-brown spores. Edible.
CAP: 3–5 in. broad. White, aging pale buff on top. Rounded, dry, smooth, with a few scales on edge. Flesh white, not changing color when bruised; thick, firm.
GILLS: White before veil breaks, then pale grayish lilac, darkening chocolate brown. Not attached to stem. Close together.
VEIL: White, thick, flaring; triangular feltlike patches on underside.
STEM: 3–5 in. tall. White, thick, bulbous; smooth, silky on upper part; tiny pointed warts just above bulbous base. About as long as cap width.
WHERE & WHEN: Grassy areas, usually near trees; fall.
LOOK-ALIKES: Often mistaken for *A. silvicola*, but doesn't bruise yellow.

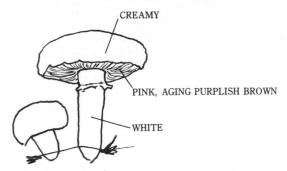

CREAMY

PINK, AGING PURPLISH BROWN

WHITE

*Agaricus campestris*

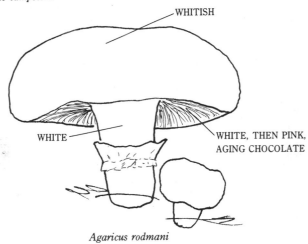

WHITISH

WHITE

WHITE, THEN PINK,
AGING CHOCOLATE

*Agaricus rodmani*

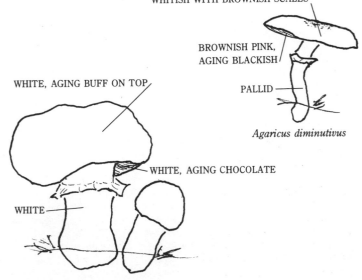

WHITISH WITH BROWNISH SCALES

BROWNISH PINK,
AGING BLACKISH

PALLID

*Agaricus diminutivus*

WHITE, AGING BUFF ON TOP

WHITE, AGING CHOCOLATE

WHITE

*Agaricus nivescens*

*Agaricus pattersonae:* Chocolate-brown spores. Edible and choice.
CAP: 2–4 (6) in. broad. Whitish, covered with patches of long, dark reddish-brown fibrils. Flesh hard, firm.
GILLS: Pinkish, aging chocolate brown with spores. Not attached to stem.
VEIL: White, double as in *A. rodmani,* leaving double ring flaring out from stem.
STEM: 2–4 in. tall. Pallid. About as long as cap is wide. Thick. Pointed base, sometimes covered with veil fragments.
WHERE & WHEN: Hard-packed soil, often in cities; fall.

*Agaricus subrutilescens;* woolly stem: Chocolate-brown spores. Edible and choice but some people are allergic to it.
CAP: 4–6 in. broad. Pallid, covered with conspicuous wine to purplish-brown fibrils over cap center, in patches around edge. Rounded. Flesh white, not changing color when bruised.
GILLS: Bright pink, aging chocolate brown. Not attached to stem. Crowded.
VEIL: White, leaving thin, white ring.
STEM: 4–8 in. tall. Pure white. Shiny above ring; densely covered below with white woolly threads and patches. Slender, long.
WHERE & WHEN: Under mixed hardwoods-conifers, Pacific Northwest; fall.

*Agaricus subrufescens* (*Psalliota subrufescens*): Chocolate-brown spores. Edible. Odor and taste of almonds.
CAP: 2–4 in. wide. Pale tawny to dull reddish brown from fibrils coating cap. Hemispherical, becoming rounded, often with wavy, irregular edge. Minutely scaly, but usually smooth and darker on center. Flesh white, unchanging.
GILLS: Whitish, then pinkish, finally blackish brown. Not attached to stem. Close together.
VEIL: Whitish with yellowish, conspicuous woolly scales and patches on underside, leaving flaring ring with same patches on underside.
STEM: 2–6 in. long. White. Smooth at top but covered with small scales and patches below ring. Somewhat bulbous at base, with white rootlike strings.
WHERE & WHEN: On rich humus, compost piles; fall.

*Agaricus crocodilinus:* Chocolate-brown spores. Edible and choice. Giant West Coast species.
CAP: Up to 18 in. broad. White to pallid covered with scales that darken to pale brown with age. Rounded, becoming expanded in age.
GILLS: Pinkish, becoming color of spores. Not attached to stem. Crowded.
VEIL: White, double, leaving conspicuous double ring.
STEM: 2–6 in. long. White, smooth, short, stout.
WHERE & WHEN: Pastures, open areas moistened by ocean fog, along West Coast; fall.
*A. californicus:* Another edible West Coast species, has 1–3-in. whitish cap tinged purplish brown at center; slightly conical, becoming rounded. Minutely hairy. Flesh whitish, does not change color. Gills pink, aging purplish, then blackish brown. Stem 1½–3 in. long, pallid to brownish, abruptly narrowing above ring. Found under oak trees, West Coast region; fall.

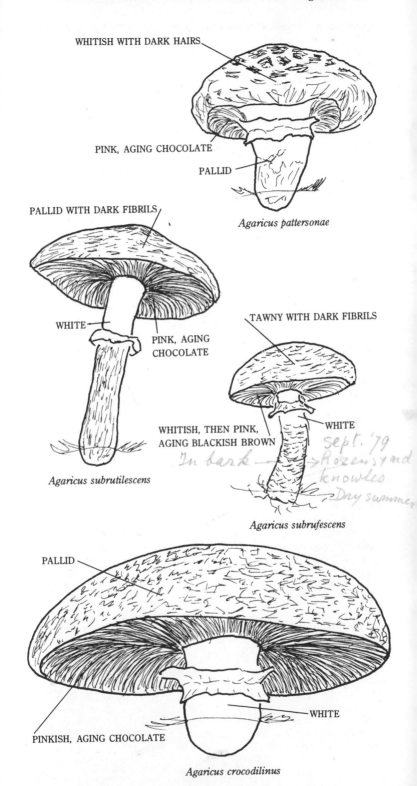

WHITISH WITH DARK HAIRS

PINK, AGING CHOCOLATE

PALLID

*Agaricus pattersonae*

PALLID WITH DARK FIBRILS

WHITE

PINK, AGING
CHOCOLATE

*Agaricus subrutilescens*

TAWNY WITH DARK FIBRILS

WHITISH, THEN PINK,
AGING BLACKISH BROWN

WHITE

*Sept. '79*
*In bark* → *Rozens and*
*Knowles*
→ *Dry summer*

*Agaricus subrufescens*

PALLID

PINKISH, AGING CHOCOLATE

WHITE

*Agaricus crocodilinus*

## AGARICUS: RED-STAINING SPECIES

***Agaricus silvaticus*** (*Psalliota silvatica, A. sanguinarius*): Chocolate-brown spores. Edible, but poisonous to some people.
CAP: 1½–4½ (6) in. broad. Tawny with pinkish-brown hairy scales, often bruising red. Egg-shaped, rounded to broadly rounded in age. Edge slightly inrolled, aging straight. Dry. Flesh white, slowly bruising reddish or remaining unchanged; thick, firm.
GILLS: Whitish, then pale grayish pink, aging to dark reddish brown. Not attached to stem. Crowded together.
VEIL: White, cottony with buff patches, leaving white ring.
STEM: 2–4 in. long. White with a few white hairs, aging dingy pinkish brown. Enlarging toward base.
WHERE & WHEN: Scattered under hardwoods, occasionally conifers; fall, occasionally spring and summer.

***Agaricus haemorrhoidarius*** (*Psalliota haemorrhoidaria*); bleeding mushroom, red-fleshed *Agaricus*: Chocolate-brown spores. Edible. Easily identified because instantly stains bloodred when cap or flesh is bruised.
CAP: 2–4 in. wide. Grayish brown to winy brown, covered with darker fibrils that may disappear in age. Hemispherical, becoming rounded to nearly flat. Edge rolled in when young. Fleshy.
GILLS: Pink, aging chocolate brown. Not attached to stem. Rather thick.
VEIL: Whitish, sometimes tinged brown, thick; leaving thick, conspicuous ring.
STEM: 2–4 in. long. Whitish, aging brownish. Narrow, hollow cavity. Some forms have short, fat stem, nearly as broad as long, slightly bulging in center.
WHERE & WHEN: Under conifers and in mixed woods, often in cities; summer, fall.

***Agaricus halophilus*** (*A. maritimus*); sea-loving *Agaricus*: Purple-brown spores. Edible. Stubby, solid species well adapted to withstand coastal storms.
CAP: 2–8 in. broad. White, aging dingy grayish brown, sometimes with reddish-brown scales. Hemispherical, then rounded, becoming nearly flat. Edge sharply inrolled in youth. Flesh white, quickly reddening when cut or bruised. Smells of the sea.
GILLS: Pinkish, aging purple brown. Not attached to stem. Crowded.
VEIL: White, delicate, leaving fragile ring that often disappears.
STEM: 1–2 in. tall. White, firm, solid. Sometimes bulbous.
WHERE & WHEN: Sandy soil near salt water, East and West Coasts; late summer, fall.
LOOK-ALIKES: Can be differentiated from *A. haemorrhoidarius*, which does not grow close to sea, has darker cap, longer hollow stem.

# AGARICUS: RED-STAINING SPECIES

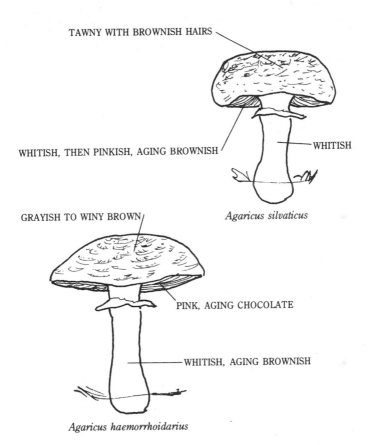

TAWNY WITH BROWNISH HAIRS

WHITISH, THEN PINKISH, AGING BROWNISH

WHITISH

*Agaricus silvaticus*

GRAYISH TO WINY BROWN

PINK, AGING CHOCOLATE

WHITISH, AGING BROWNISH

*Agaricus haemorrhoidarius*

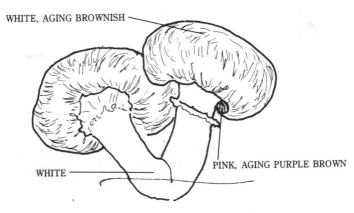

WHITE, AGING BROWNISH

WHITE

PINK, AGING PURPLE BROWN

*Agaricus halophilus*

# AGARICUS: YELLOW-STAINING SPECIES

***Agaricus arvensis*** (*Psalliota arvensis*); horse mushroom, prairie mushroom: Purplish-brown to blackish-brown spores. Edible, choice.
CAP: 3–8 in. broad. Creamy to yellowish brown, aging darker, bruising yellow. Smooth with small scales over cap center, deeply cracking in age. Spherical with slightly flattened top. Dry. Flesh white, thick, slowly turning yellowish when bruised. Sometimes with veil remnants hanging from edge. Tastes and smells like almonds.
GILLS: Whitish, then grayish pink, finally deep chocolate brown with spores. Not attached to stem. Close together.
VEIL: White, thin, double; outer layer breaks into jagged, toothed pattern, then leaves skirtlike ring on stem.
STEM: 2–8 in. long. White, bruising yellow. Smooth, dry, shining above ring; cottony, small scales below. Sometimes with bulb at base.
WHERE & WHEN: Scattered in meadows, pastures, fields, lawns, parks, usually in open, rarely under scattered trees; summer, fall.

***Agaricus silvicola*** (*Psalliota silvicola*); woodland mushroom: Chocolate spores. Edible, but poisonous to some. Similar to *A. arvensis* but grows in woods.
CAP: 3–5 in. wide. White. Rounded then flat. Smooth, silky. Flesh white, slowly staining yellow; firm.
GILLS: Pink turning purplish brown. Not attached to stem. Crowded.
VEIL: White, thick, double, with thick patches of tissue on underside, leaves thick ring on stem.
STEM: 3–5 in. long. White, bulbous, flattened at base. Some forms have large abrupt bulb at base (identified as a separate species, *A. abruptibulbus*, by some mycologists).
WHERE & WHEN: In woods, especially under conifers; occasionally in spring, but usually summer, fall. Same habitat as *Amanita*, so don't confuse them.
***A. albolutescens*** and ***A. xanthrodermus:*** Poisonous to many, resemble *A. silvicola* but instantly stain intense yellow when bruised or cut, particularly at stem base. *A. xanthrodermus* also smells of creosote.
***A. hondensis:*** Poisonous to some, resembles *A. silvicola,* grows under conifers, mixed woods, West Coast, in fall. Develops strong creosote odor and disagreeable flavor in cooking. Its ivory cap soon becomes reddish brown with beige or lilac-brown scales; stains yellowish, darkening to dingy wine. Stout, white, bulbous stem with flaring, feltlike ring.

***Agaricus augustus;*** the prince: Chocolate-brown spores. Edible, one of the best. Very large. Smells of anise.
CAP: 4–12 (17) in. wide. Creamy to yellowy tan, covered with brownish scales, bruising yellow. Large, egg-shaped with flattened top, then rounded, aging flat with low knob at center. Dry. Edge slightly inrolled in youth, soon becoming straight. Flesh white, aging yellowish, firm.
GILLS: Creamy white, then dull rose, finally purplish brown. Not attached to stem. Close together.
VEIL: White with cottony patches, leaves soft, skirtlike ring.
STEM: 3–8 in. long. White, bruising yellow. Dry. Hairless above ring; dense yellowish-brown hairs below (as on cap). Enlarged near base. Sunk deep in soil.
WHERE & WHEN: Scattered under conifers or in grassy areas, lawns, orchards, flower beds, along roads, compost heaps; spring–fall.

# AGARICUS: YELLOW-STAINING SPECIES

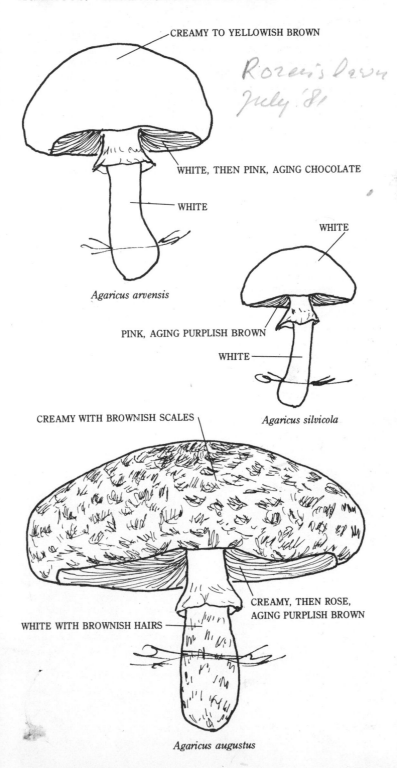

CREAMY TO YELLOWISH BROWN

*Rozen's Peak*
*July '81*

WHITE, THEN PINK, AGING CHOCOLATE

WHITE

*Agaricus arvensis*

WHITE

PINK, AGING PURPLISH BROWN

WHITE

*Agaricus silvicola*

CREAMY WITH BROWNISH SCALES

CREAMY, THEN ROSE,
AGING PURPLISH BROWN

WHITE WITH BROWNISH HAIRS

*Agaricus augustus*

## YELLOW-STAINING (CONTINUED)

***Agaricus placomyces*** (*Psalliota placomyces*); flat cap: Chocolate-brown spores. Edible for some; poisonous to others. Disagreeable odor.

CAP: 1½–3 (6) in. broad. Whitish covered with grayish to grayish-brown hairy scales, darker in the cap center, no reddish hairs typical of *A. silvaticus*. Oval, then rounded, finally nearly flat in age, sometimes with low knob at center. Edge incurved and wrinkled at first, soon becoming straight. Flesh white or dull pinkish in age, slowly staining yellow then gradually darkening to reddish brown.

GILLS: Pinkish gray, aging chocolate brown. Not attached to stem. Crowded.

VEIL: White, cottony with yellow to brown soft, flat cottony patches underneath. Leaves persistent ring on stem.

STEM: 1–3½ (6) in. long. White, aging brownish. Base slightly bulbous.

WHERE & WHEN: Under hardwoods, often clustered; late summer, fall.

PSILOCYBE   These are the smallest mushrooms in the purple-brown spore group. They have tiny bell-shaped to rounded moist caps; thin stems, usually very long; sometimes with a ring. Their gills are attached to the stem and in age turn the color of the spores. The cap edge is inrolled in youth. They are found generally on the ground or on dung. In some species, the stems stain blue; of these blue-staining species, some are hallucinogenic. In some states, possession, cultivation, or distribution of these mushrooms is prohibited by law. Several species have been used in religious ceremonies for many years by Indians in Mexico.

EDIBILITY: *Psilocybes* are too small and fragile to serve as edibles.

## YELLOW-STAINING (CONTINUED)

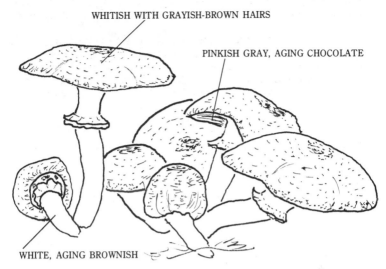

WHITISH WITH GRAYISH-BROWN HAIRS

PINKISH GRAY, AGING CHOCOLATE

WHITE, AGING BROWNISH

*Agaricus placomyces*

## PSILOCYBE

GENUS CHARACTERISTICS
- Purplish-brown to chocolate-brown spores
- Very small
- Cap conic to flat, often with knob
- Cap edge incurved in youth
- Gills age brown or purplish
- Sometimes with ring
- Stem tall, thin, sometimes stains blue
- On dung, soil, wood debris

*Psilocybe montana*

*Psilocybe semilanceata*

*Psilocybe pelliculosa*

**NAEMATOLOMA**   When you find a clump of mushrooms with purple-brown spores densely clustered on wood, you have a *Naematoloma*. Usually on top of a lower cap you can locate a spore print, made by one of the taller caps. The cap edge is incurved when young and often fringed with remnants of a veil that rarely leaves a ring on the stem. The species are usually brightly colored.
EDIBILITY: Some species are very bitter tasting, but *N. capnoides* and *N. sublateritium* are good all-purpose edibles. *N. fasciculare* is believed to be poisonous but is so bitter tasting no one would eat enough to do harm.

*Naematoloma capnoides* (*Hypholoma capnoides*): Purple-brown spores. Edible.
CAP: ¾–3 in. broad. Reddish orange to yellowish brown on top, paler and more yellow around the edge. Rounded, aging nearly flat, sometimes with small knob at center. Moist but not slimy. Smooth. Edge is inrolled at first, later fringed with buff patches of veil remnants. Flesh whitish.
GILLS: Whitish to gray, finally purple brown with spores. Attached to stem. Close together.
VEIL: Whitish, leaving an obscure zone of hairs on the stem.
STEM: 2–4 in. long. Yellowish above faint ring, tan to brownish below. Dry, hairy, hollow.
WHERE & WHEN: In clusters on conifers in fall, sometimes spring.
LOOK-ALIKES: Can be differentiated from others described here because its gills do not have olive coloration of *N. fasciculare,* and its cap is not the brick red of *N. sublateritium,* which is on hardwood, not conifers.

*Naematoloma sublateritium* (*Hypholoma sublateritium, H. perplexum*); brick cap, brick top: Purple-gray spores. Edible and good.
CAP: ¾–4 in. broad. Red-brick color over center, fading to pinky buff around edge. Rounded to rather flat, sometimes with low knob at center. Moist. Edge inrolled in youth. Flesh whitish, becoming yellowish in age or when bruised.
GILLS: White, sometimes yellowish, rarely with faint olive tint, soon changing to gray, finally smoky purplish brown. Attached to stem. Crowded.
VEIL: Yellowish white, sometimes leaving ringlike zone on stem.
STEM: 2–4 in. long, whitish above ring zone, darkening to brown below.
WHERE & WHEN: Dense clusters on hardwood logs, stumps; summer, fall.

*Naematoloma fasciculare* (*Hypholoma fasciculare*); sulphur tuft: Purple-brown spores. Poisonous, bitter.
CAP: ½–3 in. broad. Sulphur yellow over center, sometimes tinged olive, paler around edge. Conic, aging rounded, then nearly flat, sometimes with knob at center. Moist. Incurved edge at first. Veil remnants fringing edge. Flesh yellowish, bruising dark.
GILLS: Sulphur yellow to olive, finally turning purplish from spores. Attached to stem. Crowded.
VEIL: Creamy, hairy, leaving a zone of hairs on the stem.
STEM: 2–4½ in. tall, thin, white to buff above ring zone, brownish and hairy below. Tapering toward base.
WHERE & WHEN: Clustered on logs and stumps of hardwoods, conifers in spring and fall; during mild winter weather in warmer states.

# NAEMATOLOMA

GENUS CHARACTERISTICS
- Purplish-brown spores
- Cap bowl-shaped, often sulphur to reddish yellow
- Cap edge incurved when young
- Veil remnants on cap edge
- Rarely a ring
- Gills attached to stem
- Usually clustered on wood

ORANGY TO YELLOWISH; PALER EDGE

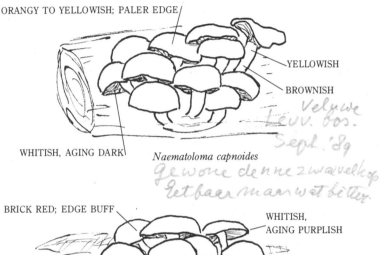

YELLOWISH

BROWNISH

WHITISH, AGING DARK

*Naematoloma capnoides*

*Veluwe*
*Leuv. bos.*
*Sept. '89*
*Gewone denne zwavelkop*
*Eetbaar maar wat bitter.*

BRICK RED; EDGE BUFF

WHITISH, AGING PURPLISH

WHITE

BROWNISH

*Naematoloma sublateritium*

YELLOWISH, AGING PURPLISH

YELLOWISH; PALER EDGE

PALLID

BROWNISH

*Naematoloma fasciculare*

**STROPHARIA** These small to medium-size mushrooms have purple-brown to violet spores; rounded caps that are slimy when wet; gills attached to the stem; fleshy to thin stems with a persistent ring; grow on manure or rich ground (barnyards, manured grass, mulch, wood chips); not in clusters. They might be confused with *Naematolomas,* which also have purple-brown spores.

EDIBILITY: *Stropharia* have not been fully tested and there are conflicting reports on their edibility. Many are considered poisonous, and the entire species is suspect, with avoidance recommended. *S. rugoso-annulata,* however, is edible and excellent, adaptable to most recipes.

*Stropharia rugoso-annulata:* Sooty violet spores. Edible.
CAP: 3–6 (8) in. broad. Dull wine red or purplish red, fading to yellowish in age. Rounded, becoming flattened. Dry. Silky. Flesh white.
GILLS: White, turning grayish violet, finally blackish violet, with white edges. Notched where they touch stem. Close together.
VEIL: Conspicuous, leaving feltlike ring with upper part ribbed; lower part with yellowish cottony patches.
STEM: 3–6+ in. tall. White or pale yellowish, stout, smooth, dry.
WHERE & WHEN: Frequently watered, cultivated areas; spring–fall.

*Stropharia semiglobata:* Purple-brown spores. Some say poisonous.
CAP: ½–1¼ in. broad. Bright straw yellow, fading to dull yellow, sometimes tinged olive. Hemispherical, becoming flattened. Slimy when wet, shiny when dry. Fleshy at center, thin at cap edge. Flesh yellowish, watery.
GILLS: Olive gray, soon deep purple brown. Attached to stem.
VEIL: Whitish, leaving fragile ring, sometimes absent. Ages dark.
STEM: 1–4½ in. long. White to buff. Base may be enlarged. Hairy above ring; slimy below.
WHERE & WHEN: On dung, manured fields; spring–fall.
LOOK-ALIKES: Might be confused with *Psilocybe coprophila,* which also grows on dung but has gray-brown cap and no ring; or with *Agrocybe pediades,* which has dull-brown spores, no ring, grows in grass.

*Stropharia coronilla* (*S. obturata*): Purple-brown spores. Suspected as poisonous.
CAP: ¾–2 in. broad, pale yellowish to yellowish brown. Rounded to nearly flat in age. Moist to slightly sticky. Flesh white, thick, soft.
GILLS: Brownish violet, with white edges. Attached to stem.
VEIL: White, leaving persistent ring, soon purple brown with spores.
STEM: 1–1½ in. tall. White. Minutely hairy.
WHERE & WHEN: Scattered in grassy places; late summer, fall.
LOOK-ALIKES: Might be mistaken for *Agaricus* but gills are not free.

*Stropharia aeruginosa:* Purple-brown spores. Suspected as poisonous.
CAP: ½–2 in. broad. Covered with bright-green slime, fading slowly to yellowish as the slime disappears. Sometimes with white veil patches adhering to cap. Rounded, becoming flattened. Flesh whitish to bluish.
GILLS: Whitish, then gray to purple brown; white edges. Attached to stem.
VEIL: Soft, leaving ring that may disappear.
STEM: 1–3 in. long. White above ring, bluish green, scaly below. Slimy.
WHERE & WHEN: Single to several, grassy areas, moist woods; late summer, fall.

## STROPHARIA

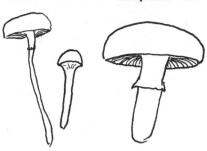

GENUS CHARACTERISTICS
· Purplish-brown spores
· Cap slimy when wet
· Gills attached to stem
· Ring on stem
· Not in clusters
· On manure, rich ground

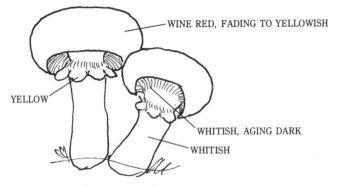

WINE RED, FADING TO YELLOWISH

YELLOW

WHITISH, AGING DARK

WHITISH

*Stropharia rugoso-annulata*

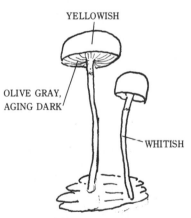

YELLOWISH

OLIVE GRAY,
AGING DARK

WHITISH

*Stropharia semiglobata*

YELLOWISH

BROWNISH
VIOLET

WHITISH

*Stropharia coronilla*

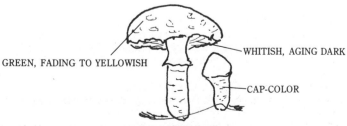

GREEN, FADING TO YELLOWISH

WHITISH, AGING DARK

CAP-COLOR

*Stropharia aeruginosa*

**COPRINUS; THE INKY CAPS**  This unique genus is identified easily by its black spores and gills that dissolve into a black inky fluid at maturity, a process called *autodigestion*. Caps are conic to bell-shaped, usually grooved from the center to edge of cap. In young stages, the cap is folded like an umbrella against the thin stem. Gills, not attached to the stem, are white or light gray at first, soon darkening upward, turning black as they liquefy.

EDIBILITY: This is a fairly large genus with over 75 species, but most are too small and short-lived to be eaten or even noticed. A few are choice edibles, however, and *C. comatus* is a favorite of mushroom connoisseurs. These mushrooms, more than any others, should be picked in their youth (while their gills are still white or light gray, before they begin to blacken and liquefy) and eaten the day they are harvested. The autodigestion is so rapid that mushrooms happily picked in the woods may be an inky mess by the time you get them home. They are very tender and well flavored, can be cooked quickly with little fuss. Especially good with eggs, cheese, fish, chicken.

· Sauté in butter, season with salt, pepper, nutmeg, squeeze of lemon.
· Stew, covered, in butter and/or cream 5–10 minutes.
· Season with salt and pepper, dot with butter, bake covered in 350° oven for 25 minutes. Add several tablespoons of cream, heat to boiling.
· Sauté gently in butter, then bake with a bit of white wine and nutmeg, topped with croutons, in a 350° oven until croutons are browned.
· Chop and cook slowly in butter for 10 minutes, then add to chicken pie or other chicken dish. Or add to any quiche—or sprinkle lavishly over the top just before serving.
· Sauté in butter and serve with fish or add to fish as it cooks.
· Season; cook, covered, for 5 minutes. Drain liquid, reserving for other purposes. Dip mushrooms in fritter batter, fry in oil.
· Brush with condensed milk, roll in flour and dry bread crumbs, broil.
· Add to scrambled eggs or omelets. Season with chopped parsley and green onions with a bit of garlic mashed with salt. Or place sliced, sautéed *Coprinus* (with their juices) on top of eggs in buttered rame-kins and bake.
· Dip in beaten egg, then in grated Parmesan. Sauté. Dust with herbs.
· *C. comatus* is delicious sliced and eaten raw in oil and vinegar salads. Try adding toasted nuts or seasoning with fresh-grated ginger root or a pinch of curry powder.
· Slice *C. comatus* in half. Steam.
· Cooking stops autodigestion, so *Coprinus* can be blanched, frozen.

*Coprinus micaceus;* glistening *Coprinus*: Blackish-brown spores. Edible.
CAP: 1–2½ in., tannish to reddish brown, covered with glistening micalike white particles that soon disappear. Oval to conic to bell-shaped in age, ribbed from near cap center to cap edge. Edges some-what wavy.
GILLS: White, becoming inky in age. Crowded. Notched at the stem.
STEM: 1–3 in. long. Silky white, hollow, slender, fragile, often twisted.
WHERE & WHEN: In dense clusters around old stumps, trees, fence posts, or on decayed, buried wood, sawdust, during cool moist weather, early spring–late fall, reappearing after rains in the same places. Usually in great numbers.
*C. hansenii:* Edible. Related to *C. micaceus,* but smaller; cap is more pointed and richer date brown with deep grooves around border. Stem tinged brownish. Doesn't show much autodigestion.

# COPRINUS

GENUS CHARACTERISTICS
· Black spores
· Cap oval to conic to bell-shaped
· Cap folded like umbrella against stem in youth
· Cap edge wrinkled or ribbed
· Gills dissolving into black inky liquid
· On wood, dung, humus, ground
· Stem thin, easily detached from cap
· Some species have fluffy scales, movable ring

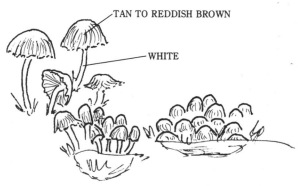

TAN TO REDDISH BROWN

WHITE

*Coprinus micaceus*

DATE BROWN

TINGED BROWNISH

*Coprinus hansenii*

*Coprinus atramentarius;* inky cap: Black spores. Edible, NOT with alcohol.

CAP: ¾–3 in. wide. Tan to grayish, conic becoming bell-shaped in age, generally smooth but sometimes with small, pale-brownish scales over center. Often covered with a marked bloom. Ribbed to wrinkled from center to cap edge. Flesh pallid, thin.

GILLS: White to gray, aging black and inky. Close together. Not attached to stem. More thick and meaty than other *Coprinus* species.

STEM: 1½–4 in. long, thin, white, upper half covered with minute, flattened white hairs, lower portion with scattered brown fibrils, hollow. Sometimes enlarged at base.

WHERE & WHEN: Densely clustered in grass, wood debris, sawdust, or from buried wood; summer and fall.

CAUTION: This mushroom contains a chemical that reacts with alcohol, causing digestive distress in some but not all people. This reaction may reoccur when more alcohol is consumed, even up to a week after eating the mushrooms. Therefore if you drink, don't eat this one; if you eat this one, don't drink.

*Coprinus comatus;* shaggy mane, lawyer's wig: Black spores. Edible, choice; one of the best. Large and easily recognized.

CAP: 2–6 (12) in. tall. White with many shaggy upturned scales, tinged brownish. Egg-shaped, expanding to bell-shaped, splitting along line of gills. Edge ribbed to wrinkled. Flesh white, then darkening, soft.

GILLS: White, shading to pink, aging black, then dripping inky fluid. Crowded. Notched at junction with stem.

VEIL: Fibrous, leaving a movable ring that often slips to base of stem, or disappears altogether.

STEM: ½–6 (12) in. long. Creamy white, bulbous, hollow, brittle, pointed base.

WHERE & WHEN: Singly or in groups on hard ground or grassy areas, garbage dumps, compost heaps, often in a row along roadsides; late summer, fall.

*C. sterquilinus:* Edible. Very similar to *C. comatus* but smaller. Scales easily removed. Stem slowly discolors when bruised. Cap edge has forked ribbing. Grows in old manure, straw, or manured ground. Has stronger flavor.

*Coprinus quadrifidus:* Black spores. Edible.

CAP: 1–2 in. tall. Narrow, oval-shaped in youth. ½–1 in. wide; expanding to 2 in. in age. Whitish, covered at first by a veil that soon breaks into woolly scales on the cap. Edge often wavy, rolling up and back.

GILLS: Whitish, then purplish brown, finally black and liquefying at the edges. Crowded. Not attached to stem.

STEM: Up to 5 in. high. White, silky, thin, hollow, growing from well-developed rootlike black strands.

WHERE & WHEN: In clusters on decaying stumps and roots; summer, fall.

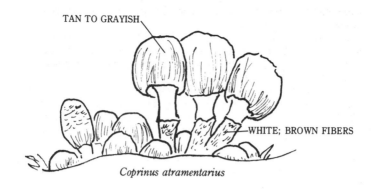

TAN TO GRAYISH

WHITE; BROWN FIBERS

*Coprinus atramentarius*

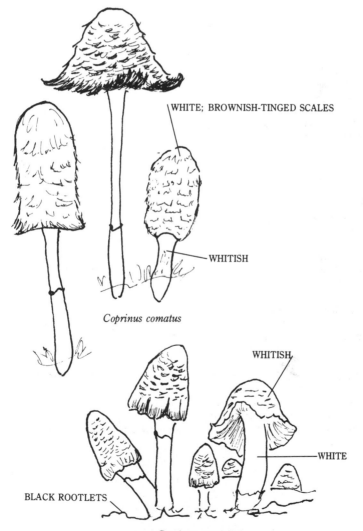

WHITE; BROWNISH-TINGED SCALES

WHITISH

*Coprinus comatus*

WHITISH

WHITE

BLACK ROOTLETS

*Coprinus quadrifidus*

**PANAEOLUS**  These small dull-colored mushrooms were rated as edible in older books but recent studies show they contain poisonous toxins and all should be avoided. As they are so small, it is no culinary loss. A few species are hallucinogenic when growing in certain areas; but growing in other regions, they are not. *Panaeolus* typically have conic grayish to brownish caps that never flatten. They have pale gills that become mottled with ripening spores, finally turning deep purple brown to purple black, although the edges usually remain white. The gills are precisely arranged close together and are attached to the stem. The cap edge extends beyond the gills. The stem is thin and rigid. Only one species, *P. separatus,* has a ring. All grow on dung or manured grass. They could be mistaken for edible *Coprinus* but do not decay into an inky liquid. The following 4 species are common:

*Panaeolus campanulatus:* Black spores. Poisonous, sometimes with hallucinogenic properties.
CAP: ½–2 in. broad. Brownish gray to olive gray. Conic to bell-shaped, slightly incurved, frilled with white veil remnants hanging from cap edge. Moist and slippery when wet. Flesh whitish to grayish, soft, thin.
GILLS: Grayish with white edges, speckled dark purple brown in age. Close together. Attached to stem.
VEIL: White, soft, leaving no ring.
STEM: 1½–4 in. Light gray at top, reddish brown to gray brown below. Brittle, rigid, slender, slightly enlarged at base.
WHERE & WHEN: Single to several on dung; spring–fall.

*Panaeolus foenisecii* (*Psilocybe foenisecii, Panaeolina foenisecii*); harvest, haymaker's, or mower's mushroom: Dull blackish-brown spores. Poisonous, sometimes hallucinogenic. Common lawn mushroom.
CAP: ½–1 in. broad. Dull brown to reddish brown when moist; dries lighter in center with darker band around edge. Conic. Flesh tan, thin.
GILLS: Pale brown with white edges, becoming dark and mottled with spores. Close. Attached to stem, rounded where they touch stem.
STEM: 1½–4 in. tall. Pale with minute hairs at top; dingy brown, hairless below. Brittle, thin, fragile, sometimes slightly enlarged at base.
WHERE & WHEN: In grass in early morning; spring–fall.

*Panaeolus retirugis;* wrinkled *Panaeolus*: Blackish spores. Poisonous.
CAP: ½–2 in. broad. Smoky and slimy when wet; tannish to creamy, covered with shiny particles when dry. Conic, veined, wrinkled, with white veil fragments hanging from edge. Flesh white, thin, soft.
GILLS: White, then mottled with spores; edges white. Close. Attached.
STEM: 2–6 in. tall. Gray reddish-brown; sometimes with band blackened with spores. Slender, thick, hollow, somewhat bulbous at base.
WHERE & WHEN: On dung or manured lawns; summer, fall.

*Panaeolus separatus* (*P. semiovatus, Anellaria separata*): Black spores. Poisonous. The only *Panaeolus* with a ring.
CAP: ½–2 in. broad. Grayish to pale tan. Conic. Slimy when wet. Edge often splits in age. Flesh white, thin, soft.
GILLS: Gray, becoming mottled with spores. Close; attached to stem.
VEIL: Membranous, leaving ring, soon blackened by falling spores.
STEM: 2½–7 in. tall. Whitish, smooth, enlarged at base.
WHERE & WHEN: On dung, manured ground; cool, moist weather; spring–fall.

# PANAEOLUS

GENUS CHARACTERISTICS
· Blackish spores
· Cap conic to bell-shaped, never flat
· Gills pale, becoming mottled with spores
· Gills attached to stem
· Stem pale, thin, rigid
· On dung or manured grass

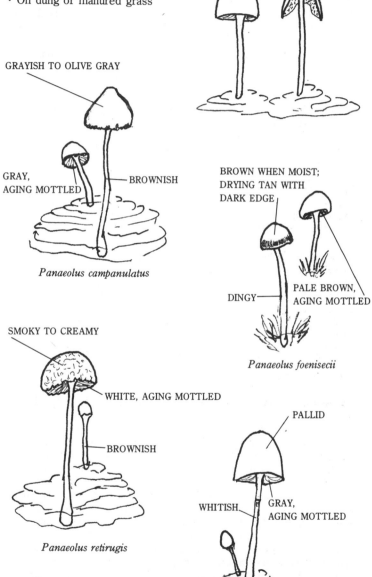

GRAYISH TO OLIVE GRAY

GRAY, AGING MOTTLED

BROWNISH

*Panaeolus campanulatus*

BROWN WHEN MOIST; DRYING TAN WITH DARK EDGE

DINGY

PALE BROWN, AGING MOTTLED

*Panaeolus foenisecii*

SMOKY TO CREAMY

WHITE, AGING MOTTLED

BROWNISH

*Panaeolus retirugis*

PALLID

WHITISH

GRAY, AGING MOTTLED

*Panaeolus separatus*

**PSATHYRELLA** The name means "fragile," aptly describing these small thin-fleshed mushrooms. Generally, they have dull-colored caps, conic to rounded to nearly flat, 1–4 in. broad, atop very slender stems, giving them a slightly top-heavy look. The cap darkens when wet, drying lighter again. The cap edge often becomes grooved when wet. In some species, remnants of a veil remain attached to the cap edge. The gills are pallid at first, then become sooty with maturing spores. They grow singly to densely clustered on wood, grass, humus.

EDIBILITY: Most species in this very large genus (400–500 species) have not been tested for edibility. Their small size, thin flesh, and fragility do not make them likely candidates for the kitchen, and the sinister reputations of related genera have discouraged experimentation. The two species described here, however, are tasty morsels, useful for a quick sauté or for flavoring other dishes, if sufficient numbers can be found.

LOOK-ALIKES: Sometimes hard to separate from *Panaeolus,* but do not have the mottled gills of *Panaeolus.* Also could be confused with *Stropharia,* which should be crosschecked.

*Psathyrella candolleana* (*P. candolliana, Hypholoma candolliana, H. appendiculatum, H. incertum*): Purple brownish-black spores. Edible.

CAP: 1–3+ in. broad. Buff, fading to whitish, with scattered small, white scales in youth. Rounded, becoming broadly rounded to upturned in age. Veil remnants may hang from cap edge. Edge often splits in age. Flesh white, thin, fragile.

GILLS: White to grayish, maturing purplish brown. Close to crowded. Attached to stem.

VEIL: White, membranous, rarely leaving ring, sometimes remaining attached to cap edge.

STEM: 1–4 in. tall. Shiny white, thin, smooth, hollow, rigid.

WHERE & WHEN: Single to clustered in grassy areas, clearings in woods, lawns, fields; spring–fall, widely distributed.

*Psathyrella velutina* (*P. lacrymabunda, Hypholoma velutina*); weeping widow: Dark purple-brown to brownish-black spores. Edible.

CAP: ½–3 in. broad. Yellowish brown, darker in center, fading to buff at edges. Covered with dense brown hairs. Rounded, with center knob in age. Edge often splitting. Flesh brownish, soft.

GILLS: Light brown with white edges, maturing dark purple brown with ripening spores. Close to crowded. Notched at the stem. Sometimes beaded with drops of moisture in wet weather, hence its common name.

VEIL: White, fibrous, becoming blackish with spores, leaving obscure hairy ring.

STEM: 1–3 in. tall, whitish above ring, light brown below. Thin, dry, hairy.

WHERE & WHEN: Single to many in grassy areas or humus; spring–fall, widely distributed.

# PSATHYRELLA

GENUS CHARACTERISTICS
· Brown-black spores, tinged purplish
· Small, fragile, dull-colored
· Cap round to nearly flat
· Small species have conic cap,
  long thin stem
· Gills pale, aging dark
· Gills attached to stem
· Stem thin, fragile
· On wood, humus, grass

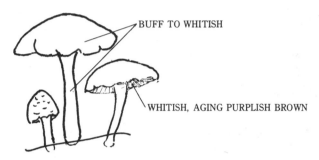

BUFF TO WHITISH

WHITISH, AGING PURPLISH BROWN

*Psathyrella candolleana*

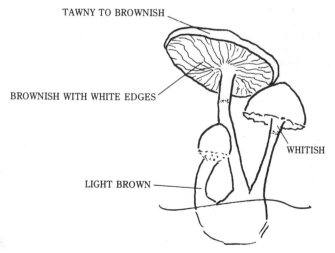

TAWNY TO BROWNISH

BROWNISH WITH WHITE EDGES

WHITISH

LIGHT BROWN

*Psathyrella velutina*

**GOMPHIDIUS AND CHROOGOMPHUS**   These closely related genera are good ones for the novice because they are easy to recognize and all species are edible. They were considered one genus, *Gomphidius,* until as late as 1964 when they were finally published as two distinct groups by Orson K. Miller, Jr.

**THEIR SIMILARITIES:** (1) Blackish spores, (2) gills that are thick, far apart, extend down the stem, (3) gills that turn grayish as they become coated with maturing spores, (4) in young mushrooms, the cap is usually connected to the stem by a thin veil that breaks as the cap expands, leaving a few fibrils, or a ring of them, on the stem, (5) all species grow under conifers, especially pine, Douglas fir, hemlock.

**THEIR DIFFERENCES:** (1) *Gomphidius* has white flesh, and its cap surface and veil are slimy to the touch, (2) *Chroogomphus* has colored flesh, a dry-to-sticky cap surface, and a dry veil.

**EDIBILITY:** All species are edible. Although not regarded as choice, they are good combined with other foods, as in stuffing, meat loaf, rice pilaf, casseroles. *C. rutilus, G. subroseus,* and *G. glutinosus* are the favored species for flavor. Peel off the sticky cap surfaces before cooking, and don't be dismayed when the flesh turns a deep wine color in the pan.

**LOOK-ALIKES:** Some people mistake these mushrooms for *Hygrophorus* (also edible), which have waxy gills extending down the stem. However, *Hygrophorus* spores are white, which ends the confusion quickly.

*Gomphidius subroseus;* rosy *Gomphidius*: Blackish-brown spores. Edible. This small colorful mushroom can be recognized quickly by its rosy-red cap and yellowing stem that is white above the ring, turning yellowish below, deepening to deep yellow at the base.

**CAP:** 1½–2½ in. broad. Pink to reddish. Rounded when young, becoming flat with age with upturned edge. Slimy when wet, covered with a thick gelatinlike surface. Flesh white, thick, firm.

**GILLS:** White, aging smoky gray from spores. Thick, fairly well separated, soft and waxy, extending down stem.

**VEIL:** Slimy, thin, leaving a colorless ring that soon blackens from spores.

**STEM:** 1½–2½ in. tall. Silky white above the ring, cream to yellow below, deep yellow at base. Tapers toward base.

**WHERE & WHEN:** Alone to many under conifers, particularly Douglas fir, often in moss; spring, summer, but mostly fall until frost.

# GOMPHIDIUS AND CHROOGOMPHUS

GENERA CHARACTERISTICS
- Smoky-black spores
- Gills thick, far apart, extend down stem, age grayish
- Veil thin, hairy
- Under conifers

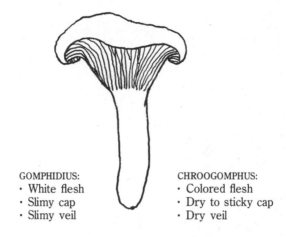

GOMPHIDIUS:
- White flesh
- Slimy cap
- Slimy veil

CHROOGOMPHUS:
- Colored flesh
- Dry to sticky cap
- Dry veil

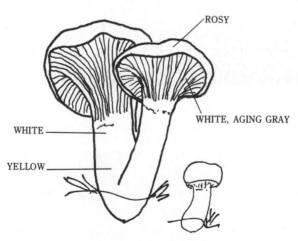

ROSY

WHITE, AGING GRAY

WHITE

YELLOW

*Gomphidius subroseus*

*Gomphidius maculatus;* spotted *Gomphidius*: Black spores. Edible. Has no veil, unlike others in this genus. Can be identified by the dark purple hairs on the stem.
CAP: 1–4 in. broad. Yellowish to reddish brown, often streaked and developing blackening blotches. Rounded when young, flattening in age. Slimy, smooth, sometimes with very fine hairs. Flesh white, except maroon under cap surface and reddish yellow at stem base; firm.
GILLS: White, aging smoky gray with spores. Extend down stem. Well separated, forked, with veins running between the gills.
VEIL: None.
STEM: 1–3 in. tall. White near cap, turning yellowish to brownish at the base, covered with purplish-black hairs.
WHERE & WHEN: Alone to many under mixed conifers, especially larch; late summer, fall, Canada, northern U.S.

*Gomphidius glutinosus:* Smoky gray to black spores. Edible.
CAP: 1–4 in. broad. Grayish to purple brown or reddish cinnamon, often with black stains. Rounded when young, flattening in age with upturned edge. Slimy to the touch, smooth. Flesh white, except pinkish beneath cap surface and yellowish in stem; soft.
GILLS: Buff turning smoky gray in age from spores. Extend down stem. Close together.
VEIL: Thin, slimy, hairy underneath, leaving a slimy ring that soon darkens from the spores.
STEM: ½–4 in. tall. Shiny white above slimy ring, yellow over lower part with blackish or purplish stains.
WHERE & WHEN: Many, under conifers; spring–fall throughout North America, particularly western U.S.
*var. salmoneus:* Orange cap; in Pacific Northwest. Edible.
*var. purpureus:* Dark-purple cap; in Pacific Northwest. Edible.
*G. smithii:* Reddish to brownish-gray cap, with little or no yellow in the stem. Edible.
*G. largus:* Large species up to 6 in. broad, pinkish to reddish-brown cap. Edible.

*Gomphidius oregonensis:* Black spores. Edible.
CAP: 1–6 in. broad. Dingy white when young, turning yellowish to reddish brown. Rounded when young, flattening in age with upturned edge. Slimy to the touch with soil particles sticking to surface. Flesh white, except cap-color beneath cap surface; thick, soft.
GILLS: White, aging smoky gray with spores. Extend down stem. Well separated, large and coarse.
VEIL: Slimy, with white hairy layer underneath, leaves slimy ring that soon becomes blackish with spores.
STEM: 2½–4¾ in. tall. White above ring, changing to light yellow below, deepening to chrome yellow at the base. Yellow within. Attached deep in soil to enlarged mass of undeveloped mushrooms.
WHERE & WHEN: In clusters under conifers; summer, mostly fall, in western states.
*G. pseudomaculatus:* Similar but without veil, in Idaho, edible.

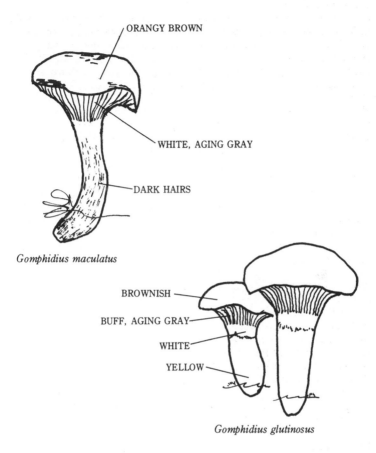

ORANGY BROWN

WHITE, AGING GRAY

DARK HAIRS

*Gomphidius maculatus*

BROWNISH

BUFF, AGING GRAY

WHITE

YELLOW

*Gomphidius glutinosus*

BROWNISH

WHITE, AGING GRAY

DINGY WHITE WHEN YOUNG

WHITE

YELLOW

*Gomphidius oregonensis*

***Chroogomphus rutilus*** (*Gomphidius rutilus, G. viscidus*); colorful *Gomphidius*, viscid *Gomphidius*: Black spores. Edible.

CAP: 1–4½ in. broad. Varies from olive brown to winy brown to orange brown to red, aging to dark wine red. Rounded with small pointed knob in center. Edge curved under when young. Smooth, sticky, but not slimy when fresh, becoming dry and shiny. Flesh light salmon or orchid-tinted, except pinkish near cap surface and yellowish near stem; firm. More slender specimens than illustrated are also found.

GILLS: Buff to dull cinnamon, becoming gray with spores. Fairly well separated, thickish. Extend down stem.

VEIL: Hairy, dry, leaving a ring of hairs that soon disappears.

STEM: 1½–7 in. tall. Tannish orange tinged with red, aging·wine red. Base often bright yellow. Tapers toward base. Dry to somewhat moist.

WHERE & WHEN: Alone to many under conifers, especially pine, after summer and fall rains.

***C. ochraceus:*** Also usually under pines and closely related to *C. rutilus,* has orange cap and stem. Edible.

***C. vinicolor:*** Hard to distinguish from *C. rutilus,* but is smaller, more orangy orchid when young, develops dark red brown as it matures. More cone-shaped than *C. rutilus* and with slimy cap. Found in fall under pines in North and West after rains. Edible.

***Chroogomphus tomentosus*** (*Gomphidius tomentosus*); woolly *Gomphidius*: Black spores. Edible.

CAP: ¾–2½ in. broad. Yellowish to orangy with firm, light-orange flesh. Rounded when young, becoming flat. Dry to the touch with a downy to woolly surface.

GILLS: Yellow orange, turning gray with spores. Extend down stem. Well separated, thick.

VEIL: Thin, hairy, leaving a few fibrils on stem as cap grows and veil breaks, but no ring.

STEM: 1½–6½ in. tall. Same color as cap, tapering toward base. Dry, smooth with scattered hairs.

WHERE & WHEN: Alone to many under conifers, particularly hemlock and Douglas fir; in fall in western states, especially in mountains.

***C. leptocystis:*** Frequently found with *C. tomentosus* but with more grayish cap, also dry and hairy. Edible.

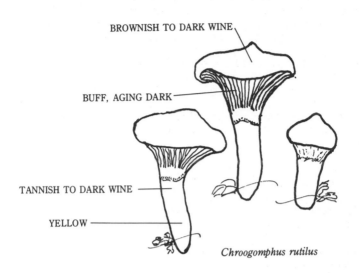

BROWNISH TO DARK WINE

BUFF, AGING DARK

TANNISH TO DARK WINE

YELLOW

*Chroogomphus rutilus*

YELLOW TO ORANGY OVERALL

*Chroogomphus tomentosus*

# PICTURE KEYS, NONGILLED MUSHROOMS

- Fleshy cap and stem or vaselike
- Blunt ridges, veins, or wrinkles instead of gills on undersurface of cap
- Stem central
- On ground under trees

CHANTERELLES, PP. 164–173

- Soft, fleshy cap and stem
- Pores (spongelike layer) instead of gills on undersurface of cap
- Stem central
- On ground

BOLETES, PP. 174–187

- Variety of shapes and sizes, often clustered, one above the other
- Pores (spongelike layer) instead of gills on undersurface
- Usually tough to woody with off-center or no stem
- If fleshy, seldom with stem
- On wood

POLYPORES, PP. 188–193

- Fleshy to tough
- (1) clusters of spinelike structures, growing on wood, or (2) cap and stem with needlelike teeth on undersurface of cap, growing on ground

TEETH FUNGI, PP. 194–199

- Cap cone-shaped; pitted and ridged like honeycomb; whitish to brown to black
- Stem central, white, often wrinkled or furrowed
- Cap and stem hollow, all one piece
- On ground, in spring only

MORCHELLA (TRUE MORELS), PP. 200–207

- Cap (1) folded into two saddle-shaped lobes or (2) a single mass, deeply wrinkled and puckered
- Stem central
- Brittle
- On ground, spring–fall

VERPA, GYROMITRA, HELVELLA (FALSE MORELS)
PP. 206–215

- Small to large
- Round to oval
- Usually without stem
- Usually on ground; a few species on wood

PUFFBALLS, PP. 216–227

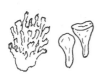

- Like ocean coral with one to many erect fingers or clubs
- Base absent to massive
- On ground, humus, wood

CORAL FUNGI, PP. 228–237

- Very small
- Colorless or yellow to orangy or reddish to brownish black
- (1) Like shallow cup, sometimes lopsided, on ground or (2) like gelatinous blobs or fingers, usually on wood.

CUP AND JELLY FUNGI, Pp. 238

- Small to medium-size
- (1) Like bird's nests with "eggs" inside, sometimes with lid, on soil, wood, dung, (2) star-shaped with spore sac in center, on ground, humus.

BIRD'S NESTS, EARTH STARS

- Small, solitary stalk, abruptly enlarged at top to club or spatula shape or with wrinkled head
- Stalk and head usually of different color and texture
- On soil, wood, debris

EARTH TONGUES

- Soft gelatinous egg, developing long stalklike or branched body
- Slimy spore-producing layer on top
- Offensive odor
- On rotten wood, humus, sawdust

STINKHORNS

# NONGILLED
# MUSHROOMS

# CHANTERELLES

One of the most famous groups of mushrooms in the world. These delicious species tend to grow in the same places each year, if conditions are right, so it pays to remember where and when you find them. Distinguishing characteristics of the three main genera are:

**CANTHARELLUS**   The test is to look at the gill surface. You won't find true gills, sharp-edged and bladelike. Instead, there will be blunt-edged ridges or veins extending down the stem, frequently forked and interconnected by smaller veins, forming an intricate network. The cap is rounded when young, then becoming depressed in the center, often funnel-shaped with wavy, irregular edges.

**CRATERELLUS**   The gills are reduced to mere wrinkles or may be entirely absent. Usually trumpet-shaped with ruffled cap edges.

**GOMPHUS**   The gills are wrinkles or irregular ridges. More vase-shaped with straighter sides, less flaring top than the above two. Although very delicious, should be tried with caution since some people are sensitive to them; observe precautions, page 7.

EDIBILITY: Chanterelles are excellent in sauces (especially flavored with Madeira), with eggs, on toast, *à la crème*, in rice pilaf, with beef, chicken, veal, chicken livers, in stuffings, or pickled. All are rather tough and most people prefer them cooked slowly for a long time. A minority faction recommends sautéing them in butter at high heat for about 10 minutes so the liquid evaporates and the mushroom doesn't stew to toughness in its own juices (pour off excess juice and use as a flavorful liquid elsewhere). Sautéing them with chopped onion, shallots, garlic, parsley is especially tasty. After this quick sauté, they can be eaten as is, or added to soup, sauce, or other dishes and simmered for a few more minutes.
· Or eat chopped raw in salad. Sensational added to a hot, wilted lettuce salad, along with bacon bits and chopped pimiento.
· For slow baking, halve or quarter, discarding stems, and bake for 2 hours with seasoned butter and chopped shallots or onions. Serve with chopped parsley.
· Or parboil in stock seasoned with lemon juice for 10 minutes, then braise, covered, in the stock spiked with Madeira or sherry and seasoned with sautéed shallots or onions, in a slow oven for 1½ hours, turning occasionally.
· Bake in layers with oysters, chopped green onions, bread crumbs, parsley, seasoning each layer with salt, pepper, nutmeg.
· Cut in half or slice, discarding stem; place with a little butter in covered saucepan or double boiler and sweat them over a low fire.
· Dip caps in egg and bread crumbs seasoned with salt and pepper; fry in hot butter or oil.
· *Cantharellus infundibuliformis* and relatives are good sautéed slowly in butter, seasoned with salt, pepper, lemon juice, grated nutmeg, then served on crackers, toast, or as a topping for quiche.
· Sauté *Craterellus cornucopioides* slowly until tender and eat as is or use its black slices as a substitute for truffles in pâté, pilaf, egg dishes, chicken, sauces, pasta.
· *Cantharelli* do not dry well. Better to sauté or parboil, then freeze.

# CHANTERELLES

GENUS CHARACTERISTICS

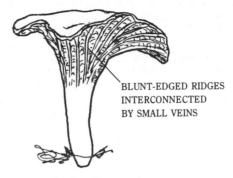

BLUNT-EDGED RIDGES
INTERCONNECTED
BY SMALL VEINS

*Cantharellus*

WRINKLED TO SMOOTH

*Craterellus*

WRINKLES OR
IRREGULAR RIDGES

*Gomphus*

*Cantharellus cinnabarinus;* red Chanterelle: Pink spores. Edible. 1–2 in. high. Its small size and cinnabar-red color distinguish it from other Chanterelles.
CAP: Vermilion red. Slightly rounded to flat to depressed in center, with irregular, wavy edge. Dry. Flesh white, very thin.
"GILLS": Pink or reddish color of cap. Blunt-edged ridges, instead of gills, with veins running in between. Rather far apart. Extend down stem.
STEM: Color of cap. Tapers toward base.
WHERE & WHEN: Under hardwoods and conifers, open woods, summer and early fall across country, particularly in Southeast and Great Lakes. Usually in large numbers, crowded together.
LOOK-ALIKES: Similar to *C. cibarius* but smaller, redder, with flatter cap, wavier edge, and blunter "gills" with more veins between them.

*Cantharellus cibarius;* French *girolle*, German *Pfifferling*, the famous Chanterelle of ancient Rome, our yellow or golden Chanterelle: Pale-yellow spores. One of the world's choicest mushrooms. Recognized by its yellow-orange color and lovely fragrance of apricots. 2–3 in. high.
CAP: Golden to orange yellow over entire mushroom. Rounded in youth, becoming depressed in the center with cap edge curling under, finally funnel-shaped with ruffled cap edge. Hairy at first, hairless in age. Flesh has the color and tough consistency of dried apricots.
"GILLS": Color of cap or paler. Narrow, blunt ridges instead of true gills. Extend down stem, well separated, repeatedly forked, with smaller veins in between.
STEM: Color of cap or near it. Dry, solid, hairless. Tapering toward base, often curved and lateral to the ground.
WHERE & WHEN: Scattered or in clusters throughout forested regions of North America—under hardwoods, conifers, and mixed woods—even at very high elevations, summer and fall.
*var. pallidifolius:* Similar but with whitish gills, pinkish spore print. Edible and good.
LOOK-ALIKES: It is traditional to warn that *Omphalotus olearius,* which can cause stomach upset, might be mistaken for *C. cibarius.* However, *O. olearius* has true gills, unbranched, while *C. cibarius* has ridges that are repeatedly forked. Anyone making the mistake simply isn't paying attention.

*Cantharellus subalbidus:* White spores. Found in the Pacific Northwest in the same places as *C. cibarius,* which it resembles except *C. subalbidus* is white. Very fleshy, delicious mushroom; one of the choicest edibles in the region. Short, stocky, 2–4 in. high and broad.
CAP: Dead white, staining orangy yellow when first bruised, then turning orange brown. Flat to depressed. Sometimes slightly scaly.
"GILLS": White, soon discoloring brown. Veinlike, close together, often forked, extend down stem.
STEM: White, staining like cap. Short, stocky, thick, often fused with other stems.
WHERE & WHEN: In groups or in immense clusters in mixed conifers, late summer and fall in the Pacific Northwest.

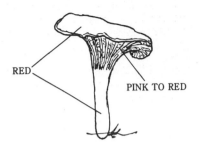

RED

PINK TO RED

*Cantharellus cinnabarinus*

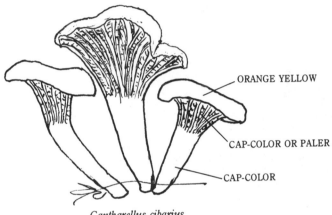

ORANGE YELLOW

CAP-COLOR OR PALER

CAP-COLOR

*Cantharellus cibarius*

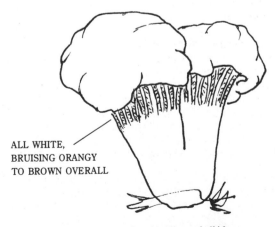

ALL WHITE,
BRUISING ORANGY
TO BROWN OVERALL

*Cantharellus subalbidus*

*Cantharellus umbonatus* (*Cantharellula umbonata, Geopetalum carbonarium*): White spores. Edible. ¾–3 in. high, 1 in. broad.
CAP: Brownish gray with olive tinge. Rounded in youth with small knob at cap center, and cap edges rolled under. Later becoming depressed with upturned edge. Flesh thin, white, changing to red when bruised.
"GILLS": White, tinged with gray. Veinlike gills more prominent than in other Chanterelles, forked, extend down stem.
STEM: Paler than cap, staining reddish brown over base, moist to the touch, thickening at base; extends deep into moss in which it grows, so firmly attached that it is impossible to pick without getting a clump of moss too.
WHERE & WHEN: Singly, in moss in summer and fall.

*Cantharellus minor;* small Chanterelle: White spores. Edible, excellent flavor makes it worth picking despite its small size. Only ½–1 in. high.
CAP: Yellow. Rounded to flat to depressed at center or with pit at center. Often with wavy cap edge. Flesh whitish to pale yellow.
"GILLS": Yellow. Far apart, seldom forked, extend down stem.
STEM: Yellow, sometimes with whitish down at base. Thin, smooth, solid when young, becoming hollow.
WHERE & WHEN: In groups or clusters, sometimes in large numbers, in thin woods, summer.

*Cantharellus tubaeformis:* White spores. Edible. ¾–2½ in. high.
CAP: Yellowish brown with small, dark-brown scales. Rounded at first, soon becoming depressed with incurved, wavy cap edge; finally goblet- or trumpet-shaped. Hole in center extends through stem to base. Flesh thin, dingy yellow.
"GILLS": Gray to lilac, veinlike, irregularly branched, well separated, extend down stem.
STEM: Slightly grayish below cap, brightening to yellow or orange near base. Hollow, smooth to furrowed, somewhat flattened. Moist to the touch.
WHERE & WHEN: Scattered or in clusters in coniferous woods on wet soil or in moist or well-decayed wood, summer and fall.

*Cantharellus infundibuliformis:* Pale-yellow spores. Edible. ¾–3 in. high.
CAP: Dark brown. Flat with a small center knob, then becoming depressed to funnel-shaped. Hole in center of cap opens into stem. Cap edge is wavy. Flesh thin.
"GILLS": Color of cap to yellowish. Ridged veins, forked and connected by cross veins, extend down stem.
STEM: Ocher in upper half, yellow below. Slightly flattened, grooved. Hollow, long and slender.
WHERE & WHEN: In groups in boggy soil, around decayed wood in coniferous woods, in fall.

*C. lutescens:* Midway between *C. infundibuliformis* and *C. tubaeformis,* with more regular, pale-orange to yellow cap, gills, stem. Edible.

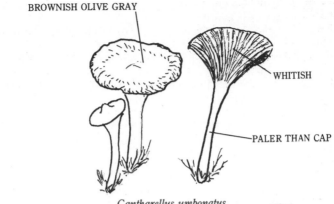

BROWNISH OLIVE GRAY

WHITISH

PALER THAN CAP

*Cantharellus umbonatus*

YELLOW OVERALL

*Cantharellus minor*

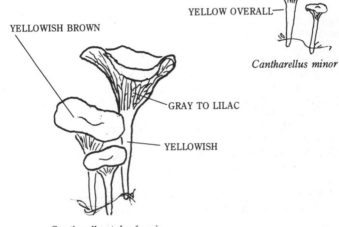

YELLOWISH BROWN

GRAY TO LILAC

YELLOWISH

*Cantharellus tubaeformis*

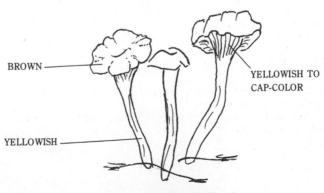

BROWN

YELLOWISH TO CAP-COLOR

YELLOWISH

*Cantharellus infundibuliformis*

*Craterellus cornucopioides;* trumpet of death, horn of plenty: Whitish spores with pale-salmon tint. Edible, despite its funereal common name, which applies only to its trumpetlike shape and dark color.
CAP: Ashy gray or brown to blackish on outside of trumpet-shaped cap; paler grayish with dry stiff hairs and small scales on inner portion. Split and wavy cap edge. Hollow at center.
"GILLS": Ashy gray to blackish, becoming whitish gray as spores ripen. "Gill" area is smooth to slightly wrinkled.
STEM: Very short, dingy brown. Hollow from fluted top of plant through stem to its base.
WHERE & WHEN: In clusters under hardwoods, old roads, trails, in exposed humus and moss beds, in summer and fall, primarily in eastern North America and along Pacific Coast.

*Craterellus cantharellus* (*Cantharellus odoratus*): Light-salmon spores. Edible and choice. 1–3 in. high.
CAP: Yellow to pinkish yellow. Rounded, often becoming depressed to funnel-shaped. Edges inrolled at first, later irregular and ruffled. Flesh firm, white.
"GILLS": Yellow, turning to salmon or orange. "Gill" surface is smooth to slightly wrinkled.
STEM: Cream yellow or "gill" color. Often hollow, tapering toward base.
WHERE & WHEN: Clustered under hardwoods in wet summer weather across country, most frequently in Southeast and South.
LOOK-ALIKES: Resembles *Cantharellus cibarius* and has same fruity odor, but is more pinkish, with thinner flesh and smooth to wrinkled gill surface (*C. cibarius* has blunt veins).

**POLYOZELLUS**   This beautiful purple Chanterelle has a genus all its own because of microscopic spore distinctions.

*Polyozellus multiplex* (*Cantharellus multiplex*): White spores. Edible and good.
CAP: Deep purple to violet black or blue black, sometimes a frosted blue to deep blue. Vase-shaped with ruffled edges, many caps growing together. Flesh soft and thick, same color as cap.
"GILLS": Pale violet. Veinlike, very close together.
STEM: Violet black. Usually fused with others in the cluster.
WHERE & WHEN: In large clusters under conifers, often in burned-over areas, in fall or other wet seasons in northern U.S. and Canada.

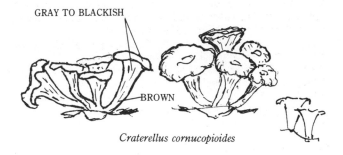

*Craterellus cornucopioides*

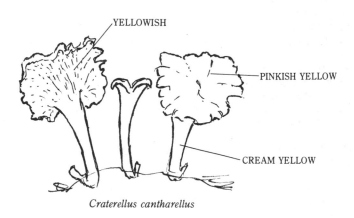

*Craterellus cantharellus*

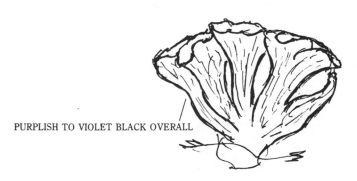

*Polyozellus multiplex*

***Gomphus clavatus*** (*Cantharellus clavatus*); pig's ears: Yellowish-orange spores. Edible, delicious. 1–4 in. broad, 3+ in. tall.

CAP: Light purplish to faded purplish brown, somewhat olive in old age. Club-shaped when young, then becoming flat to depressed at center; one side of cap generally grows larger than the other. Cap edges wavy, sometimes deeply lobed. Flesh whitish or dingy.

"GILLS": Tan or brownish, shaded purple. Not true gills but more like blunt-edged, thick veins, interconnected by smaller veins.

STEM: Color of "gill" area, but purple at base. Very short, compound, with several caps coming from one stem.

WHERE & WHEN: Usually large clusters in mossy areas under conifers, hardwoods; late summer, fall, across country, particularly abundant in mountains of western states.

***Gomphus floccosus*** (*Cantharellus floccosus*); scaly or shaggy or woolly Chanterelle: Ocher spores. Delicious but some people are sensitive to it. Follow precautions, page 7. 5–10 in. high, up to 6 in. broad.

CAP: Yellowish to dull orange, aging lighter. Vase-shaped with fairly straight sides, tapering toward bottom, with orange-red woolly scales inside that are flat in youth, becoming erect and curving inward. Flesh white, fibrous.

"GILLS": Buff to yellowish cream. Low blunt ridges, extending down stem almost to base, becoming irregular veins toward stem base.

STEM: Buff to color of gill surface; not distinct from cap; hollow, short, and rooted deeply in soil.

WHERE & WHEN: Solitary or in large groups, under conifers, deciduous and mixed woods, mossy hillsides, late summer and fall, in western and northern states.

***Gomphus bonarii*** (*Cantharellus bonarii*): Ocher spores. Edible with caution since some people are sensitive to it; follow precautions, page 7. Small western species, 1–4 in. high.

CAP: Whitish to yellowish with orangy scales. Truncate when young, becoming vase-shaped in age.

"GILLS": White becoming dingy cream. Blunt, narrow veins.

STEM: White, with lemon-yellow base. Very firm and hard, often deeply rooted or buried in deep humus. Branches into a number of caps.

WHERE & WHEN: In close clusters, often with small aborted specimens, under conifers in western mountains, in spring–fall.

***Gomphus kauffmanii*** (*Cantharellus kauffmanii*): Ocher spores. Not recommended as an edible since many people are sensitive to it. Large western species, 4–10 in. high.

CAP: Clay to brownish. Vase-shaped, with top splitting into erect or curving scales with white flesh showing through. Very brittle.

"GILLS": Yellow when young, aging pinkish buff. Shallow, ridgelike veins extending down stem almost to base, becoming crisscrossed in netlike fashion.

STEM: Whitish, somewhat narrowed at base. Solid, becoming hollow. Often deeply rooted.

WHERE & WHEN: Singly or in scattered stands under conifers, in Pacific Northwest, in fall.

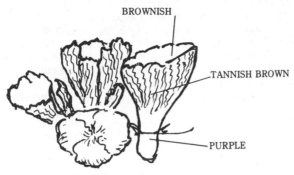

BROWNISH

TANNISH BROWN

PURPLE

*Gomphus clavatus*

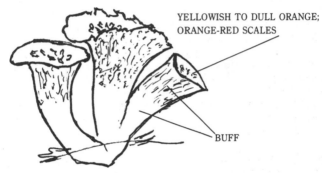

YELLOWISH TO DULL ORANGE;
ORANGE-RED SCALES

BUFF

*Gomphus floccosus*

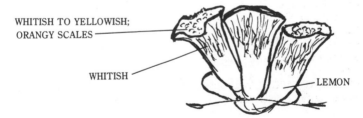

WHITISH TO YELLOWISH;
ORANGY SCALES

WHITISH

LEMON

*Gomphus bonarii*

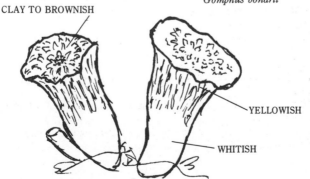

CLAY TO BROWNISH

YELLOWISH

WHITISH

*Gomphus kauffmanii*

# BOLETES

Look like gilled mushrooms with soft, fleshy cap and stem, but instead of gills have a spongelike layer with many tiny holes, called *pores*—the mouths of minute tubes where the spores are produced. Formerly, most Boletes were classified as *Boletus,* but are now divided into a number of genera as described on the following pages. You identify them by noting (1) spore color, (2) whether the cap is slimy, (3) what kind of markings are on the stem, (4) whether the flesh changes color when bruised or cut, and (5) how the tubes are arranged—randomly or in vague rows radiating from stem to cap edge.

EDIBILITY: Boletes are one of the largest and safest edible groups. A few are bitter, many are bland, but a goodly number are excellent. Until recently the rule was not to eat any species that turned blue when bruised or had red pores. Now, according to Harry D. Thiers, the American Bolete expert, most are safe and the main precaution is never to eat the red-pored ones raw and to avoid a few species such as *B. pulcherrimus, B. miniato-olivaceus,* and ones similar. Cook only fresh, young, unwormy specimens. Inspect for larvae tunnels, by cutting in half lengthwise, and discard infested areas. If cap is slimy, peel off top layer. Tube section should be removed in older specimens since it becomes slimy when cooked. Stems unless crisp and tender should also be discarded. If a specimen tastes bitter, throw it out; it will ruin any dish. Boletes are excellent in any mushroom recipe—grill or broil, bake, stuff, use in soups, sauces, stuffings, stews. Blanch and pickle, serve as cold hors d'oeuvres. Marinate in lemon-oil dressing, add to salad.

· Slice caps and cook in olive oil for 5 minutes; salt, pepper, turn, and cook 5 minutes more. Stir in chopped stems and cook another 5 minutes. Sprinkle minced shallots and parsley over top. Cook only long enough to heat through. Serve sprinkled with lemon juice.

· Slice, dip in egg beaten with milk, roll in crumbs. Sauté in butter in which you've browned half a garlic clove. Or shake in seasoned flour, sauté.

· Sauté caps, place on buttered toast, top with slice of Cheddar, broil till cheese is melted and browned.

· Sauté caps in oil, place in single layer in baking dish, cover with Cheddar cheese sauce, and brown in oven.

· Slice, sauté, serve with fish, chicken, steak.

· Spoon olive oil into each cap, grill or broil, gill side up, 15 minutes. Add butter to each cap, bake at 400° for 5 minutes. Add chopped parsley.

· Arrange caps in buttered baking dish, sprinkle with salt, pepper, chopped chives, parsley, cracker crumbs. Dot with butter. Bake 30 minutes at 375°.

· Thinly slice potatoes and Boletes. Alternate layers in baking dish, sprinkling each with onion, parsley, cheese. Pour on heavy cream, bit of water, scatter cheese, butter on top. Bake at 325° 1½ hours.

· Sauté chopped onion in butter. Add caps, cut up if large, and butter as necessary. Then (1) sauté, raising heat to evaporate juices as they accumulate. Pour in very thick cream, reduce quickly to thick coating sauce. Add thin cream to make sauce of correct consistency; or (2) don't sauté, but simmer covered in milk or cream for 10 minutes; or (3) substitute sour cream for fresh cream, stir in at serving time, serve with chopped parsley, fennel.

# BOLETES

GENUS CHARACTERISTICS

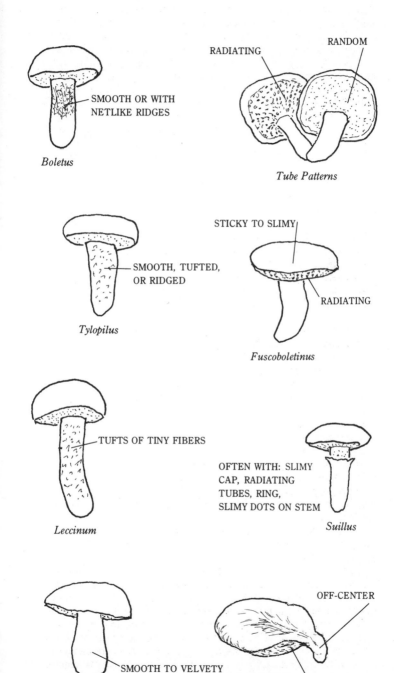

Boletus — SMOOTH OR WITH NETLIKE RIDGES

Tube Patterns — RADIATING, RANDOM

Tylopilus — SMOOTH, TUFTED, OR RIDGED

Fuscoboletinus — STICKY TO SLIMY, RADIATING

Leccinum — TUFTS OF TINY FIBERS

Suillus — OFTEN WITH: SLIMY CAP, RADIATING TUBES, RING, SLIMY DOTS ON STEM

Gyroporus — SMOOTH TO VELVETY

Boletinellus — OFF-CENTER, RADIATING

**BOLETUS**  Distinguished from other Bolete genera by its (1) moist to dry (not slimy) cap, (2) stem that is smooth or covered with a fine network of lines, especially at top, (3) small, round pores, white to yellow, not arranged in any pattern, (4) tube section easily peeled from cap, (5) spores that are yellow brown to olive brown.

*Boletus edulis;* king *Boletus*, French *cèpe*, German *Steinpilz*: Olive-brown spores. Edible, choice. Shape and color vary greatly.
CAP: 3–10 (12) in. broad. Creamy brown to reddish brown, or off-white if in shade. Broadly rounded, aging almost flat. Dry, but slightly sticky in wet weather. Hairless. Smooth. Flesh white, sometimes reddish just under cap surface; not changing color when bruised; thick, firm.
TUBES: White, aging yellow, finally yellowish green. Small. Depressed at junction with stem.
STEM: 4–8 in. tall. Whitish to dingy ivory to yellowish brown. With fine network of lines, usually at top but sometimes overall. Bulbous or sometimes enlarged just at base. Western species generally have bulbous stem; eastern species usually have straight or club-shaped stem.
WHERE & WHEN: Alone to scattered under conifers or hardwoods or mixed conifer-hardwood forests; summer, fall. *madrona*
*B. aereus:* Similar but smaller with dark-brown cap, under oak in California. Edible, choice.  *madrona*
*B. variipes:* Similar but more grayish brown, hairy to scaly cap; tubes not depressed at stem; in poor soil under hardwoods, especially oak, eastern half of U.S.; edible, choice.
*Tylopilus felleus:* Similar but with pink spores. Easily separable because very bitter tasting. Will ruin any dish.

*Boletus mirabilis:* Olive-brown spores. Edible, choice.
CAP: 2–5 in. broad. Maroon brown. Rounded, aging flat. Densely woolly. Slippery when wet. Flesh pale purplish, unchanging or sometimes reddish when bruised, firm.
TUBES: Yellow, aging darker. Irregular pores. Depressed around stem.
STEM: 3–5 in. tall. Cap-color, sometimes whitish at base. Often pitted and rough. Usually club-shaped to bulbous.
WHERE & WHEN: Scattered on or beside conifer logs, stumps; summer, fall. One of the few Boletes growing on wood.

*Boletus zelleri* (*Xerocomus zelleri*): Olive-brown spores. Edible.
CAP: 2–6 in. broad. Dark reddish brown to nearly black. Powdery at first, aging velvety. Rounded, aging flat. Dry. Flesh yellowish, unchanging when bruised or very slow change to blue.
TUBES: Yellow, aging greenish yellow. Slowly stain slightly blue. Large pores. Depressed around stem.
STEM: 2–4 in. tall. Yellowish with reddish overlay. Often yellow just at base. Dry. Hairless.
WHERE & WHEN: Scattered under or on western conifers; summer, fall.
*B. badius* (*Xerocomus badius*): Similar but smaller with red-brown to yellow-brown velvety cap, slimy in wet weather. Whitish flesh. Greenish-yellow tubes, bruising slightly blue. Stem color of cap. Growing under or on eastern conifers. Edible.

# BOLETUS

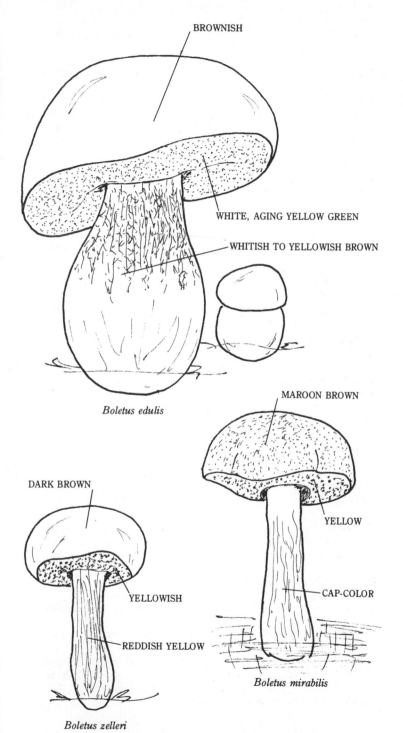

BROWNISH

WHITE, AGING YELLOW GREEN

WHITISH TO YELLOWISH BROWN

*Boletus edulis*

MAROON BROWN

YELLOW

CAP-COLOR

*Boletus mirabilis*

DARK BROWN

YELLOWISH

REDDISH YELLOW

*Boletus zelleri*

***Boletus bicolor:*** Olive spores. Edible, good.

CAP: 2–6 (11) in. broad. Reddish, fading to mottled yellow. Rounded, aging flat. Dry, sometimes sticky in wet weather. Hairless, becoming finely woolly, often cracking. Flesh yellow, staining blue when bruised, but fading back to yellow.

TUBES: Bright yellow, aging olive, bruising blue. Depressed around stem.

STEM: 2–6 in. tall. Yellow at top, deep red elsewhere, slowly bruising blue. Hairless. May have network of lines at top.

WHERE & WHEN: Scattered under hardwoods, especially oak; summer, fall, eastern half of U.S.

***B. miniato-olivaceus:*** Similar but with more yellow in cap, aging olive, spongy. Chrome-yellow tubes. Stem yellow above and orange to reddish brown below, faintly scurfy in youth, becoming smooth. Flesh yellow with much faster change to blue when bruised. Suspected. Best to avoid this and all similar species.

***Boletus luridus:*** Olive-brown spores. Labeled poisonous, although eaten by some. Never eat raw.

CAP: 2–5 (8) in. broad. Multicolored mixture of olive, yellow, red, brown, slowly turning greenish blue when bruised. Minutely hairy, matted or with minute scales. Rounded. Dry to slightly slimy in wet weather. Flesh whitish to yellowish, bruising blue (reddish in old bruises).

TUBES: Yellow to greenish yellow with reddish pores, bruising greenish blue. Small, compact pores. Depressed around stem, almost not touching it.

STEM: 2–4 (6) in. tall. Yellow, sometimes red in lower portion. Smooth or with reddish network of lines. Changing quickly to blue when touched.

WHERE & WHEN: Scattered under mixed hardwoods; summer, fall, eastern half of U.S.

***Boletus satanus:*** Olive-brown spores. Poisonous raw. Avoidance recommended. No red-pored *Boletus* should be eaten raw.

CAP: 4–8 in. broad. Buff to olive buff, sometimes pinkish around edge. Massive, rounded. Dry. Smooth. Flesh pale olive, instantly bruising blue when young.

TUBES: Deep-red pores with greenish-yellow flesh, bruising blue. Small pores. Attached to stem or shallowly depressed.

STEM: 2–3½ in. tall. Cap-color with pinkish to wine-red netlike ridges at top or overall, changing quickly to blue when touched. Dry. Bulbous.

WHERE & WHEN: Alone to scattered under oak; fall, winter, West Coast, South.

***B. pulcherrimus*** (*B. eastwoodiae*): Similar but with much less prominent bulbous base, yellow orange; cap brown to dark red brown, minutely woolly; scarlet tubes. Poisonous, suspected of containing muscarine.

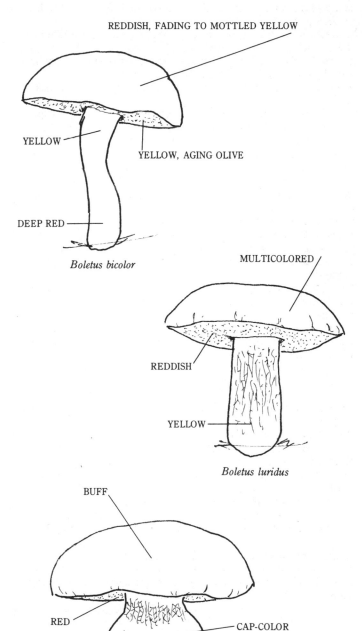

REDDISH, FADING TO MOTTLED YELLOW

YELLOW

YELLOW, AGING OLIVE

DEEP RED

*Boletus bicolor*

MULTICOLORED

REDDISH

YELLOW

*Boletus luridus*

BUFF

RED

CAP-COLOR

*Boletus satanus*

**SUILLUS** Have one or more of the following characteristics: (1) pores arranged in vague rows radiating from stem to cap edge, as in *Fuscoboletinus*, (2) slimy cap, (3) moist to slimy dots on the stem, (4) veil and ring (usually with dry cap and stem). Caps are usually yellow or reddish brown; tubes are white, aging yellow. Spores are olive brown to brown (not red brown, as in *Fuscoboletinus*). Most are associated with conifers. There are no poisonous U.S. species; several are excellent edibles.

***Suillus cavipes*** (*Boletinus cavipes*): Dark olive-brown spores. Edible, choice.
CAP: 1–4 in. broad. Rust brown to yellow brown, covered with dense, suedelike hairs with pallid tips. Round, aging flat with a low knob. Dry. Flesh white to yellow, unchanging when bruised; soft.
TUBES: Yellow, aging greenish yellow. Large, irregular. Extend down stem. Radiating in rows to cap edge.
VEIL: White to light orange red, fibrous, soon disappearing.
STEM: 1–3½ in. tall. Cap-color or paler, sometimes with netlike ridges above a thin, hairy ring. Flesh brownish when cut lengthwise. Dry. Narrowing toward base. Lower half is hollow.
WHERE & WHEN: Numerous under larch; summer, fall.
***S. pictus*** (*Boletinus pictus*): Similar but smaller, covered with wine-red hairs over yellow flesh; yellow tubes bruising reddish brown; no cavity in stem; stem yellow above ring, whitish below with patches of red threads. Whitish ring with reddish fibrils on outer surface. Edible.

***Suillus luteus*** (*Boletus luteus*); slippery Jack: Dull-cinnamon spores. Edible, choice.
CAP: 1½–6½ in. broad. Yellow brown to chocolate, streaked and spotted. Egg-shaped, becoming broadly rounded in age. Hairless. Slimy when wet, drying shiny, forming a layer that can be peeled off easily. Flesh white to pale yellow, unchanging.
TUBES: White, aging yellow with brownish tint. Edges dotted with slimy drops that age dark brown. Arranged in loose rows radiating from stem to cap edge.
VEIL: White, sticky, membranous, sheathing stem up to ring, leaving flaring membranous, feltlike ring, purplish on the underside.
STEM: 1½–4 in. tall. Yellow with netlike ridges and pinkish sticky dots above a sticky, prominent ring that ages brown. Pale yellowish to nearly white with brownish streaks below ring.
WHERE & WHEN: Scattered to numerous under pine, spruce; late summer, fall, eastern U.S. and adjoining Canada.
***S. grevillei*** (*Boletus elegans*): Similar but varying from yellow with red coloration over center to chestnut red; without slimy dots on stem; cottony white to buff ring; under larch. Edible.
***S. borealis:*** Similar but brownish-yellow cap with reddish-brown hairs; slimy dots on stem; veil but no ring; near western white pine. Edible.
***S. subluteus:*** Similar but smaller, with reddish or brownish slimy dots above and below ring; narrow whitish or brownish ring on stem. Edible.

## SUILLUS

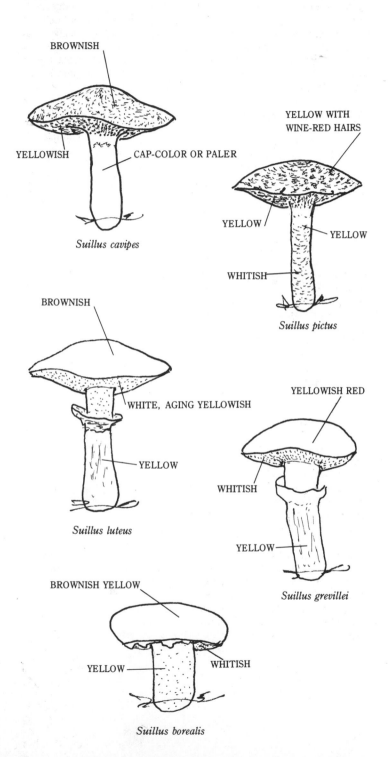

BROWNISH

YELLOWISH          CAP-COLOR OR PALER

*Suillus cavipes*

YELLOW WITH
WINE-RED HAIRS

YELLOW          YELLOW

WHITISH

*Suillus pictus*

BROWNISH

WHITE, AGING YELLOWISH

YELLOW

*Suillus luteus*

YELLOWISH RED

WHITISH

YELLOW

*Suillus grevillei*

BROWNISH YELLOW

YELLOW          WHITISH

*Suillus borealis*

*Suillus granulatus* (*Boletus granulatus*): Dingy cinnamon spores. Edible, good.

CAP: 2–6 in. broad. Buff, mottled cinnamon, aging darker, covered with a brownish slimy layer. Round, broadening in age. Flesh white to pale yellowish, unchanging.

TUBES: Creamy, aging yellowish then brownish, often spotted with red, slimy droplets. Small, irregular pores, almost extend down stem, arranged more or less in rows radiating to cap edge.

STEM: 1½–3 in. tall. Bright yellow at top; white to yellowish below. Dry. Covered with pinkish slimy dots, drying like granules of dark reddish-brown or blackish sugar.

WHERE & WHEN: Alone to many under pines, in cities as well as woods; summer, fall, northern and western U.S. and southern Canada.

*S. brevipes:* Similar but with darker cap; short, white stem, lacking slimy dots; growing under ponderosa and lodgepole pine. Edible.

*S. albidipes:* Similar but with white, cottony veil that leaves no ring on stem but clings to cap edge in a cottony roll. Lacks slimy dots on stem.

## FUSCOBOLETINUS

Like *Suillus* has pores arranged in loose rows radiating from stem to cap edge, but with pinkish to reddish-brown spores (never cinnamon to olive or olive brown). None is poisonous, although many are tasteless.

*Fuscoboletinus spectabilis:* Dark reddish-brown spores. Edible.

CAP: 1½–3 in. broad. At first coated with hairy scales of grayish veil remnants, then becoming red as scales disintegrate, revealing cap surface. Rounded. Sticky. Edge fringed with veil fragments. Flesh whitish to yellowish, bruising bright pinkish brown or yellow.

TUBES: Yellow, bruising pinkish, then finally yellow. Attached to stem or extending slightly down it. Arranged in vague rows radiating to cap edge.

VEIL: Gelatinous, leaving reddish to yellowish ring.

STEM: 1½–3 in. tall. Yellow above ring, covered with red fibers below.

WHERE & WHEN: Single to clustered under eastern larch in boggy areas; short fruiting season, late August–September.

*Fuscoboletinus aeruginascens* (*Suillus aeruginascens*): Reddish-brown spores. Edible, but mild; best used in combination with other ingredients.

CAP: 1–5 in. broad. Whitish to grayish to brownish in dry weather. Rounded, aging nearly flat. Sticky to slimy in wet weather. Flesh white, staining blue green when bruised.

TUBES: White, aging gray to brownish. Staining blue green. Small and round, elongating in age. In vague rows radiating to cap edge.

VEIL: White, membranous with cottony hairs, leaving flattened ring.

STEM: 1½–2½ in. tall. White above ring, grayish to olive to brownish below. Slimy. With netlike ridges.

WHERE & WHEN: Scattered to many under larch; spring–fall.

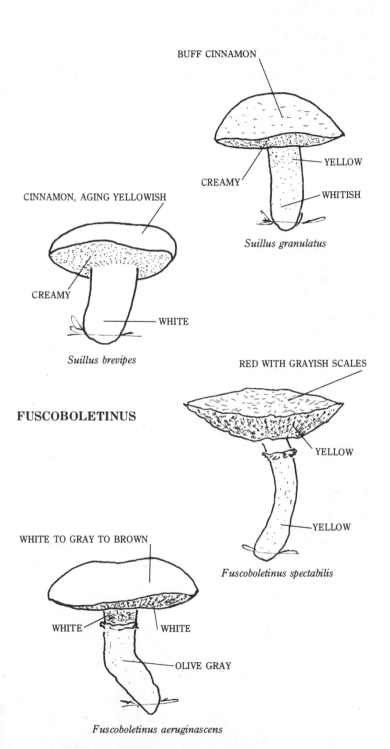

BUFF CINNAMON

YELLOW

CREAMY

WHITISH

*Suillus granulatus*

CINNAMON, AGING YELLOWISH

CREAMY

WHITE

*Suillus brevipes*

**FUSCOBOLETINUS**

RED WITH GRAYISH SCALES

YELLOW

YELLOW

*Fuscoboletinus spectabilis*

WHITE TO GRAY TO BROWN

WHITE

WHITE

OLIVE GRAY

*Fuscoboletinus aeruginascens*

**LECCINUM**   Identified by tufts of tiny fibers (scabers) dotting the dry stem. The pores, as in *Boletus,* are randomly arranged, not radiating in rows from stem to cap. Pores are whitish, aging yellow to yellow brown, never red. Cap is dry to slightly slimy when wet. The flesh often changes color when cut or bruised. Spores are yellow brown to olive brown. There are many closely related species, difficult to separate. All are edible. Some cooks prefer using them dried, believing the texture is better.

*Leccinum aurantiacum* (*Boletus aurantiacus*): Yellow-brown spores. Edible, nearly as good as *Boletus edulis.* Blackens in cooking but doesn't affect flavor. Stems good, too, when young and fresh.
CAP: 2–6 (8) in. broad. Reddish orange. Rounded, broadening in age. With flattened hairs or minutely woolly. Edge sometimes fringed with veil remnants. Dry to sticky in wet weather. Flesh white, bruising winy red, then darkening to dark bluish black; firm, thick.
TUBES: Pallid, bruising olive. Depressed at stem. Small.
STEM: 2–8 in. tall. Pallid with tufts of short whitish hairs or fibers that soon age reddish brown, finally blackish. Dry. Enlarging at base or expanding noticeably at center.
WHERE & WHEN: Scattered to many under aspen, birch, poplar, pine; summer, fall.
*L. scabrum* (*Boletus scaber*): Similar but smaller, more slender, with cap grayish brown to dirty yellow brown, often aging olive-tinted, with no veil remnants on edge. White flesh, not changing color. Under aspen, birch. Edible.
*L. testaceoscabrum:* Similar but with reddish-orange cap; flesh slowly and unevenly turning dingy pinkish lilac, usually bluish green at stem base; pallid pores aging grayish brown. Under birch, conifers. Edible.
*L. holopus:* Similar but with elongated stem; whitish to greenish-white cap; unchanging flesh; in northern conifer swamps and bogs. Edible.
*L. albellum:* Similar but with white cap. Edible.
*L. fibrillosum:* Similar but with dark liver-brown cap, with matted, black hairy scales; edge fringed with veil remnants; pallid flesh staining reddish, then dingy purplish; short, thick stem, swollen midway; under western conifers. Edible.

**TYLOPILUS**   Similar to *Boletus* and *Leccinum.* Sometimes has netlike ridges on stem, like *Boletus.* Sometimes has small hairy tufts on stem like *Leccinum.* Tubes when young are white to pallid, sometimes yellowish, randomly arranged. Spores are pallid to rusty brown, winy brown, or chocolate to purplish brown. Most species are very bitter tasting, thus inedible.

*Tylopilus chromapes* (*Leccinum chromapes*): Pinkish-brown spores. Edible.
CAP: 1½–4¾ in. broad. Pink to rose, aging tan. Rounded. Dry to sticky. Feltlike. Flesh white, except pink directly beneath cap.
TUBES: White, aging pink to pale brown. Small. Depressed around stem.
STEM: 2½–5½ in. tall. Pinkish except bright chrome yellow at base with yellowish threads (mycelium). Covered with small pinkish dots or tufts of short pinkish hairs. Often curved.
WHERE & WHEN: Scattered to numerous under hardwoods, conifers; summer, fall, eastern and central U.S.

# LECCINUM

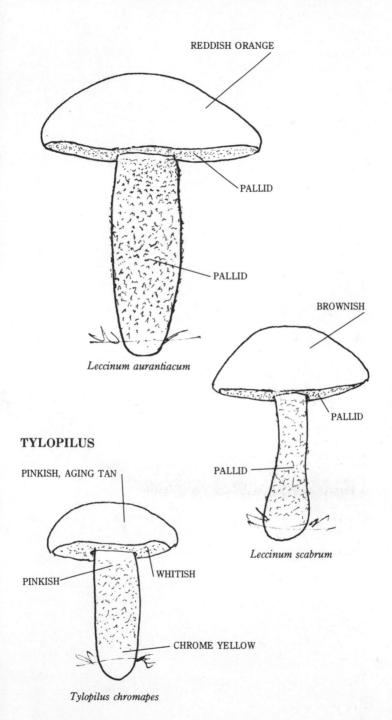

REDDISH ORANGE

PALLID

PALLID

*Leccinum aurantiacum*

BROWNISH

PALLID

PALLID

*Leccinum scabrum*

# TYLOPILUS

PINKISH, AGING TAN

PINKISH

WHITISH

CHROME YELLOW

*Tylopilus chromapes*

**GYROPORUS**   Distinguished from other Boletes by yellowish spores; dry cap; smooth to velvety stem, hollow, lacking black hairy tufts of *Leccinum*, the netlike ridges of *Boletus*, slimy dots of *Suillus*.

*Gyroporus cyanescens* (*Boletus cyanescens*): Yellow spores. Edible.
CAP: 2–4½ in. broad. Whitish to buff to yellowish, covered with brownish cottony scales or hairy patches. Round with edge incurved at first, aging broadly rounded to flat, often with wavy edge. Dry. Flesh white, instantly turning deep blue when cut, darkening to nearly black.
TUBES: White, aging yellow, instantly turning blue when bruised. Small, round pores. Depressed around stem.
STEM: 2–3 (10) in. tall. Cap-color, bruising deep blue. Somewhat hairy, like cap. Crooked. Irregularly swollen. Hollow in age.
WHERE & WHEN: Alone to scattered on gravel, sandy soil under hardwoods, conifers; spring, fall, eastern, central North America.

*Gyroporus castaneus* (*Boletus castaneus*): Yellow spores. Edible.
CAP: 1–3 in. broad. Rusty red to winy brown, or whitish at times. Rounded, aging nearly flat. Minutely velvety. Dry. Flesh white, bruising brown, not bluish.
TUBES: White, aging yellowish, bruising brownish. Not attached to stem.
STEM: 1–3 in. tall. Cap-color with a band of white just beneath tubes. Dry. Velvety. Enlarged toward base. Hollow.
WHERE & WHEN: Alone to many under hardwoods; summer, fall.

**STROBILOMYCES**   Blackish spores; coarse to fine scales on cap.

*Strobilomyces floccopus* (*S. strobilaceus*); old man of the woods, pine cone fungus: Blackish spores. Edible—some people rate it good, others say inedible. Best if you peel cap, cut tubes away with sharp knife, sauté what's left in butter, season with salt, pepper.
CAP: 1½– 6 in. broad. Whitish, covered with gray to blackish cottony scales. Rounded with veil remnants hanging from edge. Dry. Flesh white, bruising red then black.
TUBES: White, aging gray to blackish, staining like flesh. Large pores. Difficult to separate from cap.
VEIL: White to gray, soft, cottony.
STEM: 2–5½ in. tall. Cap-color. Shaggy and scaly like cap.
WHERE & WHEN: Alone to several in leaf clutter or on well-rotted wood under hardwoods-conifers; summer, eastern and central U.S.

**BOLETINELLUS**   Olive-brown spores; stem lateral, off-center.

*Boletinellus merulioides* (*Gyrodon merulioides, Boletinus meru-lioides*): Dull olive-brown spores. Edible, but needs special treatment. Remove tubes if slimy. Marinate in highly seasoned wine or lemon-oil dressing, dip in beaten egg, roll in bread crumbs, fry.
CAP: 2–4½ in. broad. Dull yellow brown to dark brown. Nearly flat to slightly depressed. Dry. Felty. Flesh yellow, usually unchanging but sometimes turning bluish green.
TUBES: Yellow, aging dingy, bruising dark olive to reddish brown. Extend down stem. Arranged in rows radiating to cap edge with ridges in between.
STEM: ½–1½ in. tall. Yellow, staining reddish over lower part in age. Growing from side, not center of cap.
WHERE & WHEN: Scattered under or near ash trees; summer, fall.

# GYROPORUS

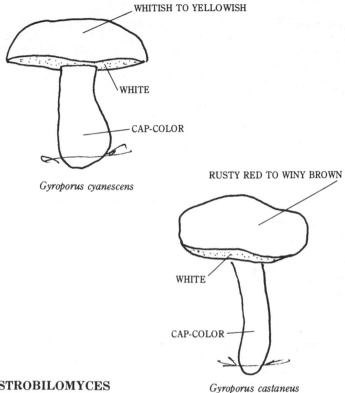

WHITISH TO YELLOWISH

WHITE

CAP-COLOR

*Gyroporus cyanescens*

RUSTY RED TO WINY BROWN

WHITE

CAP-COLOR

*Gyroporus castaneus*

# STROBILOMYCES

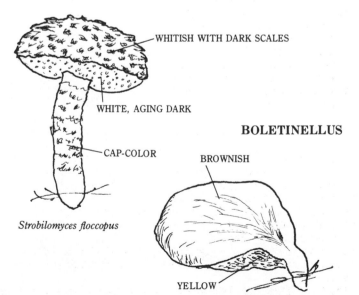

WHITISH WITH DARK SCALES

WHITE, AGING DARK

# BOLETINELLUS

CAP-COLOR

BROWNISH

*Strobilomyces floccopus*

YELLOW

*Boletinellus merulioides*

**POLYPORES** The tough, woody mushrooms you find growing on trees, usually year-round, often huge and conspicuous. The undersurface of the cap is covered with small holes (pores), instead of gills, giving the appearance of a sponge. Most have no stems, or if they do, it is short and usually sticks out laterally from the tree. This is a very large family that has been split into several genera, but most people still call all of them Polypores.

EDIBILITY: Most are too tough or woody to eat so are of little interest to the mushroom pothunter who shrugs them off: "Oh, that's just a Polypore." The four described here, however, are delicious and eagerly sought when young. Use only the fresh, young, tender portions, discarding any stem or cap sections that are tough. They all require long, slow cooking, covered.

· Slice thin and sauté slowly, serve as is, or creamed, or scramble with eggs.

· Slice thin, simmer in stock or water 30–60 minutes. Use immediately (or refrigerate with the liquid for later use) as a vegetable with lemon or wine sauce, in stews, creamed, with a cheese sauce, in a mushroom loaf or croquettes, or chill and slice into salad.

· For tougher specimens, cut into small uniform pieces. Parboil for a few minutes or soak for 30 minutes in tepid water. Discard water and simmer mushrooms covered, for 40 minutes, adding stock or water as necessary. Serve creamed, seasoned with salt, pepper, nutmeg, chopped parsley.

· Sauté small uniform pieces, or cut fine, in butter until most of the butter has been absorbed. Sprinkle with flour and add cream (about 1 tablespoon flour to 1 cup cream) and simmer until sauce thickens. Season and serve on hot toast.

· Serve sautéed or stewed (or use in a casserole) with beef, chicken, or fish; particularly good cooked with shrimp.

*Polyporus frondosus* (*Grifola frondosa, Polypilus frondosus*); hen of the woods (so called because it resembles a chicken ruffling its feathers): White spores. Edible and superb when cooked long and slow. If young, entire plant may be used; if old, use only caps. Composed of many small, overlapping caps, each on a slender stem, forming a large mass, up to 24 in. across, arising from one bulbous trunk.

CAP: Gray to gray brown, with circular bands of light and dark color, the individual caps 1–3 in. broad. Fan or spoon-shaped, wrinkled, lobed, with irregular, wavy cap edge. Dry, hairless to velvety. Flesh white, firm, brittle.

PORES: White, aging yellowish, small, rounded, often torn and gaping open. Extend down stem.

STEM: White, large, bulbous, compound with many smaller stems, each bearing a single cap.

WHERE & WHEN: Usually solitary, around but not on stumps and snags of oak or other hardwoods, rarely around conifers; in fall throughout U.S., but mostly in eastern half.

# POLYPORES

*Examples of Polypores too woody to eat*

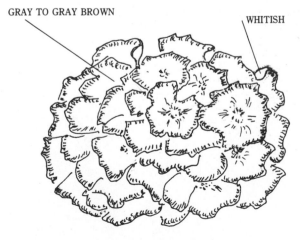

GRAY TO GRAY BROWN

WHITISH

*Polyporus frondosus*

***Polyporus umbellatus*** (*Grifola umbellata, Polypilus umbellatus*); sunshade Polypore: White spores. Edible and choice when young and tender. Similar to *P. frondosus,* but with smaller, rounder caps, only ½–1½ in. broad, forming a conspicuous cluster up to 12 in. high and wide.

CAP: Sooty to grayish brown, rounded, then depressed in center (almost funnel-shaped) with wavy, somewhat cracked edges. As many as 100 caps, overlapping each other in a huge tuft. Flesh white, tender, brittle.

PORES: White, very small, extend down stem.

STEM: White with pinkish to orchid tinge; irregular, compound, buried tuber with many branches arising from it.

WHERE & WHEN: On buried, decaying roots or around stumps or old trees from May to November throughout northern U.S. and southern Canada. Infrequent except in very rainy seasons.


***Polyporus sulphureus*** (*Laetiporus sulphureus, Grifola sulphurea*); sulphur shelf, chicken mushroom, chicken of the woods (so called because young caps have texture—not flavor—of chicken when cooked): White spores. Edible if you use only the tender edge of young caps; the rest is tough and tasteless. This flashy mushroom is like a neon sign in the woods with its bright sulphur-yellow and red coloration shining through the leaves. Consists of clusters of shelflike caps, overlapping one above the other on a tree trunk or along a log.

CAP: Cream-colored when very young, soon developing bands of brilliant tangerine, sulphur yellow, and cream. As the cap expands, the edge becomes thinner, lobed, and wavy. Flesh white to yellowing; soft on the edge, tough in the center. Fleshy and watery when young, punky with age.

PORES: Bright sulphur yellow to cream (no other species has this sulphurous color).

STEM: White to yellowish, very short or absent, merely an attachment for the spreading growth.

WHERE & WHEN: In large clumps, singly or many together on logs or stumps or decayed places in living hardwoods and conifers, starting in early summer but most common in late summer and fall. Widely distributed. Since it is a long-lasting plant, you can break off only what you need, taking only the tender cap edges, returning for other meals all through summer until winter.

*var. semialbinus:* Similar, but with rosy-orange cap with no yellow tones, and pale-yellow to white pore layer. Grows in large rosettes, 12–16 in. in diameter but only about 6 in. high, in layers with each shorter than the one underneath. Lobes are thinner than *P. sulphureus,* with sharper edges. Grows early spring at base of tree or on stumps, roots, throughout North America. Edible.

SOOTY TO GRAYISH BROWN

WHITE

*Polyporus umbellatus*

BANDS OF TANGERINE, YELLOW, CREAM

SULPHUR YELLOW
TO CREAM

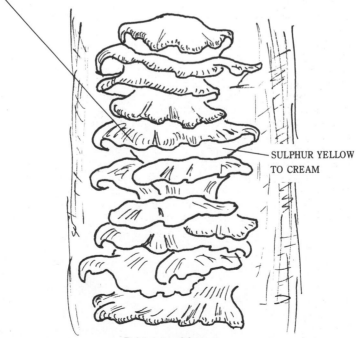

*Polyporus sulphureus*

*Polyporus ovinus* (*Albatrellus ovinus*); sheep *Polyporus*: White spores. Edible when young (parboiling advised). Usually grows in large clusters of small caps, 1½–5 in. broad.

CAP: White, becoming creamy or brownish, sometimes tinged pinkish or violet. Usually circular, but irregular if growing close together in large masses, sometimes with caps joined together. Rounded when young, then flat to depressed, uneven with wavy edge. Flesh whitish then yellowish, thick, firm, brittle.

PORES: White, yellowing in age; very small, extend down stem unevenly.

STEM: Color of cap with a few dark spots; 1–3 in. long, ½–1 in. thick; short, squat, tapered at base, sometimes curved.

WHERE & WHEN: Solitary or in large groups or tufts, on humus in coniferous woods, especially pines, in summer, in eastern North America, Great Lakes, and conifer belt of western mountains, widely distributed in Canada.

*var. violaceous:* A violet-brown to brownish-gray variant found in Idaho mountains. Edible.

**FISTULINA**   In this genus, the tubes are separate from each other, hanging down like individual pipes, instead of looking like holes in a sponge, as in Polypores and Boletes.

*Fistulina hepatica;* beefsteak fungus, ox-tongue fungus: Salmon-brown spores. Edible and good. Easily recognized as it sticks out from tree like a large red tongue, 4–8 in. long, 4–12 in. broad.

CAP: Bloodred to liver-colored. Fan-shaped like an ox tongue. Sticky on top when moist. Flesh somewhat mottled with white to reddish zones, oozing a reddish juice. 1½–2½ in. thick; soft, turning fibrous in age.

TUBES: Yellowish, staining reddish. Surface looks like a very fine sponge, with short, crowded tubes, separate from each other like pieces of individual tubing.

STEM: Same color as cap, 1½–3 in. long, ½–1 in. thick. Extends laterally from tree like handle of a fan. The mycelium stains the tree wood a deep, rich brown.

WHERE & WHEN: Grows from cracks on hardwood stumps or living trees, usually oak and chestnut, after rains in late summer and fall. Widely distributed.

EDIBILITY: Good raw or cooked. This is one mushroom that can be seasoned highly with onion, garlic, spices, herbs.

• To eat raw, cut in thin slices, rub with garlic, toss with lettuce or other greens and an oily dressing made with mustard and very little vinegar or lemon.

• Slice, sauté in hot butter, season with salt, pepper, and optional herbs. Or with soy sauce and ginger.

• Dice and cook slowly, covered, with a little water and plenty of butter, for 20 minutes. Season highly.

• This fungus has a slightly acid taste that some like, others don't. To get rid of it, discard tubes and outer layer of cap, marinate in seasoning and oil (no vinegar or lemon) for several hours. Drain well, reseason, and eat raw or prepare as above.

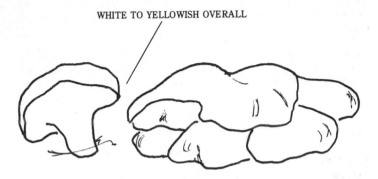

WHITE TO YELLOWISH OVERALL

*Polyporus ovinus*

# FISTULINA

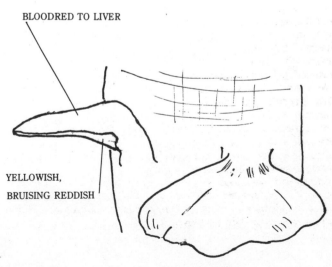

BLOODRED TO LIVER

YELLOWISH,
BRUISING REDDISH

*Fistulina hepatica*

# TEETH FUNGI

So called because they produce their spores on needlelike teeth or spines. Some consist of clusters of spines, hanging down like icicles. Others look like a regular mushroom with a cap and stem but the undersurface of the cap is covered with tiny needlelike teeth or "prickles" as the English call them. All were once classified as *Hydnum* but have since been divided into several genera. Most are too woody or bitter to eat, but the following genera include some choice species (use only fresh, tender parts; cook slowly, well):

**DENTINUM**   White spore sprint. Small, have cap and stem but instead of gills have thin needlelike teeth on the underside of the cap.
· *D. repandum* is considered one of the choicest edibles, ranking with *Boletus edulis* and the morels. It and *D. umbilicatum* (also good) can be used in almost any mushroom dish. Try this fricassee: Slice, sauté in butter, thicken with a bit of flour, moisten with stock (a splash of Madeira too), season sparingly with spices (mace and nutmeg or cayenne and mace) and much chopped parsley, then bind with cream and egg yolks.
· Or slice thin and sauté or stew very slowly until tender.

**HYDNUM**   Brown spore print. Medium size, have cap and stem but with teeth instead of gills. Larger than the above *Dentinum,* with coarser teeth and a scaly or cracked cap.
· Eat only fresh young specimens of *H. imbricatum.* Other species are bitter. Most cooks discard the teeth. Many prefer dried *Hydnum* to the fresh. May be prepared the same as Chanterelles, cooking slowly with plenty of liquid. If rather tough or bitter, cut into uniform pieces, parboil 5–6 minutes, discard water.
· After parboiling, place in casserole, stir in milk and cream, season, sprinkle with bread crumbs and/or small dabs of butter. Bake uncovered at 350° until tender, about 20 minutes; garnish with parsley.
· After parboiling, dice, dredge in flour, sauté in butter, season.
· After parboiling, dip in bread crumbs, sauté, serve with fried onions.
· Without parboiling, cut into small uniform pieces, stew covered in water or stock, 30–40 minutes, season with butter, pepper, salt.
· With or without parboiling, slice thin, sauté with one or several vegetables for 5 minutes, add a spoonful of stock, and simmer covered for a minute or two.
· Or just slice thin and sauté in butter for a crunchy treat.

**HERICIUM**   White spore deposit. Large, do not have the usual cap and stem, but consist of clusters of white spines, hanging down like icicles, attached to a tree or log by a fleshy tuber.
· All *Hericium* are edible and choice. Use only fresh white portions, discard yellowed parts, which are sour tasting. Most cooks parboil *Hericium* a few minutes in boiling salted water until almost tender, discarding the water.
· After parboiling, sauté in butter and serve as a vegetable.
· After parboiling, stew until tender and serve with a cheese sauce.
· After parboiling, marinate in a garlicky vinaigrette dressing with chopped parsley or other fresh herbs for several hours or overnight.

# TEETH FUNGI

GENUS CHARACTERISTICS

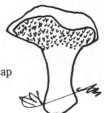

· Small size
· Tiny teeth under cap

*Dentinum*

· Medium size
· Scaly, cracked cap
· Teeth under cap

*Hydnum*

· Large size
· No cap or stem, but cluster of spines growing on wood

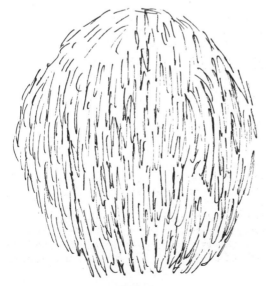

*Hericium*

***Dentinum repandum*** (*Hydnum repandum*); hedgehog mushroom, the French call it rubber brush or pig's trotter: White spores. Edible and choice. Up to 4 in. tall, cap ½–4 in. broad. Varies greatly in color and shape even in same environs.

CAP: Usually buff to faded orange, but a white variant is also common. Rounded in youth, then flat to depressed, often irregular and lopsided. Usually hairless and dry, but sometimes minutely velvety. Flesh white to light yellowish, slowly turning yellow when bruised, thick, soft.

TEETH: Whitish to cream-colored, turning cap-color. Flesh soft at first, then becoming brittle. Round to slightly flattened, ¼–½ in. long with various lengths intermixed, extend slightly down stem.

STEM: White, sometimes colored like cap or paler, ¼–2 in. thick. Sometimes enlarged at base. Often grows off to one side of cap. Dry, solid, smooth.

WHERE & WHEN: Single to numerous under hardwoods, conifers, mixed woods, in summer and fall; early winter in northern California and southern states.

*var. album:* All-white variety, best tasting of the *repandums.*
*var. rufescens:* Orange with white stem. Edible.

***Dentinum umbilicatum:*** White spores. Edible. Small, 1–3 in. tall, 1–2 in. broad.

CAP: Orangy to reddish buff, usually irregular and wavy with depression in cap center, often with dark-colored center and lighter border around cap edge.

TEETH: Buff-colored, up to ¼ in. long with various lengths intermixed.

STEM: Paler than cap, bruising darker. Slender, under ½ in. thick.

WHERE & WHEN: Many together in boggy, swampy areas under conifers, particularly spruce, cedar, in eastern and north-central U.S.; summer, fall.

***Hydnum imbricatum*** (*Sarcodon imbricatus*); shingle cap, scaly *Hydnum*: Brown spores. Edible. 2–5 in. tall and broad.

CAP: Dark brown, covered with coarse scales that are erect in cap center, overlapping like shingles on a roof. Edge is often cracked. Flesh dingy white to tannish, brittle.

TEETH: Ashy white to brownish, ¼–1 in. long, mostly of equal length, blunt. Extend unevenly down stem.

STEM: Light brown, ½–1¼ in. thick, enlarged at base, dry, smooth.

WHERE & WHEN: Single to several under hardwoods and conifers in summer and fall, widely distributed.

LOOK-ALIKES: *H. scabrosum* (*Sarcodon scabrosum*) is similar but with bitter taste; smaller, brownish yellow, scales not as coarse with more red coloration. Stem is short and ash-colored with bluish to black base. Spines are dingy rust color with whitish tips.

CAUTION: The other Teeth Fungi with cap and stem are too tough or bitter to eat.

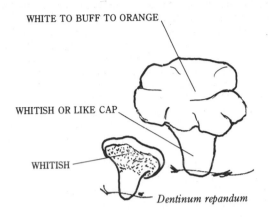

WHITE TO BUFF TO ORANGE

WHITISH OR LIKE CAP

WHITISH

*Dentinum repandum*

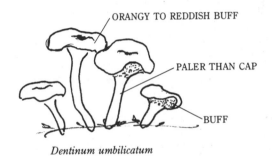

ORANGY TO REDDISH BUFF

PALER THAN CAP

BUFF

*Dentinum umbilicatum*

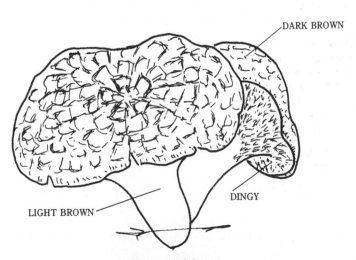

DARK BROWN

DINGY

LIGHT BROWN

*Hydnum imbricatum*

*Hericium coralloides* (*Hydnum coralloides*); coral *Hydnum*: White spores. Edible, 4–11 in. high, 6–18 in. across.

CHARACTERISTICS: Glistening white, aging dark cream. Composed of many interlacing branches, ½ in. wide at base, tapering to a point, with corallike clusters of delicate white teeth hanging down from the underside of the branch tips. Flesh white, fibrous. Attached to wood by thick, stout stalk.

WHERE & WHEN: On standing or fallen decaying timber (hardwood and conifer) in moist, shady locations, from August until frost. Widely distributed through Northeast, central states, Pacific Northwest.

*Hericium ramosum* (*Hydnum laciniatum*, *Hydnum caput-ursi*); bear's head: White spores. Edible.

CHARACTERISTICS: White, aging brownish. Irregular clusters of dainty milk-white teeth, growing in tiers, resembling a miniature frozen waterfall. Similar to *H. coralloides* but with teeth all along branches, not just underside of branch tips.

WHERE & WHEN: On fallen, decaying deciduous logs in the fall. Widely distributed.

*Hericium abietis* (*H. weirii*): White spores. Edible. Very large, up to 30 in. high, 16 in. wide.

CHARACTERISTICS: Salmon buff when young, aging paler. Starts as a fleshy tuber, gradually develops many short branches covered with short teeth.

WHERE & WHEN: On standing and fallen conifers, both living and dead, in Pacific Northwest in fall.

*Hericium erinaceus* (*Hydnum caput-medusae*, *Hydnum erinaceum*); Medusa's head, satyr's beard: White spores. Edible. 2–20 in. across.

CHARACTERISTICS: White, aging grayish or yellowish brown. Large, round fleshy mass of crowded slender spines, 1–3 in. long, hanging like icicles. No branches. Attached at top to the tree by fleshy unbranched tuber.

WHERE & WHEN: Grows from crotches or wounds of living hardwoods, especially oak, but also beech, locust, etc., late summer, fall in eastern and central U.S. and Pacific Coast; winter in Florida.

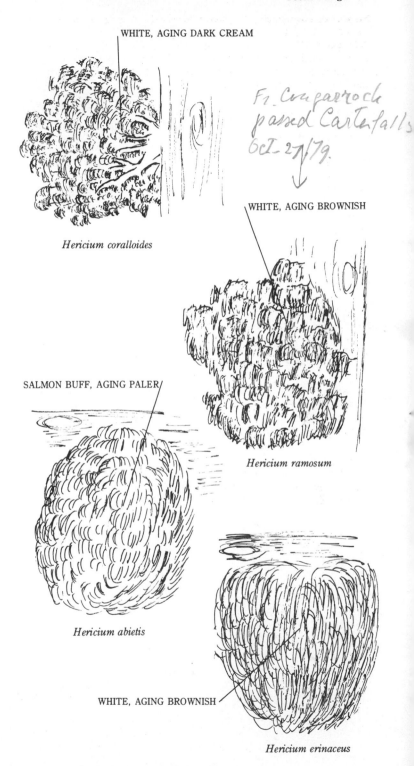

WHITE, AGING DARK CREAM

*Hericium coralloides*

WHITE, AGING BROWNISH

*Hericium ramosum*

SALMON BUFF, AGING PALER

*Hericium abietis*

WHITE, AGING BROWNISH

*Hericium erinaceus*

**MORCHELLA** True morel, French *morille:* Rank among the world's choicest mushrooms. Easily recognized by their cone-shaped caps that are pitted and ridged like a honeycomb. As they push through the earth, they give the appearance of pinecone-strewn ground. The cap and stem are hollow and fused together in one continuous piece. The stems are brittle, thin-walled, often wrinkled and furrowed, sometimes enlarged at the base. Morels are the spring mushrooms, starting in January in southern California, in March in the South and Southwest, then following the spring rains across the country. They grow in a wide variety of habitats and tend to reappear in the same places when growing conditions are right. When you find one morel, you're apt to find bushels. Morel spores are yellowish in color, borne on the pitted surface of the cap. Morels are so easy to recognize, however, that noting spore color is not necessary for identification.

EDIBILITY: Always cut a morel in half lengthwise to inspect for insects. Wash carefully to remove grit from the pits and stem, then dry thoroughly. The San Francisco Mycological Society recommends precooking them in butter with a few drops of lemon for 7 to 8 minutes to remove excess moisture before final preparation. Long, slow cooking is best. Morels are delicious sautéed, stewed, baked, stuffed, *à la crème,* with chicken, fish, or steak. Excellent frozen or dried. In fact, many cooks prefer them dried rather than fresh, rehydrating them in milk or cream.

CAUTION: Some unfortunate people are allergic to morels, so when tasting them for the first time, eat only a small portion (see page 7). Never eat morels raw.

LOOK-ALIKES: Always be on guard lest through carelessness you mistake a *Gyromitra* for a morel. Remember, morels have definite pits and ridges; *Gyromitra* are folded into convolutions like a brain—they bulge outward, while morels are pitted inward.

*Morchella esculenta* (*M. rotunda, M. vulgaris*); sponge morel, common morel, yellow morel: Edible, choice. Best known of the morels. 2–6 in. high, about half as wide as tall.

CAP: Grayish to brownish pits, fading with age. Ridges paler than pits. Does not blacken like *M. angusticeps.* Usually conical with rounded top, but sometimes oval or even round in shape. Pits are irregular and broader and rounder than in other morels.

STEM: Whitish or yellowish, lighter than cap, browning with age. Covered with a white, persistent, powdery coating. Almost smooth when young, faintly grooved or wrinkled when old.

WHERE & WHEN: Under deciduous trees; in old orchards, particularly apple, peach, cherry; near roots of dead or dying elms; grassy, swampy areas; at the edges of aspen and birch forests; in the ashes of burned-over woodlands or areas fertilized with ashes. Appears in spring after *M. angusticeps,* when oak leaves are size of "mouse ears" and apple trees are in blossom.

*Under cottonwoods*
*April - May*

# MORCHELLA

GENUS CHARACTERISTICS

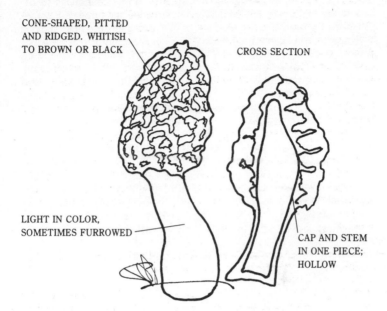

CONE-SHAPED, PITTED
AND RIDGED. WHITISH
TO BROWN OR BLACK

CROSS SECTION

LIGHT IN COLOR,
SOMETIMES FURROWED

CAP AND STEM
IN ONE PIECE;
HOLLOW

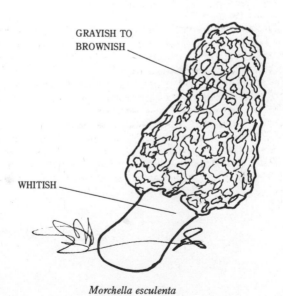

GRAYISH TO
BROWNISH

WHITISH

*Morchella esculenta*

*Morchella crassipes;* thick-footed morel, gigantic morel: Considered by some mycologists as a giant form of *M. esculenta,* which it closely resembles when young. Eagerly sought since it is not only the most delicious morel but the largest, reaching a height of 9 in. or even 1 ft.
CAP: Brownish, usually cone-shaped but sometimes misshapen. Large, shallow, roundish, irregular pits, up to ¾ in. long, yellowish at bottom of pit with thin, meandering ridges.
STEM: Whitish or yellowish, sometimes flesh-colored, stout, enlarged at base, often wrinkled and furrowed.
WHERE & WHEN: In rich garden soil, under oak, beech, maple, ash, dead or dying elms; edges of woods; open areas; in spring after the last of *M. esculenta.*

*Morchella deliciosa;* white morel: Typically small, only 1½–3 in. high, but very delicious, as its name indicates. Considered by some as a variant of *M. esculenta,* for which it is often mistaken.
CAP: Grayish to brownish pits, outlined by white to pallid ridges that do not darken. Pits are narrow and long. Cap is usually cylindrical, narrowed toward the top, with blunt apex. Often curved.
STEM: Whitish to yellowish, shorter or about same height as cap, up to two-thirds as thick as cap, often enlarged at base.
WHERE & WHEN: Moist grassy places, usually at edge of mixed woods, elm, red maple, ash, etc. One of the last morels to appear in the spring, after *M. angusticeps* and *M. esculenta.*

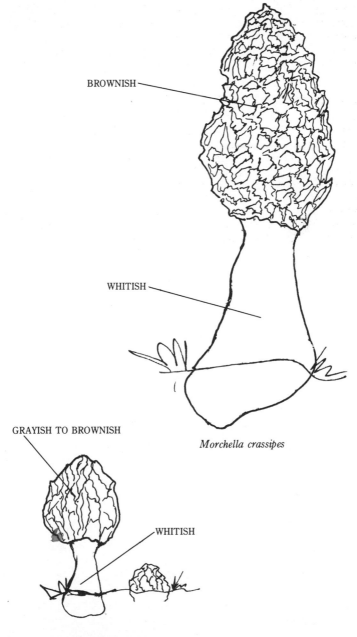

BROWNISH

WHITISH

*Morchella crassipes*

GRAYISH TO BROWNISH

WHITISH

*Morchella deliciosa*

***Morchella angusticeps*** (*M. elata*); black morel, narrow-headed or slender-capped morel: 2–4+ in. high. Edible with caution.

CAP: Grayish to grayish-tan pits, outlined by darker ridges that turn black before the mushroom matures. Narrow, cone-shaped, tapering upward to a rounded top. Pits are longer than they are wide; arranged one above the other in vertical rows, intersected by small connections.

STEM: Buff to grayish, flaky surface, nearly as wide as cap, often wrinkled or uneven at base. Sometimes curved.

WHERE & WHEN: Sandy and clay soils in thin mixed woods, borders of woods (oak, hickory, birch, maple, etc.) or conifer forests, in ashes of burned-over ground. In mid-spring, shortly after *Verpa bohemica* and usually before *M. esculenta,* when white violets are in bloom and bracken fern are still curled in fiddlehead stage.

CAUTION: Eat only young, perfect specimens. Discard any that have a completely blackened head and have begun to shrink.

*Large variant:* A large black variety grows to 7 in. tall, 3–4 in. broad; particularly in the Pacific Northwest but also found in the Great Lakes, Midwest, and East. Black even in youth with large conic cap rounded at top. Fruits shortly after *M. angusticeps*. Exercise caution in eating since some people are allergic to it. Eat only young, perfect specimens, never old or even slightly deteriorated ones.

***Morchella conica:*** 3–5 in. tall, regarded by some as a slender variant of *M. esculenta.* Edible.

CAP: Grayish to yellowish brown with lighter ridges, conical or oblong conical with wide irregular pits, arranged more or less one above the other.

STEM: Paler, longer, and more slender than cap, often curved. Somewhat scurfy on surface, occasionally slightly wrinkled at base.

WHERE & WHEN: Coniferous and light mixed woods, grassy clearings in mid-spring, particularly in South and Southwest. Abundant in coastal southern California in rainy January.

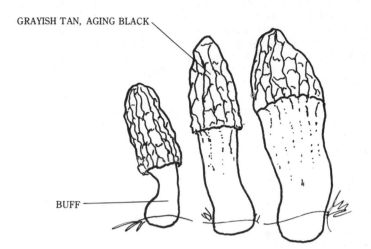

GRAYISH TAN, AGING BLACK

BUFF

*Morchella angusticeps*

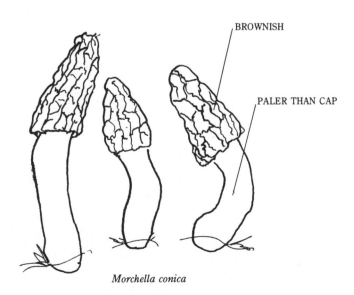

BROWNISH

PALER THAN CAP

*Morchella conica*

*Morchella semilibera* (*M. hybrida, Mitrophora semilibera*); the half-free morel: The least tasty of the morels but better than none at all. Differs from other morels in that the stem is attached for half the length of the cap. Thus it is midway between a morel, which has the cap continuous with the stem, and a *Verpa,* which has the cap attached only to the top of the stem. 2–4 in. high.
CAP: Light to dark brown with olive tinge. Bell-shaped. Pits longer than broad. Ridges in vertical rows, discoloring to blackish brown with age. Cap becomes smaller and more bell-shaped with age.
STEM: Off-white at first, aging slightly brownish yellow or pinkish. Long and thin, becoming enlarged at base. Slightly grooved at base, ribbed above, minutely mealy. At least twice cap height.
WHERE & WHEN: Damp, mixed woods on rich soil, under oak, beech, cottonwood, alder, in spring, usually after leaves are out. About 2 weeks after *V. bohemica,* about a week earlier than other morels.

**VERPA**   Differs from *Morchella* in that cap is attached only to top of stem.

*Verpa conica* (*V. digitaliformis*); false morel: Edible but only of fair quality. 2–5 in. high, smaller and smoother than *V. bohemica.*
CAP: Olive to umber brown, conic to bell-shaped, nearly smooth, attached to top of stem only, hangs around stem like a skirt, often upturned showing whitish underside.
STEM: Whitish with incomplete reddish-yellow circles, slightly scaly.
WHERE & WHEN: In deciduous woods, moist shady ravines; May–August.

*Verpa bohemica* (*Morchella bispora*); false morel, early morel, two-spored morel: Edible with caution. 3–8 in. tall.
CAP: Pale to dark yellow brown, white underneath. Thimble-shaped with vertical wrinkles. Cap is attached to top of stem only, hangs around it like a tiny skirt. Edge is often upturned and wavy.
STEM: Whitish to cream, finally pale tan. Long, hollow or loosely stuffed with cottony substance. Surface slightly granular. Fragile, easily separating from cap, often slightly curved. Base covered with cottony tufts, easily rubbed off.
WHERE & WHEN: Very early spring among fallen leaves in areas wet from spring drainage, in rich, wet woods before trees have leafed out.
CAUTION: Although most people eat it with no ill effects, a few suffer severe reactions. Never eat in large quantities or for several days in succession as toxic qualities accumulate until body can no longer tolerate them. Follow precautions, pages 7 and 208.

*Morchella* CAP AND
STEM CONTINUOUS

*M. Semilibera* CAP
"HALF-FREE" FROM STEM

*Verpa* CAP ATTACHED
TO TOP OF STEM ONLY

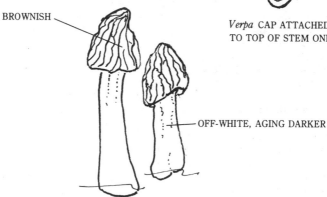

BROWNISH

OFF-WHITE, AGING DARKER

*Morchella semilibera*

**VERPA**

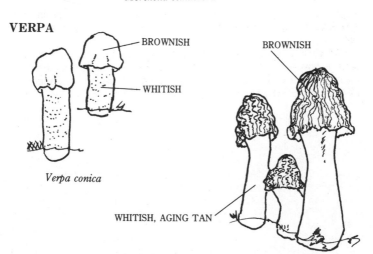

BROWNISH

WHITISH

*Verpa conica*

BROWNISH

WHITISH, AGING TAN

*Verpa bohemica*

**GYROMITRA AND HELVELLA**   False morels, German *Lorchels*: All were once grouped under *Helvella*, and mycologists still differ on how to classify them. Distinguishing characteristics between the two genera are technical and microscopic. The rule of thumb is that *Helvella* species are generally white, or pallid gray to black, while *Gyromitra* species are yellow or tan to brown. Also, a *Gyromitra* cap is generally composed of one single gnarled mass while a *Helvella* cap is folded into two segments or saddle-shaped lobes. In the few cases where a *Gyromitra* is saddle-shaped like a *Helvella*, it does not have a white stem, which *Helvella* has. *Gyromitra* and *Helvella* spores are white to yellowish but the spore color is not necessary to note for identification purposes.

EDIBILITY: These are controversial, dangerous genera that are eaten, particularly in Europe and the Pacific Northwest, although fatal poisonings have been reported. It is now known that certain species of *Gyromitra* contain deadly monomethylhydrazine (MMH) used in rocket fuels, and all species are suspected of containing it. Therefore, it is recommended that no *Gyromitra* be eaten, even though many people have eaten them for years. The situation is further complicated by the fact that for reasons still unknown, toxicity varies within a species, particularly by locality. For example, while *G. esculenta* poisonings have been reported in Europe and the eastern U.S., none has been reported west of the Rocky Mountains, where it is a popular mushroom in the Pacific Northwest. It has long been known that species of *Gyromitra* were poisonous raw or without parboiling. Recommended preparation was to dissipate the toxins by parboiling the mushrooms for 5 to 6 minutes in an uncovered pan in a well-ventilated room, taking care not to inhale the fumes and to discard the cooking water before final cooking. Some people parboiled them several times, discarding the cooking water each time. However, it is now known that parboiling isn't sufficient, and that there is only a fine line between no effect and a lethal dose. Thus, one person may be unaffected after eating a *Gyromitra* species, while someone else eating a larger amount will be stricken. *Helvella* and *Verpa* should not be eaten raw, and although widely eaten, are poisonous to some people even if cooked. Small quantities only should be eaten, never twice in the same day nor several days in succession and only fresh, young specimens with no trace of spoilage or discoloration.

*Gyromitra gigas* (*Helvella gigas*); snow morel: 4–8 in. high, a heavy, solid mushroom. This and *G. fastigiata* are the famous snow mushrooms, both formerly considered edible and excellent after parboiling as above, but now known to contain MMH and no longer recommended.

CAP: Ocher yellow to yellow brown, sometimes dark red brown in age. Large top-heavy cap, deeply wrinkled and puckered, folded closely around stem, almost reaching ground. Brittle.

STEM: White or light-colored. Big, bulky, furrowed with many interior cavities, nearly as thick as cap, often nearly hidden by cap.

WHERE & WHEN: Early spring, near melting snowbanks in rich humus.

# GYROMITRA AND HELVELLA

GYROMITRA CHARACTERISTICS
· Cap yellow to tan to brown, deeply wrinkled, folded
· Stem whitish to brownish

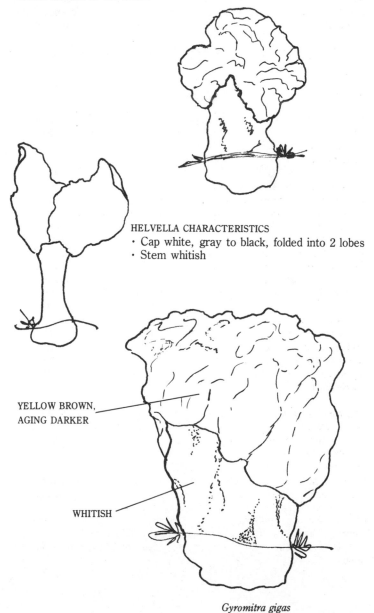

HELVELLA CHARACTERISTICS
· Cap white, gray to black, folded into 2 lobes
· Stem whitish

YELLOW BROWN, AGING DARKER

WHITISH

*Gyromitra gigas*

***Gyromitra fastigiata:*** One of the snow mushrooms, commonly confused with the other snow mushroom, *G. gigas*. Formerly considered edible but no longer recommended.

CAP: Dull yellow to tan, wavy and folded, edge often upturned. Doesn't hang down over stem as far as in *G. gigas*.

STEM: Whitish, stout, very short with interior folding.

WHERE & WHEN: Near melting or melted snowbanks in conifers, June–early July throughout Northwest.

***Gyromitra esculenta;*** brain mushroom, Arkansas morel: As its name, *esculenta,* indicates, this has long been considered edible, but is now considered poisonous (see page 208). Averages 2–8 in. high with great variations in size, color, and texture.

CAP: Pale yellowish to grayish tan to dark reddish brown, smooth at first, later becoming deeply wrinkled (not pitted) and folded into many convolutions like lobes of the brain. About fist-size or smaller. When cut in sections, shows many irregular cavities. Cap edges usually curl inward.

STEM: White or brownish, smooth although sometimes grooved, pithy to hollow. Sometimes two stems are fused together at base.

WHERE & WHEN: On humus soon after snow melts until mid-May in conifer, aspen stands or in open, at same time and location as black morels.

***Gyromitra brunnea*** (*G. underwoodii, Elvela underwoodii*); brown *Gyromitra*: Poisonous, although eaten when fresh and young by many, particularly in the Midwest. Best to avoid. Up to 5 in. high, 2–3 in. broad.

CAP: Reddish to chocolate brown with irregularly lobed cap overhanging stem. Saddle-shaped, brittle.

STEM: White, large, stuffed or hollow, sometimes fluted, enlarged base.

WHERE & WHEN: On rich humus in low woods, clustered around stumps of living trees, along rotting logs, hardwood forests, in late spring, early summer.

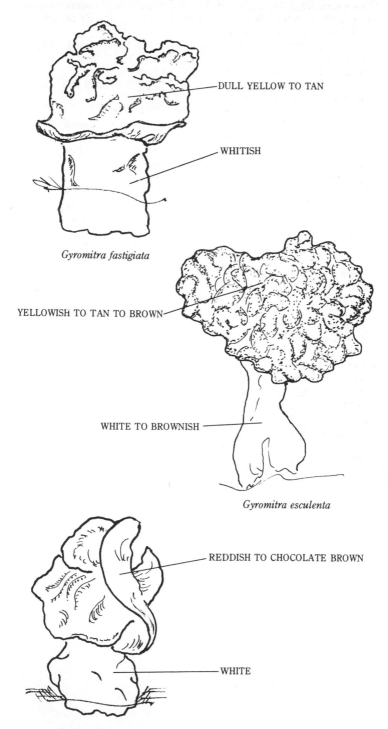

DULL YELLOW TO TAN

WHITISH

*Gyromitra fastigiata*

YELLOWISH TO TAN TO BROWN

WHITE TO BROWNISH

*Gyromitra esculenta*

REDDISH TO CHOCOLATE BROWN

WHITE

*Gyromitra brunnea*

***Gyromitra californica*** (*Helvella californica*): Regarded as poisonous by authorities. 3–6 in. high, often broader than wide.
CAP: Tan to olive, aging reddish brown. White underneath. Lobed with undulating folds, sometimes saddle-shaped or broad and rounded, edges rolled in. Brittle, thin flesh.
STEM: White, usually staining rose or purplish at base, deeply ridged, thin flesh, brittle.
WHERE & WHEN: Under conifers or open areas in western states in spring and summer.

***Gyromitra caroliniana:*** Authorities recommend avoidance. Averages 6 in. high, stout and heavy, easily confused with *G. brunnea*.
CAP: Brownish black with solid, white flesh, very large, about as high as wide, wrinkled and convoluted.
STEM: White, large, furrowed, enlarged at base.
WHERE & WHEN: On rich humus in oak or other deciduous woods, moist hardwoods in East, Midwest, South, March–early May.

***Gyromitra infula*** (*Helvella infula*); bay *Gyromitra*, hooded *Helvella*: Poisonous. 2–5 in. high.
CAP: Dirty yellow to reddish brown. Lobed and folded down the middle into saddle shape. Smooth to slightly wrinkled but not convoluted. Attached to top of stem only. Brittle.
STEM: Buff to light purplish brown to dull reddish brown. Hollow, usually smooth, although sometimes grooved or folded.
WHERE & WHEN: In wood debris from moist, rotted conifers or hardwoods, in shade, summer and fall, rarely in morel season.

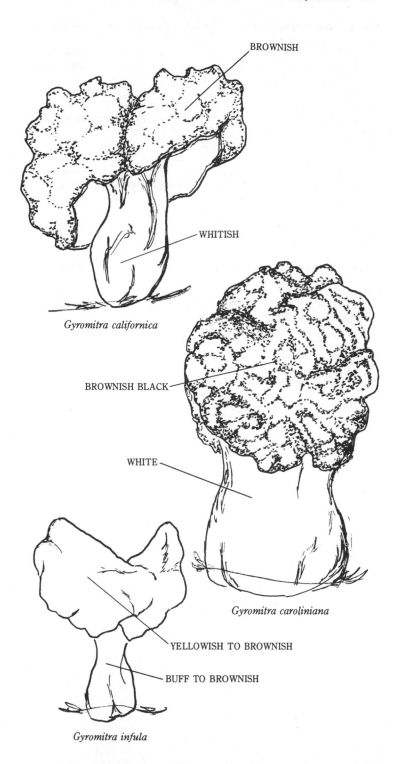

BROWNISH

WHITISH

*Gyromitra californica*

BROWNISH BLACK

WHITE

*Gyromitra caroliniana*

YELLOWISH TO BROWNISH

BUFF TO BROWNISH

*Gyromitra infula*

***Helvella lacunosa;*** bishop's miter, black-capped *Helvella*, elfin saddle: Young, fresh specimens eaten by many (observe precautions on page 208), but poisonous to some, so great caution is necessary. Never eat raw. Tastes rather like a morel when sautéed in butter; tough stems require long cooking. 3–6 in. high. Variable in size and shape, often overlooked.

CAP: Gray brown to ashy black. Two or more irregular lobes, folded and convoluted. Edge of cap attached to stem in places. Brittle.

STEM: White or shaded smoky black, usually lighter than cap, sometimes lighter at stem base. With deep pits and vertical grooves. Flexible.

WHERE & WHEN: After rains in thin mixed woods, Douglas fir, June until frost. About same places as *H. crispa.*

***Helvella crispa*** (*Elvela mitra*); white saddle, saddle-back false morel: Poisonous to some; observe all precautions, page 208; rather delicate flavor. Never eat raw. 2–5 in. high.

CAP: Whitish to yellowish white; underside light cinnamon. Irregularly shaped and folded lobes attached to top of stem. Thin, brittle.

STEM: Milky white, deeply fluted. Its whitish cap and stem distinguish it from *H. lacunosa.*

WHERE & WHEN: In deciduous woods, along paths, in pastures, summer until well into autumn. About same places as *H. lacunosa.*

***Helvella elastica*** (*Leptopodia elastica*); smooth-stem gray *Helvella*: Poisonous to some; observe precautions, page 208. Never eat raw. 2–4 in. high.

CAP: Smoky gray, sometimes brownish; undersurface opaque white. Generally 2 drooping, irregular lobes, centrally attached but edges free from stem. Very thin, brittle. Covered with minute white down.

STEM: Whitish. Slender, cylindrical, pliable, narrowing slightly at top. Nearly smooth, base slightly flattened with short groove at each side. Stuffed with cottony fibers, covered with fine white bloom.

WHERE & WHEN: In deciduous and coniferous woods, August–October.

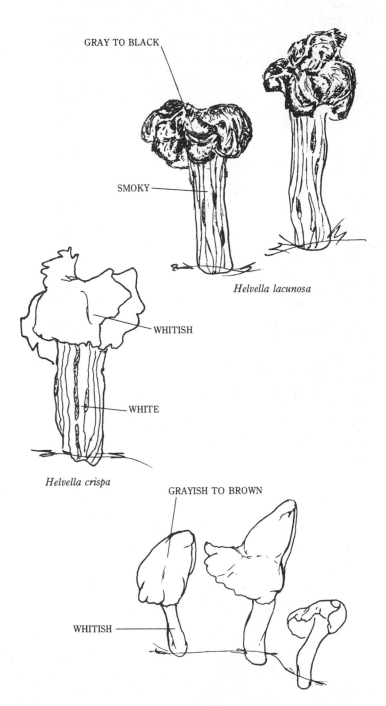

GRAY TO BLACK

SMOKY

*Helvella lacunosa*

WHITISH

WHITE

*Helvella crispa*

GRAYISH TO BROWN

WHITISH

*Helvella elastica*

# PUFFBALLS

Easiest to recognize of all fungi, the puffballs are just what their name implies: round balls (ranging from small to very large) that puff out their spores in a powdery dust at maturity. They are the most advanced fungi because they produce and protect their spores inside a completely enclosed ball until ready to be discharged into the world on their own. Main classifications are:

**CALVATIA** Medium to large to very large. At maturity, the upper part disintegrates, releasing the spores. The base is usually hollow and does not produce spores (hence called a *sterile* base); often remains like a ragged cup or bowl long after the spores have blown away. Most have an outer and inner wall, often of different colors. Often classified as *Lycoperdon* in older books.

**LYCOPERDON** Small, often growing in dense clusters. At maturity, a small hole opens at the top and the spores puff out when the puffball is pressed or as the walls wrinkle and collapse. The spores are produced in the round top while the narrower base is hollow and sterile (not producing spores).

**BOVISTA** Small, anchored to the ground by numerous fibers, breaking away from earth at maturity to be blown about by the wind, distributing spores through an irregularly torn hole at the top. Often persist through winter into spring, still full of spores.

**SCLERODERMA** Small, thick-skinned, too bitter to eat; easily distinguished by their thick, hard rind or outer wall and purplish interior, which is hard and solid, not spongy like the *Lycoperdons*.

EDIBILITY: Most puffballs are edible if pure white inside. Always slice each one and discard any that have turned color, even if only slightly yellowish. It is also important to ensure you haven't picked a gilled mushroom still in the button stage by mistake; some people have tragically eaten poisonous *Amanita* buttons for puffballs, so always slice through, starting at bottom and cutting up to the top. If you see the embryo of a gilled mushroom, you do not have a puffball.
· Puffballs are good raw, fried, stewed, pickled, canned, dried; in stews, gravies, sauces, salads. Discard small puffballs that are insect-ridden. In large species, cut out areas that have insect tunnels. If dirty, scrub with vegetable brush under cold running water, dry with towel. If outer skin is tough, most cooks prefer to peel it off.
· Slice or chop raw in salads alone or combine with raw vegetables. *Calvatia* is especially good cut into cubes, drenched with dressing, then added to salad.
· Slice ⅓–½ in. thick (or use small ones whole), dip into beaten egg and fine cracker or bread crumbs or flour; sauté in hot butter or olive oil, 1 minute per side until golden brown. Salt.
· Cut in strips, ½ × 4–5 in. long (like French fries) and deep-fry a few at a time 4–5 minutes until golden but not brown. Drain. Salt.
· Cut in pieces, stew gently in milk until tender. Serve with white sauce made from resultant juices, seasoning with lemon juice.
· Hollow out large *Calvatia*, chop center part, mix with any dressing recipe (very good with sage and onion), stuff mushroom shell, drape with bacon strips, wrap in foil, bake at 325° for 1 hour.

# PUFFBALLS

GENUS CHARACTERISTICS

- Top disintegrates, distributing spores
- Base often remains as ragged cup or bowl

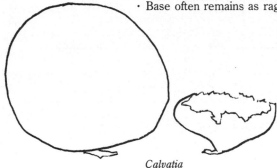

*Calvatia*

- Spores puff out top

*Lycoperdon*

- Blown about by wind, distributing spores

*Bovista*

- Tough outer rind
- Purple interior

*Scleroderma*

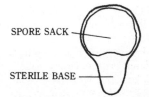

SPORE SACK

STERILE BASE

CROSS SECTION: PUFFBALL

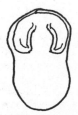

CROSS SECTION: GILLED MUSHROOM BUTTON

*Lycoperdon perlatum* (*L. gemmatum, L. nigrescens*); devil's snuff-box, gemmed puffball: Olive-brown spores. Edible, good. Diameter 1–3½ in. Whitish, then grayish brown. Shaped like a pestle or upside-down bottle. Covered with small, round, pointed spines that break off with age, leaving round scars. White interior ages olive to dark brown as spores mature. Narrow hollow base, chambered, sterile (no spores).
WHERE & WHEN: Single or in tight clusters around wood and leaves under hardwoods and conifers: summer, fall, across country.

*Lycoperdon curtisii* (*L. wrightii*): Olive spores. Edible. Diameter ½–1½ in. Pure white. Round, slightly flattened on top, covered with tiny cone-shaped warts or spines, easily rubbed off, leaving velvety surface.
WHERE & WHEN: In dense clusters in short grass in pastures, lawns; summer, fall, widely distributed.

*Lycoperdon candidum* (*L. calvescens, L. cruciatum, L. marginatum*): Olive-brown spores. Edible. Diameter ½–1½ in. Oval. White outer skin covered with sharp spines, sometimes fused together, cracking and flaking off in patches at maturity, revealing thin layer of minute yellowish scales. White interior ages olive or gray brown as spores mature. Hollow sterile base (not producing spores) in lower third, chambered, white.
WHERE & WHEN: Scattered or in small clusters in grassy open areas, pastures, golf courses; summer, fall, widely distributed.

*Lycoperdon pedicellatum*: Olive spores. Edible. Diameter ¾–2½ in. Whitish or ashy, aging smoky gray. Rounded, narrowing into stem-like base. Shaggy appearance because of dense spines that fall away, exposing pitted undercoat, dull brown to grayish. White interior ages olive to dull cinnamon as spores mature. Well-developed sterile base (no spores) chambered, pallid to brownish, numerous cordlike roots.
WHERE & WHEN: Scattered to many on humus or very rotted wood; in fall, particularly in eastern North America, but also in West.

*Lycoperdon echinatum* (*L. constellatum*): Purple-brown spores. Edible. Diameter ¾–2 in. Round to pear-shaped. White outer skin densely covered with long white spines that fall off revealing brown underskin. White interior ages yellowish, finally purplish as spores mature. Small, hollow, sterile base (no spores), dingy white to purplish gray.
WHERE & WHEN: Single to many on moss, humus, or wood debris; late summer, fall, in eastern and central states.

*Lycoperdon pulcherrimum* (*L. frostii*): Brownish-purple spores. Edible, but not the best. Diameter 1–2 in. Oval. Covered with long white spines that soon fall off, revealing purple-brown inner skin, slightly scarred. White interior ages dark purple brown. Hollow sterile base (no spores) occupies lower third, chambered. Cordlike root.
WHERE & WHEN: Single or in clusters on humus in hardwoods, fields, edges of woods; summer, fall, eastern and southern states.

WHITISH, AGING
GRAYISH BROWN.
ROUND POINTED SPINES

*Lycoperdon perlatum*

WHITE. TINY
CONE-SHAPED WARTS

*Lycoperdon curtisii*

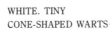

WHITE. SHARP SPINES
FLAKE OFF, REVEALING
TINY YELLOW SCALES

*Lycoperdon candidum*

WHITISH, AGING GRAYISH.
SPINES FALL OFF,
EXPOSING DARKER SKIN

*Lycoperdon pedicellatum*

WHITE. LONG SPINES
FALL OFF, EXPOSING
BROWN UNDERSKIN

*Lycoperdon echinatum*

WHITE. LONG SPINES
FALL OFF, EXPOSING
PURPLE-BROWN SKIN

*Lycoperdon pulcherrimum*

*Lycoperdon pyriforme;* pear-shaped puffball: Olive spores. Edible. Diameter 1–2 in. Off-white when growing in shade; tan to brown in sunlight, aging rusty brown. Smooth, then covered with minute granules. Rather tough skin. Small, hollow sterile base (no spores), occupies lower third, chambered. White interior ages olive as spores mature. Conspicuous white cords at base.

WHERE & WHEN: Single to dense clusters, on rotted wood (uprooted trees, stumps, sawdust piles), abundant late summer and fall throughout U.S. and Canada. Old spore sacs remain on wood throughout the year.

*Lycoperdon coloratum:* Dingy olive spores. Edible. Diameter ½–1½ in. Yellow when young, slowly becoming bronze to dull brown. Rounded, pinched off at base. Covered with harsh, darker warts and nodules, which tend to fall off. White interior ages olive to brown as spores mature. Poorly developed sterile base (no spores). Cordlike roots.

WHERE & WHEN: Single to many on humus and debris; summer, fall, eastern U.S.

*Lycoperdon umbrinum* (*L. asterospermum, L. glabellum, L. hirtum, L. muscorum, L. turneri*): Dull-brown spores. Edible. Diameter ½–3 in. Honey to clay-colored, aging dull brown. Pear-shaped with outer skin covered with short, slender, velvety spines and granules. White interior ages olive to purplish brown as spores mature. Hollow sterile base (no spores) in lower half, chambered.

WHERE & WHEN: Scattered to clusters on humus, usually under conifers; summer, fall, widely distributed, primarily eastern, southeastern, central states.

*Lycoperdon rimulatum*: Brownish-purple spores. Edible. Diameter ½–2 in. Egg-shaped. Grayish smooth outer layer breaks into a network of fine lines, finally flaking off, revealing purplish-gray to brownish underlayer. White interior becomes purplish as spores mature.

WHERE & WHEN: Generally in groups in or on edges of woods, uncultivated fields, sandy areas; late summer, fall, primarily in East, but also in West.

*Lycoperdon pusillum* (*L. ericetorum*): Olive spores. Edible. Diameter ¼–1 in. Round. White, aging brownish, with minutely roughened surface. White interior ages olive then deep brown as spores mature. No sterile base.

WHERE & WHEN: Single to gregarious in lawns, pastures; summer, fall, widely distributed.

*Scleroderma aurantium* (*S. vulgare*); common *Scleroderma*: Purple spores. Inedible because of strong bitter taste. Used as an aromatic seasoning in eastern Europe, often in sausage and to adulterate dried truffles. Diameter 1–3 in. Dingy to brownish yellow with purplish interior, aging almost black as spores mature. Easily distinguished by its thick, hard, outer skin with flattened warts arranged in a definite pattern.

WHERE & WHEN: On humus and very rotted logs in conifers and hardwoods; late summer, fall, primarily in eastern half of U.S.

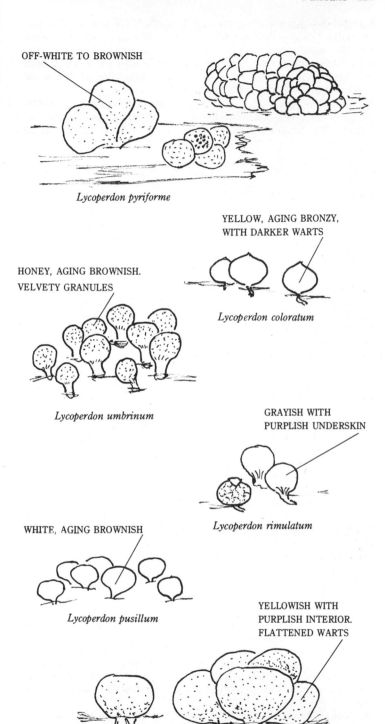

OFF-WHITE TO BROWNISH

*Lycoperdon pyriforme*

YELLOW, AGING BRONZY, WITH DARKER WARTS

*Lycoperdon coloratum*

HONEY, AGING BROWNISH. VELVETY GRANULES

*Lycoperdon umbrinum*

GRAYISH WITH PURPLISH UNDERSKIN

*Lycoperdon rimulatum*

WHITE, AGING BROWNISH

*Lycoperdon pusillum*

YELLOWISH WITH PURPLISH INTERIOR. FLATTENED WARTS

*Scleroderma aurantium*

*Calvatia gigantea* (*C. maxima*); giant puffball: Olive spores. Edible, choice. Diameter usually 8–24 in., but with published reports of larger ones weighing 30 lbs.! Whitish, aging grayish to yellowish or olive. Round and smooth at first with kid-glove texture, then frequently cracking into small areas. White interior ages yellow then olive brown as spores mature. Attached to ground by short, cordlike root.
WHERE & WHEN: Single to several in rich wet humus or grass, in the open, along edges of streams, ditches, pools, meadows. Fond of hillsides, likes to nestle in grass; late summer, fall, across country.

*Calvatia booniana;* western giant puffball: Edible, choice. Diameter 4–24 in. Dull white to buff or tannish. Egg-shaped but flattened on top, outer skin sculptured at first with tannish markings, then breaking into large, flat, polygonal scales. White interior turns olive brown as spores mature. Thick cordlike root.
WHERE & WHEN: Single to a few in sagebrush country of West after summer rains; sometimes in or near old corrals but usually near or under sage; spring, summer, Rocky Mountains, Pacific Northwest, Pacific Southwest.

*Calvatia bovista* (*C. uteriformis, C. caelata*): Olive-brown spores. Edible. Diameter 2–5 in. Egg-shaped with tapered narrow base. Whitish outer skin cracks, showing dark olive-brown inside at maturity. Hollow sterile base (no spores) comprises lower half, remains as hollow ragged bowl after top disintegrates.
WHERE & WHEN: In poor soil under scrub oak, on hillsides, brushy areas; in Southwest and east of Rocky Mountains, summer, fall.

*Calvatia cyathiformis* (*C. lilacina*); pasture puffball, lilac puffball: Purple-brown spores. Edible, choice. Diameter 3–8 in. Whitish to light pinkish tan, aging brown. Rather pear-shaped with egg-shaped top and short, thick, stemless base. Outer skin soon breaks into a network of cracks, showing purple stains from spores. Thick sterile base (no spores) occupies lower third, chambered, white to dingy yellowish, remains as large ragged cup long after top of mushroom has disappeared.
WHERE & WHEN: Scattered to numerous in grassy pastures, open prairies; late summer, fall, after heavy rains, same places as *Agaricus campestris*. Widely distributed, particularly in Midwest.

*Calvatia lepidophora*: Olive-brown spores. Edible, good. Diameter 2–8 in. Nearly round, depressed on top. Dull white, aging tan or dull yellowish brown. Outer skin cracking, forming irregular scales. White interior ages olive brown as spores mature. Small sterile base (no spores), white, aging yellowish.
WHERE & WHEN: Single to scattered in arid sage or prairie areas; spring–early fall, central and western states.

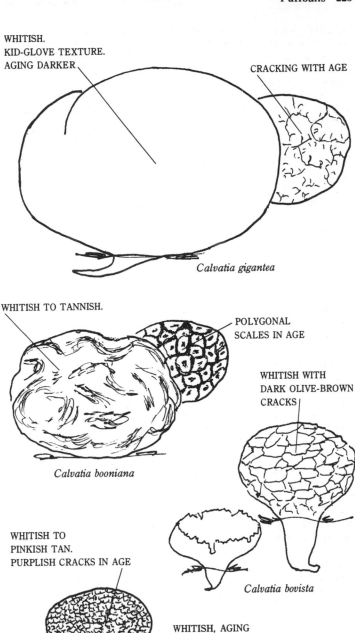

WHITISH.
KID-GLOVE TEXTURE.
AGING DARKER

CRACKING WITH AGE

*Calvatia gigantea*

WHITISH TO TANNISH.

POLYGONAL
SCALES IN AGE

WHITISH WITH
DARK OLIVE-BROWN
CRACKS

*Calvatia booniana*

WHITISH TO
PINKISH TAN.
PURPLISH CRACKS IN AGE

*Calvatia bovista*

WHITISH, AGING
BROWNISH. IRREGULAR
SCALES IN AGE

*Calvatia cyathiformis*

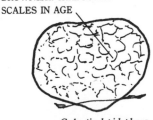

*Calvatia lepidophora*

*Calvatia sculpta*: Olive-brown spores. Edible, choice. Diameter 3–6 in. White, pear-shaped, very unusual looking with top covered with conspicuous, pointed, pyramid-shaped warts, some erect, others bent over or even joined at the tip with other warts. White interior ages deep olive brown as spores mature. Small sterile base (no spores).
WHERE & WHEN: Single to several, usually near conifers at high elevations in Rocky Mountains, Pacific Northwest, Pacific Southwest; spring, summer.

*Calbovista subsculpta:* Yellowish-brown spores. Edible. Diameter usually 2–6 in., but up to 12 in. in wet seasons. White, nearly round, but flattened on top. Covered with low, cone-shaped warts with brownish hairs at center of each. Large sterile base (no spores) occupies lower third of mushroom. White interior ages dark brown as spores mature. (This species is put in a genus of its own, *Calbovista*, because of microscopic differences. However, to the casual collector, it looks like a *Calvatia*.)
WHERE & WHEN: Single to several, usually near conifers in middle and higher elevations of western mountains, often along old roads; late spring, summer. Common western mountain puffball.

*Calvatia pachyderma*: Olive spores. Edible. Diameter 2–8 in. Variously shaped, ranging from round to egg-shaped, often irregular. White to brownish, smooth to slightly roughened rindlike outer skin, often peeling in thin patches. Inner skin, tan to dark olive brown. White interior ages olive brown as spores mature. No sterile base. Thick cordlike root.
WHERE & WHEN: Singly in arid regions of the Southwest and California; summer, fall.

*Calvatia rubro-flava;* orange puffball: Yellowish-olive spores. Edible. Diameter 1½–3 in. Whitish to pinkish tan at first, instantly bruising yellow, then becoming orangy red to orangy brown. Thin outer skin breaks up and falls away. After maturity, top of mushroom breaks into fragments and disintegrates. Interior is yellow to olive orange. Sterile base (no spores) occupies lower third.
WHERE & WHEN: On cultivated ground, widely distributed, particularly in the South; summer, fall.

*Calvatia subcretacea:* Olive-brown spores. Edible, good. Diameter 1–4 in. Egg-shaped. White, thick outer skin, covered with small, pointed warts with dark gray tips that break away, one by one, at maturity. White interior ages dark olive brown as spores mature. Very small or no sterile base (no spores).
WHERE & WHEN: Single to scattered in conifer forests at high elevations in western mountains; spring–fall.

*Calvatia fumosa*: Brown spores. Inedible because of bitter taste. Diameter up to 4 in. Smoky gray to gray brown, round with thick, smooth outer skin. White interior ages brown as spores mature. No sterile base.
WHERE & WHEN: Single to numerous under conifers at high elevations in Pacific Northwest, often with *C. subcretacea*; spring, summer.

WHITE. PYRAMID-SHAPED
WARTS

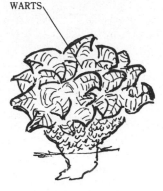

*Calvatia sculpta*

WHITE. LOW CONE-SHAPED
WARTS WITH BROWNISH HAIRS

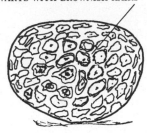

*Calbovista subsculpta*

WHITE TO BROWNISH.
PEELING IN THIN PATCHES

*Calvatia pachyderma*

WHITISH TO PINKISH TAN.
BRUISING YELLOW,
THEN DARK ORANGY

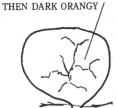

*Calvatia rubro-flava*

WHITE. POINTED WARTS
WITH GRAY TIPS

*Calvatia subcretacea*

SMOKY TO GRAY BROWN.
CRACKING IN AGE

*Calvatia fumosa*

*Calvatia craniiformis* (*Lycoperdon delicatum*); skull-shaped puffball: Greenish-yellow spores. Edible. Diameter 3–8 in. Whitish to grayish, sometimes with reddish tinge. Somewhat skull-shaped, depressed at top. Outer skin, smooth, thin, fragile, easily peeled off. White interior ages yellow green as spores mature. Stemlike sterile base (no spores) with cordlike root.
WHERE & WHEN: In woods or brush, in Southwest, east of Rockies; fall.

*Calvatia elata*: Brown or greenish-brown spores. Edible. Diameter 1½–6 in. Pale to brownish, aging darker. Round, often slightly depressed, abruptly contracted into long, slender stemlike base that is round, often pitted, anchored to ground by fibrous threads. Top is coated with minute granules. Inner skin, white to cream, becoming olive to brownish, thin and fragile, breaking off and falling away. White interior ages olive or brown as spores mature.
WHERE & WHEN: Mossy, brushy areas, especially boggy or swampy places; eastern half of U.S.; summer, fall.

*Calvatia excipuliforme* (*C. saccata*): Dingy olive-brown spores. Edible, good. Diameter 2–4 in. White to creamy, becoming brown or olive brown. Round with depressed top on long round stemlike sterile base. Rough with minute persistent mealy granules.
WHERE & WHEN: Pastures, mossy, brushy areas, especially swamps; late summer, fall.

*Bovista pila* (*B. montana*, *B. nigriscens*): Dark-brown spores. Edible. Diameter 1–3 in. Round. White outercoat with mealy fuzzy surface, soon wearing off, exposing thin, papery undercoat that is grayish brown to bronze, aging purplish. White interior ages dark purplish brown as spores mature (no sterile base). Attached to soil by thin root. Entire body breaks away at maturity to be blown about by the wind, distributing spores through ragged pore at top. Often persists all winter, found in spring as blackish ball still full of spores.
WHERE & WHEN: Single to numerous in cow pastures, stables, open woods; late summer, fall. Widely distributed.

*Bovista minor*: Olive-brown spores. Edible although small. Diameter ½–1¼ in. White outercoat (usually dirty since it grows underground in early stages) flakes off, revealing wrinkled reddish-brown undercoat. White interior ages olive brown as spores mature. Numerous fibers at base.
WHERE & WHEN: Usually under conifers in damp shade; fall, Great Lakes southward.

*Bovista plumbea;* lead-colored *Bovista*: Dark-brown spores. Edible if inner skin is still tender. Diameter ½–1¼ in. White outercoat shrinks, creating white patches that flake off showing lead-color undercoat. White interior ages dark brown as spores mature. Base attached by mass of fibers.
WHERE & WHEN: Pastures, golf courses, parks, lawns, after rains; summer, early fall. Widely distributed.

WHITISH TO GRAYISH,
OFTEN TINGED REDDISH

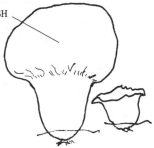

*Calvatia craniiformis*

CREAM TO BROWNISH

WHITISH, AGING BROWNISH

*Calvatia elata*

*Calvatia excipuliforme*

WHITE OUTERCOAT.
RED-BROWN UNDERCOAT

WHITE OUTERCOAT. BROWN
TO BRONZE UNDERCOAT

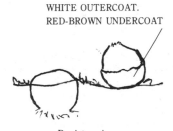

*Bovista pila*

*Bovista minor*

WHITE OUTERCOAT.
LEAD UNDERCOAT

*Bovista plumbea*

# CORAL FUNGI

Like ocean coral, which they resemble, Coral Fungi come in many sizes, shapes, and colors. All were formerly classified as *Clavaria*, later were divided into a number of genera. Most people still refer to all as *Clavaria*. They are simple, primitive mushrooms, low on the evolution scale. They have no gills, but bear their spores on the surfaces of their branches. The main genera are:

**CLAVARIADELPHUS**   Small, simple, club-shaped.

**CLAVULINOPSIS**   Small, graceful, fingerlike.

**CLAVICORONA**   Small, with many slender, upright branches, each tipped with tiny spikes forming a minute crown, or *corona*, as the Latin name indicates. Grow on wood.

**CLAVULINA**   Small, with thin, delicate branches, often irregular, with pointed, toothed tips.

**RAMARIA**   Medium size, profusely branched, large, fleshy base.

**SPARASSIS**   Very large, whitish to yellowish, like a huge bouquet of ruffled lettuce leaves; large, deeply rooted stem.

EDIBILITY: Most *Clavaria* are edible and delicious. A few are too tough or bitter to be eaten—if they taste very bitter raw, don't try cooking them. Use only fresh, young, insect-free specimens; older ones are apt to be tough and disagreeable tasting. Corals are hard to clean because of their many branches. Wash briefly in salted water to drive out the insects (a soft brush helps dig out the grit); rinse well in running cold water. Drain and blot dry. Use only the tender tips and branches for cooking, save the tough stems for drying.
· Eat tender tips raw in salads: slice thin and add to lettuce dressed with mayonnaise or a vinaigrette made with lemon juice.
· Or try sliced coral tips dressed with a vinaigrette, tossed with chopped parsley and chives, then with lettuce, watercress.
· Simmer chopped *Clavaria* in soup, gravies, spaghetti sauce.
· Sauté sliced or whole tender tips till crisp. (*Clavariadelphus*, sliced and sautéed until done, are like puffballs in texture but with much better flavor.)
· Sauté until well done, then add milk or cream, thicken with flour, season highly, adding salt at end so it won't toughen mushrooms.
· Sauté diced *Clavaria* with a bit of minced onion or shallots and serve with broiled fish.
· Stew in a little water over low heat until tender (a double boiler works well). Chop fine, if rather tough like *Clavulina*.
· Simmer tough parts with good flavor in water for 1 hour and then discard mushrooms. Use broth in soup or to cook rice.
· Dry and pulverize for a handy mushroom seasoning.
· Divide *Sparassis* into pieces and clean. Dredge with flour. Sauté gently until almost tender in butter seasoned with minced onion, salt, pepper. Transfer all to casserole, top with seasoned bread crumbs and bake in moderate oven until tender (slow cooking is best for *Sparassis*).
CAUTION: Beware *R. formosa* and *R. gelatinosa*, page 234—they're drastic laxatives. A few delicate stomachs may find all corals act like laxatives, so observe the usual precautions, page 7.

# CORAL FUNGI

GENUS CHARACTERISTICS

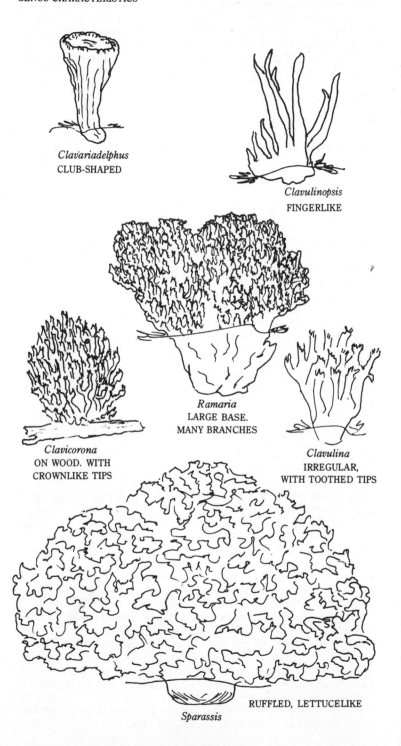

*Clavariadelphus*
CLUB-SHAPED

*Clavulinopsis*
FINGERLIKE

*Ramaria*
LARGE BASE.
MANY BRANCHES

*Clavicorona*
ON WOOD. WITH
CROWNLIKE TIPS

*Clavulina*
IRREGULAR,
WITH TOOTHED TIPS

RUFFLED, LETTUCELIKE

*Sparassis*

*Clavariadelphus truncatus* (*Clavaria truncatus*): Yellowish to orangy spores. Edible. Club-shaped, 2–6 in. high, 1–3½ in. thick, often with flattened, truncated top that breaks open revealing hollow interior. Wrinkled near top, smooth at base.
COLOR: Yellow to golden to orangy yellow. Sometimes brownish at base. White hairy coating over base. Flesh thin, white.
WHERE & WHEN: Grows scattered in needles under conifers; summer, fall, widely distributed.
*C. borealis*: In northwestern conifer forests; looks like *C. truncatus* but has white spores. Has disagreeable taste, so avoid.

*Clavariadelphus pistillaris* (*Clavaria pistillaris*); Indian clubs, little war clubs, pestle-shaped *Clavaria:* White to buff spores. Edible and good. Simple club-shaped, 1–5 (8) in. high, 1–2 in. broad at top, tapering down to a very slender base. Frequently grooved or wrinkled. Top is rounded or blunt, often puckered or depressed.
COLOR: Variable, ranging from chocolate or slate to yellow or orangish with white stem. Flesh whitish, soft, marshmallowlike in youth, often becoming hollow at maturity.
WHERE & WHEN: Grows singly, but often with several in a group in leaf clutter in moist woods; July until frost, widely distributed.

*Clavariadelphus ligula* (*Clavaria ligula*): White spores. Edible. Slender, club-shaped, 2–4 in. high.
COLOR: Pale puff to salmon to brownish. White downy base. Flesh white, firm.
WHERE & WHEN: Grows in clusters in needles of conifer forests, especially pine, after heavy fall rains, often in great numbers.

*Clavulinopsis fusiformis* (*Clavaria fusiformis*); spindle coral: Pale-yellow spores. Edible, very tender with good flavor. Thin, spindle-shaped with pointed tips, up to 4 in. high, only 1/16 in. wide. Soon becomes hollow.
COLOR: Canary yellow, translucent, smooth; tips are slightly darker.
WHERE & WHEN: Grows clustered in groups of 4 or 5 united at base, in wooded ravines, woods, pastures; summer, fall.
*C. aurantio-cinnabarina*: Similar but rosy color with orangy-red tips, white base. Edible.

*Clavaria vermicularis*: White spores. Edible, although very small, only 1–2½ in. high, quill-shaped, brittle.
COLOR: White.
WHERE & WHEN: Densely clustered in thin grassy woods, lawns, moist ravines, July–October.

*Clavaria purpurea;* fairy clubs, purple tongues: White spores. Edible. Thin, rounded, brittle blades, 1½–4 in. high, less than ⅓ in. thick.
COLOR: Dark violet when young, fading to winy buff or brownish.
WHERE & WHEN: Grows in a cluster on wet soil near conifers; common in Rocky Mountains, summer and fall.
*C. fumosa*: Similar but smoky gray, aging sooty black at tips. Edible.

YELLOW TO ORANGY

*Clavariadelphus truncatus*

BROWN TO SLATE TO ORANGY

*Clavariadelphus pistillaris*

BUFF TO SALMON TO BROWNISH

*Clavariadelphus ligula*

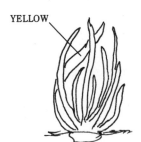

YELLOW

*Clavulinopsis fusiformis*

WHITE

*Clavaria vermicularis*

VIOLET, FADING IN AGE

*Clavaria purpurea*

***Clavicorona pyxidata*** (*Clavaria pyxidata*); crowned or cup-bearing *Clavaria*: White spores. Edible. 2–5 in. high, 1–4 in. broad.
BRANCHES: Creamy white to pale yellow when young, pale pinkish to tan to brown as it ages or is bruised. Many branches, each tipped with 6–9 spikes forming a tiny crown or cup. Flesh firm, white. Fragile. Waxy.
STEM: Whitish to pinkish brown over base.
WHERE & WHEN: Gregarious or in clusters on dead wood, especially aspen, poplar, and willow logs; spring–fall. Widely distributed throughout forested areas of U.S. and Canada.

***Clavulina cristata*** (*Clavaria cristata*); crested *Clavaria*: White spores. Edible and good. 2–5 in. high and broad.
BRANCHES: Whitish to grayish to pinkish. Irregular branches, somewhat flattened; toothed or crested at tips. Tips age brown or blackish brown. Flesh white, tough. Sometimes hollow.
STEM: Short with many branches, brittle.
WHERE & WHEN: Grows singly or several together in fields or moist shady woods, hardwoods and conifers; late summer–winter. Widely distributed, common in Pacific Northwest. Look for them after warm summer rains in rich leaf mold.
CAUTION: Frequently parasitized by another fungus and turns black; discard any that are blackened.

***Clavulina cinerea*** (*Clavaria cinerea*); gray or ashen *Clavaria*: White spores. Edible. 2–5 in. high.
BRANCHES: Smoky gray, sometimes bluish gray or brownish in age. Compact in shape with short, often wrinkled branches, many pointed, often toothed tips.
STEM: Whitish to smoky gray, rather stout, often gnarled and bent, much branched, wrinkled, brittle.
WHERE & WHEN: Grows singly or scattered, often abundant in moss and decaying debris under conifers or mixed woods; late summer, fall. Widely distributed. Found from beginning of warm weather until frost along Pacific Coast.

***Clavulina amethystina*** (*Clavaria amethystina*): Pale brownish-yellow spores. Edible. 1–4 in. tall.
BRANCHES AND STEM: Beautiful amethyst color all over, yellowing when dried. Thick, short, irregular branches forked at tips. Very short stem.
WHERE & WHEN: Among grass, in pastures, open woods; summer, fall.

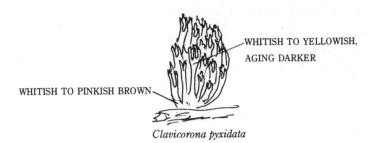

WHITISH TO YELLOWISH, AGING DARKER

WHITISH TO PINKISH BROWN

*Clavicorona pyxidata*

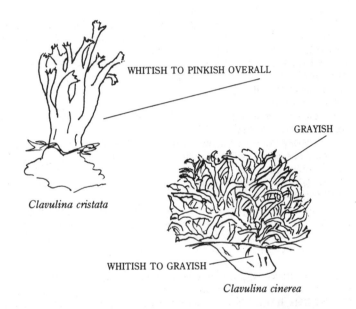

WHITISH TO PINKISH OVERALL

GRAYISH

*Clavulina cristata*

WHITISH TO GRAYISH

*Clavulina cinerea*

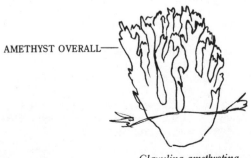

AMETHYST OVERALL

*Clavulina amethystina*

**Ramaria aurea** (*Clavaria aurea*); golden *Clavaria*, deer mushroom: Yellowish spores. Edible, tender. 2–5 in. tall, 6–7 in. wide.
BRANCHES: Golden to tawny. Do not turn color when bruised. Slightly toothed at tips. Flesh white.
STEM: White, thick, solid, brittle, pointed at base.
WHERE & WHEN: Grows singly or in clusters in conifer and mixed woods; summer, fall. In peak seasons, can be gathered by the bushel.

**Ramaria flava** (*Clavaria flava*); pale-yellow *Clavaria*: Yellowish spores. Edible. 2–6 in. tall, 4–10 in. across.
BRANCHES: Pale to dingy yellow with brighter yellow tips. Turn brownish when bruised. Toothed, pointed tips. Flesh white, soft.
STEM: White, round, thick, short, much branched.
WHERE & WHEN: In tufts on well-rotted logs (unlike other *Ramaria*) in moist woods and open places; late summer, fall.

**Ramaria sanguinea** (*Clavaria sanguinea*): Yellowish spores. Edible, very delicious. 2–5½ in. tall, 1½–6½ in. wide.
BRANCHES: Yellow with brighter yellow tips, bruising reddish wine.
STEM: Whitish to yellowish, bruising reddish wine. Short.
WHERE & WHEN: Singly or in groups under hardwoods and mixed woods; summer, fall.

**Ramaria botrytis** (*Clavaria botrytis*); purple or red-tipped coral, grape coral: Yellowish spores. Edible but must be well cooked. Eat only young specimens. 2–8 in. tall, 4–12 in. wide.
BRANCHES: Whitish to tannish with pink to red to purplish tips, fading in age. Flesh white, somewhat brittle.
STEM: Whitish, short, thick, bulbous, fleshy, often buried with only the dense head visible.
WHERE & WHEN: Grows scattered to abundant on soil under hardwoods and conifers, especially hemlock, often in moss; summer, fall (late spring–fall in South). Widely distributed.
**R. subbotrytis**: Similar, but with brilliant pink to reddish branches (no yellow tips), growing from large white base. Edible.

**Ramaria formosa** (*Clavaria formosa*); yellow-tipped coral: Yellowish-brown spores. Poisonous (drastic laxative). Bitter tasting. 2½–9 in. tall, 1–12 in. broad.
BRANCHES: Salmon to rosy pink with lemon-yellow tips. Flesh white, bruising red brown to black.
STEM: Whitish.
WHERE & WHEN: Scattered to many on humus or in soil under hardwoods and conifers; late fall, winter, occasionally early spring.

**Ramaria gelatinosa** (*Clavaria gelatinosa*); gelatinous *Clavaria*: Ocher spores. Poisonous to many. 6–12 in. tall and wide.
BRANCHES: Cream to pinkish to orangy, sometimes with yellowish tips.
STEM: Creamy, with pockets of semitransparent, gelatinous flesh.
WHERE & WHEN: Singly or several in mixed hardwood and conifer forests; summer in Southwest, fall in Northwest.

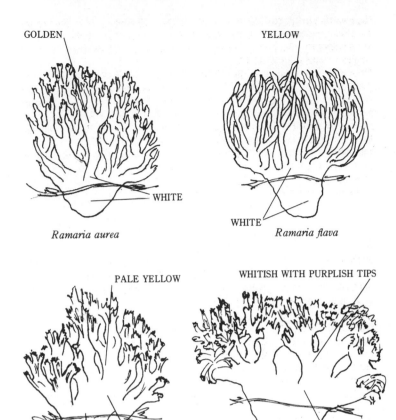

GOLDEN

WHITE

*Ramaria aurea*

YELLOW

WHITE

*Ramaria flava*

PALE YELLOW

WHITISH,
BRUISING REDDISH

*Ramaria sanguinea*

WHITISH WITH PURPLISH TIPS

WHITISH

*Ramaria botrytis*

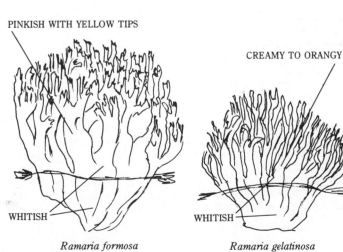

PINKISH WITH YELLOW TIPS

WHITISH

*Ramaria formosa*

CREAMY TO ORANGY

WHITISH

*Ramaria gelatinosa*

*Sparassis radicata*: White spores. Edible and choice. This very large, conspicuous fungus is a thrill to find since it grows up to 2–3 ft. across and weighs up to 40 lbs. It looks like a large rounded mass of white to yellowish leaf lettuce.

BRANCHES: Whitish to pale yellowish. Thin, ruffled, and folded like lettuce leaves. Flesh white, firm.

STEM: White, large, deeply rooted, pointed at base.

WHERE & WHEN: Grows singly under old-growth conifers. Base is usually attached to base or root of tree, in fall in western states. Most common in Pacific states and Rocky Mountains. Do not pull up entire mushroom, but cut off at ground level, leaving base in the ground so it can fruit again.

*Sparassis crispa* (*S. herbstii, S. spathulata*): White spores. Edible and choice. Smaller than *S. radicata*. 3–12 in. high, 4–24 in. wide.

BRANCHES: Whitish to yellowish with shorter, thicker branches than *S. radicata*. Wavy and folded.

STEM: White, large.

WHERE & WHEN: Grows singly in deciduous woods, usually attached to base or root of tree; July, August, eastern and southern states. Cut off at ground level, rather than pulling up entire mushroom, so it can fruit again.

WHITE TO YELLOWISH

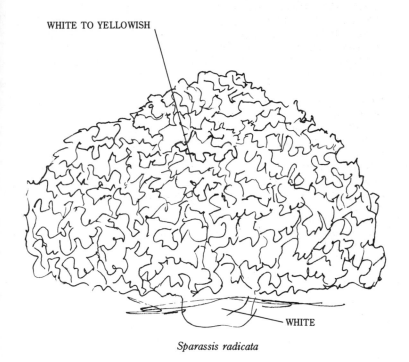

WHITE

*Sparassis radicata*

WHITE TO YELLOWISH

WHITE

*Sparassis crispa*

# CUP AND JELLY FUNGI

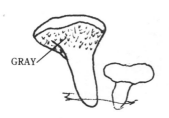

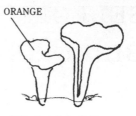

*Phlogiotis helvelloides*

*Pseudohydnum gelatinosum*

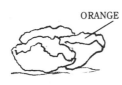

*Aleuria aurantia*

*Auricularia auricula*

**CUP AND JELLY FUNGI**   Small, often overlooked, disappearing in dry weather. Eaten more as a curiosity than a gourmet treat.

*Phlogiotis helvelloides* (*Gyrocephalus rufus*); apricot jelly mushroom: Edible when fresh and young. Eat raw in salads. Pickle in vinegar. Candy by simmering briefly in sugar syrup, cool in syrup, drain, roll in crushed hard candy or colored sugar.
CHARACTERISTICS: 1–3 in. tall. Apricot to rosy to red. Gelatinous, shining, elastic, smooth. Funnel-shaped except open on one side.
WHERE & WHEN: Scattered on duff under conifers; late summer, fall.

*Pseudohydnum gelatinosum*: Edible. Eat raw with sugar and cream, or roll in crushed hard candy or cake decorations. Marinate in French dressing and serve in salad.
CHARACTERISTICS: 1–3 in. tall. Colorless to translucent gray. Gelatinous. Spatula-shaped with minute spines (like *Hydnum*) on lower surface.
WHERE & WHEN: On conifer twigs, logs; cool, wet fall weather.

*Aleuria aurantia*: Edible raw in salads or sautéed.
CHARACTERISTICS: ½–3 in. broad. Bright orange with whitish bloom on outside. Saucer- to cup-shaped. Thin, brittle, becoming wrinkled.
WHERE & WHEN: Scattered to clusters on hard ground, in open, often newly disturbed soil, along roads; summer, fall.

*Auricularia auricula;* Judas' ear, the Orient's cloud ears (*ung nge*) or wood ears (*muk nge*): Edible, particularly in oriental food; dry and use as flavoring, especially in soup.
CHARACTERISTICS: ½–4 in. broad. Grayish to brown, drying brownish black. Shaped like a cup or ear. Tough, gelatinous, elastic.
WHERE & WHEN: On wood, usually hardwoods, but common on western conifers; near melting snow in spring, cool wet weather, late summer, fall.

# SELECTED
# BIBLIOGRAPHY

Bandoni, R. J. and Szczawinski, A. F. *Guide to Common Mushrooms of British Columbia*. Victoria, B.C.: Provincial Museum, 1964, 1976.

Bartelli, Ingrid. *Mushrooms Grow on Stumps, May Is Morel Month in Michigan, Best of the Boletes, Wood Waste Makes Wonderful Mushrooms*. (Cooperative Extension Service Bulletins) East Lansing, Mich.: Michigan State University.

Coker, William Chambers and Beers, Alma Holland. *Boleti of North Carolina*. New York: Dover Publications, 1974.

Duffy, Thomas and Vergeer, Paul. *California Toxic Fungi*. San Francisco: Mycological Society of San Francisco, 1977.

Graham, Verne Ovid. *Mushrooms of the Great Lakes Region*. New York: Dover Publications, 1970.

Groves, J. Walton. *Edible and Poisonous Mushrooms of Canada*. Ottawa: Canada Department of Agriculture, 1962.

Hard, Miron Elisha. *Mushrooms, Edible & Otherwise*. New York: Dover Publications, 1976.

Harris, Bob. *Growing Wild Mushrooms*. Berkeley, Cal.: Wingbow Press, 1976.

Hesler, L. R. *Mushrooms of the Great Smokies*. Knoxville, Tenn.: University of Tennessee Press, 1960.

Kauffman, C. H. *Gilled Mushrooms of Michigan and the Great Lakes Region*, 2 vols. New York: Dover Publications, 1971.

Kleijn, H. *Mushrooms and Other Fungi*. New York: Doubleday, 1965.

Kreiger, Louis C. *The Mushroom Handbook*. New York: Dover Publications, 1967. Originally published as *A Popular Guide to the Higher Fungi of New York State*.

Lange, Morten and Hora, F. Bayard. *A Guide to Mushrooms & Toadstools*. New York: E. P. Dutton, 1963.

Lincoff, Gary. *A Guide to the Poisonous Mushrooms in the Greater New York Area*. New York: New York Mycological Society, 1976.

Lincoff, Gary and Mitchel, D. H. *Toxic and Hallucinogenic Mushroom Poisoning*. New York: Van Nostrand Reinhold, 1977.

McIlvaine, Charles and Macadam, Robert K. *One Thousand American Fungi*. New York: Dover Publications, 1973.

McKenny, Margaret. *The Savory Wild Mushroom*. Revised by Daniel E. Stuntz. Seattle: University of Washington Press, 1962, 1971.

Menser, Gary P. *Hallucinogenic and Poisonous Mushroom Field Guide*. Berkeley, Cal.: And-Or Press, 1977.

Miller, Orson K., Jr. *Mushrooms of North America*. New York: E. P. Dutton, 1972.

Miller, Orson K., Jr., and Farr, David F. *An Index of the Common Fungi of North America*. Vaduz, Liechtenstein: Bibliotheca Mycologica, J. Cramer, 1975.

Orr, Robert T. and Orr, Dorothy B. *Mushrooms and Other Common Fungi of the San Francisco Bay Region.* Berkeley, Cal.: University of California Press, 1962.

Orr, Robert T. and Orr, Dorothy B. *Mushrooms and Other Common Fungi of Southern California.* Berkeley, Cal.: University of California Press, 1968.

Rinaldi, Augusto and Tyndalo, Vassili. *The Complete Book of Mushrooms.* New York: Crown Publishers, 1974.

Rumack, Barry H., M.D., and Emanuel Salzman, M.D., editors. *Mushroom Poisoning: Diagnosis and Treatment.* West Palm Beach, Fla: CRC Press, Inc., 1978.

Savonius, Moira. *All Color Book of Mushrooms and Fungi.* London: Octopus Books, 1973.

Smith, Alexander H. *Mushroom Hunter's Field Guide.* Ann Arbor, Mich.: University of Michigan Press, 1958, 1963.

Smith, Alexander H. *Field Guide to Western Mushrooms.* Ann Arbor, Mich.: University of Michigan Press, 1975.

Smith, Alexander H. and Smith, Helen V. *How to Know the Non-Gilled Fleshy Fungi.* Dubuque, Ia.: Wm. C. Brown, 1973.

Smith, Alexander H. and Thiers, Harry D. *The Boletes of Michigan.* Ann Arbor, Mich.: University of Michigan Press, 1971.

Stubbs, Ansel Hartley. *Wild Mushrooms of the Central Midwest.* Lawrence, Kan.: University Press of Kansas, 1971.

Thiers, Harry D. *California Mushrooms: A Field Guide to the Boletes.* New York: Hafner Press, 1975.

Thomas, William Sturgis. *Field Book of Common Mushrooms.* New York: G. P. Putnam's Sons, 1928 and 1936.

Tosco, Uberto and Fanelli, Annalaura. *Color Treasury of Mushrooms & Toadstools.* London: Orbis Publishing, 1972.

Watling, Roy. *Identification of the Larger Fungi.* Amersham, England: Hulton Educational Publications, 1973.

Wells, Mary Hallock and Mitchel, D. H. *Mushrooms of Colorado and Adjacent Areas.* Denver, Col.: Denver Museum of Natural History. 1966.

*Note:* Various mushroom cookbooks are published by local mycological societies, including those of Colorado, San Francisco, and Washington, obtainable directly from the societies:

Colorado Mycological Society, 909 York St., Denver, Colorado 80206

Mycological Society of San Francisco, Inc., P.O. Box 904, San Francisco, California 94101

Puget Sound Mycological Society, 200 Second Avenue North, Seattle, Washington 98109

# INDEX

**Major genera are in boldface.** Specific mushrooms are alphabetized under their species names, e.g., Agaricus campestris is listed as campestris, Agaricus.